HARTFORD

AMERICAN HISTORICAL PRESS
SUN VALLEY, CALIFORNIA

HARTFORD

CONNECTICUT'S CAPITAL

AN ILLUSTRATED HISTORY

Glenn Weaver & Michael Swift

OPPOSITE PAGE: Harriet
Stark Eastman painted this
View of Hartford from the
east side of the Connecticut
River in 1846 or 1847. The
craft at the center of the picture
is a "horse-powered" ferry. To
propel the vessel, a horse walked
along the treadmill connected
to paddle wheels. (CHS)

PAGE SIX: This Kellogg
brothers lithograph from the
mid-19th century is the cover
of a piece of sheet music entitled
"Foot Guard Quick-Step." The
subject is the First Governor's
Foot Guard, assembled in front
of the State House. (CHS)

© 2003 American Historical Press
All Rights Reserved
Published 2003
Printed in the United States of America

Library of Congress Catalogue Card Number: 2003096193
ISBN: 1-892724-39-1

Bibliography: p. 237
Includes Index

Contents

CHAPTER

I
=

Settlement in the Wilderness

~HARTFORD, MASSACHU-
SETTS? CONNECTICUT WITHOUT HARTFORD, THE CITY
THAT HAS CONTRIBUTED SO MUCH TO THE STATE'S
character, traditions, and prosperity?

Only 11 years after the landing of the Pilgrims, the
nucleus of America's renowned Insurance City was res-
tive in Newtown, Massachusetts, on the north bank of
the Charles River and on the future site of Harvard
University.

There, in one of the Massachusetts Bay Colony's more
affluent towns, its inhabitants enjoyed the services of the
skilled craftsmen essential to material comfort in a small
community and also those of two learned clergymen: the
Reverend Thomas Hooker, the pastor of the church, and
the Reverend Samuel Stone, the teacher, as the assistant
minister was then called.

But all was not well in this little palisaded village. The
low-lying land was not particularly fertile, and the
town's restricted territory was inadequate to its farming

and grazing needs. Furthermore, Hooker had become involved in a theological controversy with the Reverend John Cotton of the Boston church. Cotton insisted that faith went before good works. This was sound Calvinist doctrine, but Cotton saw fit to make Hooker his foil by charging that the Newtown pastor had made too much of teaching. Nor could Hooker accept Cotton's idea that only the "regenerate" could be admitted to the church and, ultimately, to the franchise. Both Cotton and Hooker had what were regarded as excellent credentials—academic and spiritual—and the 17th-century historian William Hubbard observed that "nature did not allow two suns to shine at the same time."

The parting of the ways came soon, for on March 15, 1634, the Massachusetts General Court granted the Newtown people permission "to seek out some more convenient place." The Newtown leaders investigated several sites within the territory assigned to the Bay Colony by the Charter of 1628. None was found satisfactory, and attention turned to the Connecticut River Valley. In July of 1635, six Newtown men journeyed westward to a place the Indians called Sukiaug, at the confluence of the Connecticut and Little rivers.

Although the Dutch had already established a trading station (1633), The House of Good Hope, on the south bank of the Little River, there were overwhelming considerations in the site's favor. Some five miles to the north, the Plymouth Colony also had established a trading post that year. Close by, people from Newtown's neighbor, Dorchester, were already beginning the settlement that would become Windsor; and five miles to the south, John Oldham had begun what was to become Wethersfield. Thus, there would be friendly neighbors among the English. The Dutch settlement would be of little cause for concern, as that was intended solely as a trading operation. Furthermore, the Indians were peaceful and were eager to work out an arrangement in regard to possession of the land and for trade in furs and corn.

During the summer of 1635, the Newtown people were able to sell out to a group of Englishmen led by the Reverend Thomas Shepard. A complete transfer of property was arranged, and the new community, set up by Shepard's people, was, in February, 1636, decreed by the Massachusetts General Court to be the Town of Cambridge.

Meanwhile, during the late summer of 1635, 12 men had gone to Sukiaug to make the first preparations, and in October of that year a larger band of some 60 Newtown men, women, and children followed. Fall was in the air, and the first need was to provide shelter for the winter. On a site just upstream from the Dutch fort, these pioneers set themselves to the construction of dugout huts along the steep riverbank.

Winter came early, and it was severe. By mid-November the Connecticut River had frozen over. Food became scarce, and the chilled little band barely survived on roots, acorns, and small game. Thirteen men decided to return to Massachusetts. Of these, one died on the way back to Newtown, but the other 12 made it safely, certainly to be much berated by Thomas Hooker.

Those who remained kept busy. On Sunday all attended religious services, and on all other days, weather permitting, home lots were surveyed and mapped in anticipation of the arrival in the spring of the larger body. For themselves, these original settlers laid out lots along the south bank of the Little River. For those yet to come, lots were plotted on the north bank. A large central common (now State House Square) or Meetinghouse Yard was set off some quarter of a mile to the north. Also included in the surveying project was the laying out (on paper, at least) of the first streets. Between stints at surveying, all able-bodied men in the settlement worked at

John Winthrop, Sr. (1588-
1649), top, was the first
governor of the Massachusetts
Bay Colony. His son, above,
John Winthrop, Jr. (1606-
1676), served as governor of
Connecticut in 1636-1637,
1657, and 1659-1676. From
Cirker, Dictionary of
American Portraits, Dover,
1967

putting up a crude palisade for protection against both the Indians and the Dutch.

The settlement had been made far below the southern boundary of Massachu-setts, as had the Dorchester and Oldham settlements. They were actually "squat-tings," made outside any effective jurisdiction. Realizing the precariousness of their situation, the leaders of the three communities sought some sort of legal foundation. Some suggested that they seek recognition by the Plymouth Colony, as, according to one reading of that colony's land patent from the Council for New England, the set-tlements would fall within Plymouth territory. When it was agreed that this grant was of questionable validity and that Plymouth itself was little more than a squatting colony, attention turned to the Warwick Patentees.

On March 19, 1631/2, the Earl of Warwick, president of the Council for New England, had transferred certain loosely defined New England lands to a group of English Puritan gentlemen and nobles, including Lord Saye and Sele, Lord Brook, and Lord Rich. Anticipating a civil war in England, the patentees were hopeful of setting up a refuge in the New World, should the Puritans in the Mother Country come under serious disadvantage. John Winthrop, Jr., had been sent to America in late 1635 with the title of governor and with instructions to erect a fort at the mouth of the Connecticut, and here was where the interests of the Connecticut River settle-ments, the patentees, and the Winthrop family converged.

John Winthrop, Sr., then deputy governor of the Bay Colony, prevailed upon the governor, Sir Henry Vane, to make an accommodation. A plan was devised whereby the river settlers would recognize Winthrop, Jr., as governor for one year, and the Connecticut people would maintain an informal relationship with Massachusetts.

On March 3, 1635/6, the Massachusetts General Court commissioned eight men to carry on the functions of government in the new settlements, allowing them to hold courts of law, adopt local ordinances, and declare war. These magistrates were to serve for one year, and after that the "plantation" would be free to adopt any form of government it would choose. Of the eight magistrates—Roger Ludlow, William Phillips, William Pynchon, Henry Smith, John Steele, William Swaine, Andrew Ward, and William Westwood—five met in Newtown to swear in Samuel Wakeman as constable.

All was now ready for the final move from Newtown on the Charles to New-town on the Connecticut. On May 31, 1636, about 100 men, women, and children started westward by land, taking with them some 160 head of cattle.

Each head of family proceeded to his designated land, where a small dugout or similar makeshift was provided. And as it was still not yet midsummer, all began set-ting up more comfortable structures. Within the year, the last of the dugouts had been filled in, and soon householders were adding second rooms, lean-tos, and even second stories.

While these simple homes were being built, the mansion under construction for entrepreneur George Wyllys must have seemed something of an anachronism. That Wyllys was a personage was evident in the fact that his lot (bounded by present Main, Charter Oak, Governor, and Wyllys streets) was roughly four times the size of the largest of the others. Wyllys was of gentle birth and had been lord of the manor of Fenny Compton in Warwickshire. He was also one of the wealthiest men in all New England, and although a freeman of Newtown, Massachusetts, he was so involved in the Indian trade on the Maine coast that he was unable to accompany the settlers to the new Newtown in 1636. He did, however, signify his intention to move to the colony (which he ultimately did in 1638) by commissioning his steward,

ABOVE: *The first meetinghouse was a very plain structure, both inside and out.* (CHS)

ABOVE RIGHT: *There were no photographers present when the Newtown congregation arrived, but the dedication of Hartford's new stone bridge in 1908 was occasion for a reenactment. President W. Douglas Mackenzie of the Hartford Theological Seminary took the part of Thomas Hooker.* (CHS)

William Gibbons, to build a replica of his English manor house. With the assistance of 20 indentured servants, Gibbons, beginning in the summer of 1636, erected a splendid nine-room residence, set off by formal gardens and surrounded by stables, barns, and various other outbuildings. The Wyllys mansion was unquestionably the most elegant in New England.

Although the more modest homes were hardly as comfortable, most of them, too, were soon surrounded by barns, sheds, shops, and "necessary houses." Within the simple dwellings were equally simple furnishings—chests, benches, tables, and beds, some brought from England, and some homemade. Pewter substituted for silver, and wood for chinaware. Especially lacking were chairs. Usually there was one for the master; the rest of the family had to be satisfied with benches or stools.

Next, having provided shelter for both man and beast, all hands turned toward completion of the meetinghouse. This framed structure was 36 feet by 23 feet, with thatched hip roof, board shutters, and a door of heavy plank. Inside, it was totally without ornament, and its only furnishings were a pulpit and a series of rough benches. The first meetinghouse soon proved to be too small, and in 1638 it was replaced by a larger structure, located just west of the first one, which was then given to Thomas Hooker for use as a barn. The new meetinghouse was made more commodious by the addition of a gallery in 1646.

The congregation had been in existence since 1632, and there was no problem in keeping the society (as congregations then were called) afloat. All residents, members or not, were at first required to attend the two Sunday services as well as the Thursday lecture. Attendance was never a problem, but the question of where one would sit within the meetinghouse was quite a different matter. Each New England congregation was expected to "seat the meeting" every few years, when a committee would reassign seats "according to the dignity of the family." The first seating took place on March 13, 1640/1, and although we do not have any contemporary record as to the results, it may be assumed that there was probably a mixture of joy and gloom, according to where one placed on this primary indicator of social standing.

When the magistrates turned to making an arrangement with the Indians, Sequassin, the Sukiaug Chief, granted lands extending from present Manchester to six miles west of the Connecticut River. Although the Indians were not familiar with the English concept of landholding, and although the purchase price was small, the agreement apparently met with their satisfaction.

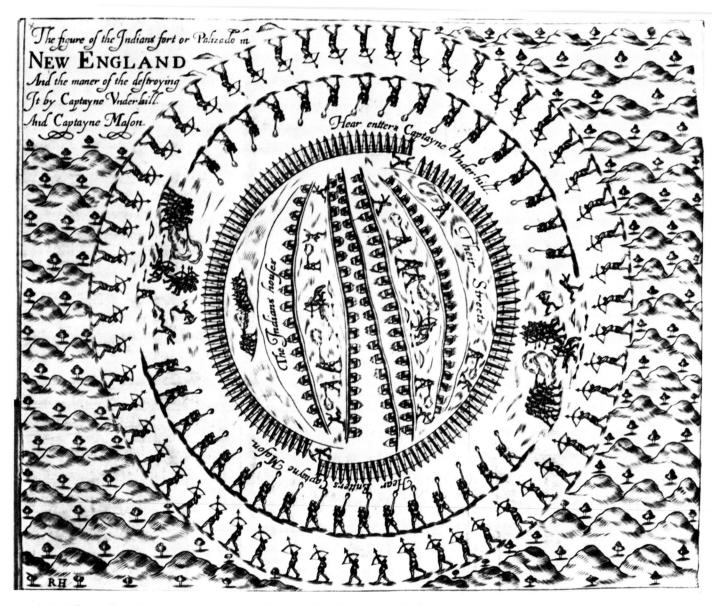

The figure of the Indians fort or Palizado in
NEW ENGLAND
And the maner of the destroying
It by Captayne Vnderhill
And Captayne Mason.

Hear enttera Captayne Vnderhill

Their Streets

The Indians houses

Hear Enttera Captayne Mason

RH

*In 1637 Captain John Mason
was sent from Hartford in
command of troops who faced
the task of clearing out the
Pequot fort at Underhill, near
Mystic. This was the plan for
capturing the Indian
stronghold and "the manner
of destroying it." (CHS)*

During the first year, all functions of government were carried out by the magistrates and the constable. Even the influence of John Winthrop dwindled rapidly, and the magistrates seemed oblivious of the fact that there was indeed still a governor.

On February 21, 1636/7, the magistrates changed the name of Newtown to Hartford, after the English home of the Reverend Samuel Stone. The name of Dorchester was also changed, to Windsor, and that of the Oldham settlement (Watertown) to Wethersfield.

The magistrates had also given much care to the matter of defense. A trainband (or militia corps) was organized for each of the settlements, and Major John Mason of Windsor was appointed to drill all males over 16 years of age at the monthly training day.

From the beginning the magistrates, or the commission, had existed as both a legislative body and, as they had tried several small cases under Massachusetts law, as a judicial body. But the commission and Winthrop's nominal term as governor were to expire on March 3, 1636/7, and a new arrangement would have to be made. On

March 28, 1637, the magistrates outlined a new plan of government whereby the inhabitants would elect a new body of eight magistrates (later to be called assistants), and each of the towns would send their committees, or deputies, as they would be known, to comprise a General Court for the entire plantation.

On May 1, 1637, the elected delegates assembled in the meetinghouse at Hartford as the first Court of Election. One of its first acts was to define the franchise: "admitted habitation" (i.e., the enjoyment of privilege within the town) would demand no religious test—all that would be required was a minimal property holding. The first General Court also fixed the price of Indian corn, declared wampum to be legal tender, awarded a monopoly for the fur trade, and declared war against the Pequot Indians.

The Pequot War grew out of a series of small clashes between the Pequots and the English, the culmination of which was the attack in February, 1636/7, upon Wethersfield. Connecticut's declaration of war was something of an accommodation to the Sukiaug Indians, a minor tribe subject to tribute to the larger and fierce Pequots. Also, the war represented the first instance of cooperation among the several New England colonies, as troops were sent from Connecticut, Massachusetts, and Plymouth.

Connecticut raised a force of 90 men, under command of John Mason, and, with Stone as chaplain and "Dr." (a courtesy title) John Olmsted as surgeon, Hartford alone sent 61. A band of Sequassin's braves accompanied the whites.

The Pequot War was brief but bloody, consisting of little more than the burning of two Pequot villages, one on the Mystic River, where some 600 Indian men, women, and children were slaughtered as they attempted to flee the Puritan firepower, and the other at present Southport, where, in "the Great Swamp Fight," the Mystic-massacre scene was repeated. Those who survived were taken as slaves. The adult males were sold in the West Indies, and the children and adult females were divided among the victorious military leaders.

The Sukiaugs were grateful to the English for the Pequot defeat, and in appreciation they ceded the portion of the North Meadows that had been retained by them according to the agreement of 1636 and moved their village to the South Meadows. This land was then divided into field lots for the returned Hartford veterans, and this low-lying section was long known as Soldiers Field.

The Pequot War left the colony with a debt of £620, and it was at this point that the General Court imposed its first general tax. Although Hartford's share of £251.2 might seem excessive by modern standards, there was an acceptance of the tax as an investment in a corporation in which dividends ultimately were to be realized in the form of additional grants from the town's still undivided lands.

In this, the Hartford homeholders were not to be disappointed. As Hartford's town government was being set up with the selection of townsmen (later selectmen) and the beginnings of town meetings in 1639, one of the principal functions of government at the local level was that of dividing and apportioning landholdings from what was still held in common by all members of the town.

One of the first divisions beyond the original town lots was made for the Adventurers, those heroes of the settlement's start—John Barnard, Richard Goodman, Stephen Hart, Matthew Merriam, James Olmsted, William Pantry, Thomas Scott, Thomas Stanley, John Steele, John Talcott, Richard Webb, and John Westwood. This tract, roughly in the vicinity of present Albany Avenue and Garden Street, was intended for the planting of field crops. Then, too, there was the Soldiers Field grant, also intended for farming purposes beyond what one could carry out on

Known as King Philip, this Indian was the second son of Massasoit. He later became Sachem of the Wampanoags, and he was greatly feared by the colonists when he ranged up and down the Connecticut Valley. (CHS)

his home lot. Other divisions followed, and in most cases all holders of home lots were entitled to outlying lots in each new division.

Perhaps the best interpretation of the rule of division was given by William DeLoss Love in his *Colonial History of Hartford* (Hartford, 1914, p. 122) as having been "according to one's estate, social standing, occupation, family, public service, convenience, and ability to improve the land."

Ever since the arrival of Hooker and his party, there had been a steady stream of newcomers from Massachusetts and from England. All who demonstrated that they were of good character were given lots, as old roads were extended and new ones were laid out, although newcomers were given home lots of one acre, half the size of the original lots.

In 1639 a Body of Proprietors was created to determine who had a right to share in the undivided lands. Those found to have such a claim were those who had shared the financial burden of the plantation's founding and who had paid taxes on real or

ABOVE: *Members of the Hartford Canoe Club, in appropriate costume, portray the Indians who may have "greeted" the Hooker congregation. (CHS)*

ABOVE RIGHT: *In 1636 Hooker's congregation crossed the Connecticut River several miles upstream from this spot, but for purposes of the bridge pageant, the group was rafted over from East Hartford. (CHS)*

personal property on a regular basis. This was simply to say that those who had participated in the earlier land division had closed the doors against the newcomers. Although later arrivals had no legal claim to land—even to a home lot—those possessed of talent in the skills and crafts then wanting in the community were given land "by the town's courtesy."

Obviously, the possession of land was a mark of status. It must be remembered, too, that land was essential to survival, as the community was entirely dependent upon itself for food and clothing, necessities that could be provided only by field and flock.

On each house lot there was a kitchen garden, and often there was an orchard. Each household had its own cattle that were branded and kept in the common cow yard; hay was cut in common from the meadows under the direction of the hay ward, and sheep were kept in the common flock by the town shepherd. Indian corn was the chief field crop, although there were small plantings of English wheat, rye, and peas. But even corn was in short supply during the early years, and much of that consumed by the settlers had to be purchased from the Indians. This crop, too, was soon recognized by the General Court as legal tender (or "commodity money"), and thus its value was fixed by law. In 1638, corn was priced (or fixed) at 5s. per bushel. In 1642, it fell to 2s. 6d., which remained the standard for several years.

In this early economy, every person farmed, few of them full-time but all of them part-time. Whatever one may have listed as his primary occupation, farming was his second, and whether he actually worked with his hands or whether he employed the services of servants or slaves, each householder, from the Reverend Thomas Hooker on down, farmed. While these part-time farmers were engaged in this subsistence type of agriculture, each was busily pursuing his primary "calling." John Barnard was a maltster; John Bidwell and Gregory Wolterton were tanners; Nicholas Clark was a carpenter; Nicholas Disbrow was both carpenter and cabinet-maker; John Cole was a cooper; Philip Davis was a tailor; Thomas Lord was a

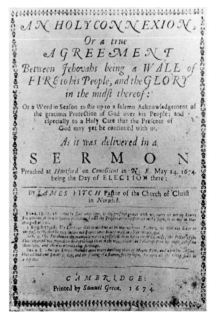

ABOVE: *This sermon was the first of the famous series of election sermons delivered to the General Assembly at the opening of the annual session in 1674. From Clark,* A History of Connecticut, *1914*

ABOVE LEFT: *This photograph, taken circa 1904, shows the general area of what was once Thomas Hooker's house and land.* (CHS)

blacksmith; and George Grove and John Baysey were weavers.

Each of these artisans held a variety of public offices. John Baysey, for example, rose from chimney viewer in 1649, surveyor of highways in 1652, constable in 1656, and fenceviewer in 1667, to townsman in 1669. Others held such posts as hay ward, juror, and rate and list maker (for purposes of taxation). In addition, each man took his turn at nighttime street patrolling, and each served in the trainband. Also, as every householder was required to keep both a fire ladder and fire bucket in readiness, these men constituted a volunteer fire department. And each was obligated to two days of service a year for repairs on the town roads.

Larger industrial undertakings that employed journeymen workers in addition to the master were sawmills, quarries, gristmills, and brick kilns. The sawmill, or saw pit, was a simple operation carried on by two men, and from the beginning of settlement several pits were producing boards and beams for houses and barns. Late in 1637, a brick kiln was opened on the site of the present railroad station. Foundation stones were quarried at the falls of the Little River not far from the brickyard.

Matthew Allyn built the first mill, which stood along the Little River. When Allyn moved to Windsor in 1644, he turned the mill over to his son, John. The younger Allyn had several partners in succession, and the Allyn partners formed other partnerships after John Allyn's death. The mill operated well into the 19th century, during which it was known as Imlay's Mill.

The town mill, called Hopkins' Mill for Edward Hopkins, the first operator, was built in 1640 and cost the town £120. Members of the town were assessed shares according to the size of their landholdings. These shares passed from hand to hand, and controlling interests were purchased by the individuals by whose names the town mill came to be known—"Brent's Mill" for Bela Brent, and later, "Todd's Mill" for Ira Todd.

These larger industries—milling, brickmaking, and quarrying—employed journeymen at wages, and thus a working class existed in Hartford from the very beginning. Quite early the matter of wage earning came before the Connecticut General Court, and in 1640 it passed "The Order Concerning Artificers and Laborers for Wages." When the men intended to be covered by the act began charging what were reported as exorbitant wages, the General Court on June 7, 1641, ordered that carpenters, plowwrights, wheelwrights, masons, joiners, smiths, and coopers should receive no more than 20d. for a day's work between March 10 and October 11, nor above 18d. for the remainder of the year. Hours of labor for these men were fixed at 11 for summer and 9 for winter. This was an early example of wage control, and its unworkable nature was demonstrated in its repeal on March 20, 1649/50, at which time the ceiling price on corn was also removed.

Nothing in Hartford during these early decades even remotely resembled a retail shop or general store. In 1643, the General Court granted authority for a weekly market in Hartford. This market, held in an open building on the southeast corner of Meetinghouse Yard, was something of a combination of English cattle fair, 20th-century flea market, and roadside vegetable stand. Two years later, Hartford was granted authority to hold two fairs each year. The fair differed from the market only in that it was conducted on a larger scale and was attended by buyers and sellers from other towns.

Although Hartford's early artisans were able to care for the day-to-day needs of the people, it was imperative that there be an external trade—both with the Indians and with the larger European world of commerce. Henry Stiles of Windsor got trade with the Indians off to a bad start when he exchanged some sort of firearm to the Indians for a quantity of corn. The General Court of April 26, 1636, ordered Stiles to make recovery "in a faire & legall waye, or else this corte will take [it] into further consideration." Stiles was unable to recover the weapon, but the incident prompted the Court to declare that any person who traded with the Indians "any piece or pistol or gun or powder or shott" would be dealt with severely.

In 1638, William Whiting and Thomas Stanton were given the Hartford monopoly on the Indian trade in corn and beaver skins. Two years later, Edward Hopkins was given license to trade with the Indians in Massachusetts, and, as corn soon became an exportable commodity, Hopkins and Whiting were given the sole privilege of sending corn to Plymouth and the Massachusetts Bay.

Whiting was then Hartford's leading merchant and was engaged in trading operations from the Piscataqua to Virginia. Whiting died in 1647, leaving the remarkably large estate of £2,854. His inventory revealed that he had then in his possession several hundred pounds' worth of furs and tobacco, a large supply of uten-

This two-story building with belfry is the second meetinghouse, pictured in 1640. The structure was built in 1638 next to the first meetinghouse, and a gallery was added in 1646 to further increase its size. (CHS)

sils intended for the Indian trade, and a sizable stock of hardware, clothing, spices, and miscellaneous household articles.

Thomas Stanton came to the colony from Virginia in 1639. Stanton always kept up his Virginia connections, sailing on numerous occasions to the First Colony in the interests of the tobacco trade, often in partnership with other Hartford men. Stanton's father-in-law, Thomas Lord, Hartford's first blacksmith, may have been a minor partner, but it was the blacksmith's son, Captain Richard Lord, who formed partnerships first with Stanton and later with Samuel Wyllys, the son of George Wyllys. Captain Richard Lord built Hartford's first warehouse, in which he stored grain, soap, salt, lime, and a great variety of what might be called general hardware. Lord died in 1662 and left an estate of £1,539. The captain's son, Richard Lord, Jr., was even more expansive, as he traveled frequently between Hartford and England. His estate came to a princely £5,786.

Samuel Wyllys had his own particular business interests, including part owner-ship in several sugar plantations in Antigua. Edward Hopkins was both an exporter of corn and beaver skins and an importer of English goods. Samuel Wakeman, perhaps the last of the first generation of Hartford merchants, was shot and killed in 1641 in the Bahamas, where he had gone in the hope of purchasing cotton. One of the most interesting early Hartford merchants was Thomas Olcott, who traded in tobacco with Virginia, transshipped the tobacco to Boston, and brought English goods back to Hartford. Olcott prospered in this form of triangular trade, and at his death in 1654 he left an estate of £1,466. 8s. 5d. His widow carried on the business for another 40 years and made her own small fortune as a sort of informal banker, lending money on mortgage security.

This early trade operated under considerable disadvantage. The sandbar at the mouth of the Connecticut River provided only 12 feet at high water. This limited the river traffic to vessels of 60 to 80 tons, and in extremely dry weather a sandbar at Middletown made that town the head of navigation for the small sloops and pinnaces in which Hartford's trade was carried on.

In Hartford these small vessels could sail up the Little River, perhaps as far as present Main Street, but quite early a landing place was established on the Connecticut, just south of the foot of present State Street. Here were built the earliest warehouses, and from this point was operated the ferry across the river.

The home of Thomas Hooker, a simple frame dwelling with the second story slightly overhanging the first, stood on School (now Arch) Street. (CHS)

II
=

Of Puritans, Dutchmen, and Regicides

~WHILE HARTFORD WAS BEING TRANSFORMED FROM A CRUDE FRONTIER SETTLEMENT TO A SELF-SUFFICIENT AGRICULTURAL village, Connecticut was undergoing the metamorphosis from plantation to colony. A General Court had been set up and was operating under the English Common Law, Massachusetts precedent, and a nominal authority of the Warwick Patentees. There was, however, no single document of constitutional force to limit and regularize the functions of government.

No one was more aware of this than Thomas Hooker, and on May 31, 1638, Hooker preached the famous sermon in which he declared that the foundation of governmental authority must always lie in "the free consent of the people." Hooker's words have often been misconstrued to the extent of making him a "democrat," but Hooker's "people" were not the people of the 20th century—far from it. To Hooker, "the people" were responsible, property-holding males.

It would be easy to think that Hooker's sermon provided the inspiration for the constitution that was to be drawn up, but work had already been begun on the Fundamental Orders, and Hooker was giving a preview of what was to come. The document was largely the work of Roger Ludlow of Windsor, the only man in the river towns with training in the law. The document was adopted on January 14, 1638/9, although it is uncertain whether ratification was by the magistrates and committees, by the freemen, or by all adult males.

The Orders provided for a form of government not much different from that already in operation. Two regular meetings of the General Court were to be held each year, one in September for the enactment of legislation and another in April, the so-called Court of Election, at which were to be chosen magistrates and colony secretary, treasurer, governor, and deputy governor. John Haynes was elected the first governor, and Roger Ludlow the deputy.

At about the same time that Haynes was elected governor, he purchased a lot across the Little River from George Wyllys' lot, and there he erected a handsome mansion of his own. Although not so elegant as that of Wyllys, it was an L-shaped structure that formed two sides of a "great court," as Haynes described it, the rectangular enclosure completed by attached barns, outhouses, stables, sheds, and a brew house.

Relations between the Hartford people and their Dutch neighbors had always been quite strained. Although the Dutch had never made any claim to the land north of the Little River, they were incensed when the earliest lots were extended to the very walls of the Dutch fort.

Actually, their House of Good Hope was a rather imposing facility, surrounded by a fortification of logs, reinforced at the corners with brick and stone. Inside, there were a two-story blockhouse, several sheds, a kitchen garden, and a cherry orchard — all within an enclosure of little more than an acre. Outside the wall there was a small burial ground.

At first, the two communities had largely ignored each other. When the Hartford people began planting fields near the Dutch fort, however, the Dutch tried to drive them off, and the Hartford men beat them with cudgels. Gysbert Opdyck, the Dutch commissary in charge, protested to Governor Haynes, and although Haynes met with Opdyck, no agreement could be reached. The following spring it was the Dutch who began to plow the land in question, whereupon Constable Thomas Hosmer appeared on the scene with 12 armed deputies. Although no blows were struck, the shouting of the Hartford men frightened the horses, which, breaking their traces, ran away. When they had gathered their animals, the Dutch finished planting the field of corn. That night the Englishmen replanted the same field, and the question might well be raised as to who was fooling whom.

From that point on, the situation deteriorated rapidly. Dutch horses strayed into Englishmen's fields, and Hartford homeholders impounded the strays. Englishmen were accused of stealing cattle from the Dutch, and the Reverend Samuel Stone reportedly took a cartload of meadow hay that had been cut on Dutch lands.

In the spring of 1641, the English built a fence to separate their own lands, or their own lands as they saw them, from those of the Dutch. The Dutch promptly tore it down, and the English retaliated by again attacking a Dutch plow team. However unbelievable these childish actions of otherwise staid Calvinist gentlemen might seem, blood had been shed at the last encounter, and Governor Edward Hopkins promptly called a halt to the antics. From then on, the English policy would be one of restraint.

ABOVE: Thomas Hooker's statement of the reason for the emigration from Massachusetts to Connecticut is surrounded by four Connecticut seals. Clockwise from upper left: seal of 1784, seal of 1622-1787, seal of 1711-1784, and English seal of colonial days. From Clark, A History of Connecticut, *1914*

ABOVE RIGHT: George Wyllys (1710-1796) served as Colony State Secretary from 1735-1796. His father, Hezekiah, held the office from 1712-1735, and George's son, Samuel, served from 1796-1810. This service of almost 100 years from a single family is an example of Connecticut's "steady habits." From Cirker, Dictionary of American Portraits, Dover, *1967*

For almost a decade thereafter there was an unsteady truce. Although the English took no further physical action, they did lodge complaints that the Dutch were urging Hartford servants to run away from their masters, receiving stolen goods, and performing marriages for couples whose unions had not been permitted by the Hartford authorities.

When the English Civil War broke out in 1642, the four New England Puritan colonies—Massachusetts, Plymouth, New Haven, and Connecticut—fearing that the Mother Country would no longer be able to provide for colonial defense, formed the Confederation of New England. The purpose of the Confederation (set up in 1643) was to promote the shared religious ideals, to improve commerce, and to provide for defense against both the Indians and the Dutch.

On September 19, 1650, commissioners from the Confederation of New England met with Dutch representatives in Hartford and signed a treaty that set the boundary line between New Netherland and Connecticut and confirmed the Dutch right to operate the House of Good Hope without interference from the English. But even the Treaty of Hartford did not provide for a working relationship between the two groups, and the situation was further aggravated with the outbreak in 1652 of the First Dutch War between England and Holland.

By 1653 Governor Peter Stuyvesant was again protesting "scores" of English depredations against the Dutch fort and its inhabitants. Late in June of that year, Captain John Underhill, acting for Providence Plantation, and without the blessing of either Connecticut or the Confederation of New England, seized Fort Good Hope. This was an embarrassment to Connecticut, and on April 6, 1654, the Connecticut General Court ordered the sequestering of the entire Dutch interest in Connecticut.

The Dutch had presented a threat from the outside, but there were also internal threats—moral threats—to Hartford's well-being that were, in their way, even more serious.

Much has been made of the fact that only a small portion of the people in any of the Puritan colonies were active church members, but the fact remains that all who came knew the rules of the game in advance, and most of them, initially at least, must have had some intention of abiding by them.

Connecticut Puritans were convinced that God would punish the sins of a colony by its destruction, and that punishment of the offending individual had to be both swift and vigorous. All New England statute books had long listed adultery, sodomy, and bestiality as capital offenses, and in each Puritan colony, executions for one or more of these crimes were carried out. Whippings were common, doubtless because of the small expense involved and because they provided examples of the wages of sin. Lesser offenses were punished by fines. Imprisonments were both rare and brief.

It would seem that few moral offenses were committed by the responsible adults of the first generation. There were, of course, exceptions, such as the prodigious example of promiscuity by the wife of proprietor Nicholas Disbrow, who was convicted in 1640 of "wanton dalliance" with three men. One of the three was none other than Nicholas Olmsted, one of the original settlers. For his part, Olmsted was fined £20 and ordered to stand in the pillory in Meetinghouse Yard.

"Single fornication" seems to have been the most common offense, and its extent must have been even greater than the available records would indicate. Only such cases were brought to light as those involving the birth of bastard children or couples who had their first child less than seven months after marriage. At times, the cases involving fornication seemed to dominate the docket. In the earlier years the punishment was invariably whipping, even though marriage followed, and there was always, of course, the public confession in the meetinghouse, after which the guilty parties were admonished and sometimes excommunicated.

The "natural" offenses against morality were bad enough, but with witchcraft what was involved was not the natural, but the supernatural. In 1655 Nathaniel Greensmith and his wife arrived in Hartford. Neither was very popular from the beginning, and charges of witchcraft were soon brought. Both were found guilty. The wife was hanged in Meetinghouse Yard in late 1662, and the husband met a similar fate on January 25, 1662/3. The trial and execution attracted wide attention throughout New England, and it might be noted that Hartford's first witches were executed exactly 30 years before the more famous, or infamous, witchcraft trials at Salem, Massachusetts.

The most stable influence during these unstable times was, of course, the church. The "Congregational Way" presented an entirely new concept of "the church"—not The Church as "the Body of Christ," but "the church" as the covenanted body of all believers. Thus, the church was made up of those who through their conversion experience had first covenanted with God and then covenanted with other covenanted believers.

The church was totally autonomous, dependent only upon itself and holding no relationship to any other congregation. Having rejected the Anglican doctrine of Apostolic Succession, it was autonomous to the extent of ordaining its own officers, including the minister, the ruling elder, and the deacon, and both admitting to its fellowship those who had "owned the covenant" and excommunicating those who had broken the covenant with God and the congregation. Both men and women were admitted to membership, and soon the women were outnumbering the men, although, despite their superior numbers, women were allowed neither to hold office nor to speak at meetings. Newcomers to the town were admitted by letter of transfer

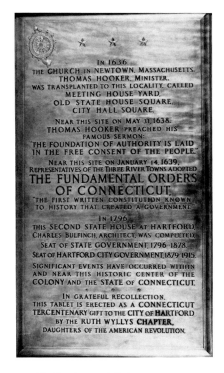

The Fundamental Orders are commemorated by this plaque, placed on the wall of the Old State House in 1935. (CHS)

21

Thomas Hooker's grave has never been found, but some believe he was buried in a part of the Ancient Burying Ground near the pulpit end of Center Church. (CHS)

from another congregation—and no questions asked. Even servants, free or bond, were admitted, provided the master would serve as spiritual overseer.

Hooker was less given to hellfire-and-damnation sermons than were the other ministers in the river towns, nor did Hooker seem to place any particular limits as to the exact nature of the conversion experience. Perhaps Hooker was satisfied that all were required by law to attend meeting, and, with the penalty for absence being 5s., the pews were always filled. Hooker preached in the morning, and Stone gave the afternoon discourse. Psalms were droned out, and prayers were fervent, long, and homemade. Sunday was a holy day but not a Holy Day, and, as the Congregationalists had completely rejected the Church year, Christmas, Easter, and the lesser Christian feasts and fasts were ignored.

During the summer of 1647 the Connecticut Valley was struck by an epidemic, the nature of which is not precisely known. The General Court took what measures it could, ordering that all meat offered for sale be inspected carefully, and also putting an end to the practice of throwing garbage upon the streets to be devoured by the town hogs. Despite those official precautions, there were several fatalities in Hartford, and among the victims was Thomas Hooker, who died on July 7.

With the passing of Hooker, church leadership fell to Samuel Stone, who proved immediately to be a difficult person with whom to deal. When Elder William Goodwin married Hooker's widow, the congregation split into two factions—those who sided with Stone and those who favored Goodwin. The division at first was one of personalities, but doctrine, too, was soon to widen the breach, and the particular point was the conversion experience and admission to the church.

The Massachusetts congregations had adopted the "Half-Way Covenant," whereby those who had not had the conversion experience were admitted to a sort of halfway membership—at least to the extent of having their children baptized, even though they were not themselves admitted to the Holy Communion. Stone accepted the principle, but a considerable portion of the congregation found it unacceptable.

It was on the matter of the selection of a colleague minister for Stone that most of the congregation's infighting occurred. A series of young candidates (all Harvard men) presented themselves to preach trial sermons: Jonathan Mitchell (1649); Michael Wigglesworth, later to write the famous poem *Day of Doom* (1653 and 1654); John Davis (1655); and John Cotton, Jr. (1659). In the case of Wigglesworth, Stone even refused to allow the congregation to vote on his candidacy. The possibility of having the younger John Cotton in Hartford was too much for Elder Goodwin, and he led a small group of the dissidents to settle in Hadley, Massachusetts.

Even this did not end the turmoil, and the General Court, in 1657 and again in 1659, appointed a Council of Ministers to investigate. The second Council suggested that the Hartford church adopt the Half-Way Covenant.

By 1660 there was sufficient harmony within the congregation to elect John Whiting, the son of Hartford's Major William Whiting, as colleague minister to Samuel Stone. When Stone died in 1663, Joseph Haynes, a son of the former governor, was selected as Stone's successor. The two young men proved to be a quarrelsome pair.

Haynes and a majority of the congregation insisted upon admitting according to the Half-Way Covenant. Whiting and an equally determined minority held to the "visible saints" idea, firmly insisting, with logic on their side, that there could be no such thing as a Half-Way Christian. On February 12, 1669/70, Whiting led 31 of his followers in organizing Second Church.

The separation was certainly not an amicable one. The Town Meeting cut off Whiting's salary, and the Proprietors refused to provide land for a meetinghouse; nor would the First Church allow the Second to use their building for worship. In 1672 the Town Meeting voted that taxes collected on the South Side be used to pay Whiting's salary, but on the matter of land there was no accommodation, and the congregation was obliged to purchase the first South Meetinghouse lot at the corner of present Sheldon and Main streets. The Second Congregation worshiped at first in private houses, but within a few years a South Meetinghouse was erected, an almost exact replica of that of First Church.

While these horrendous religious disputes were tearing the Hartford community apart, an old familiar name — that of John Winthrop, Jr. — was being tossed about. Although Winthrop lived in New London and also had a house in New Haven, Hartford leaders felt that were Winthrop to be attracted to Hartford, he would provide the leadership needed to bring calm to the troubled community. Hartford was also well aware of Winthrop's reputation as a medical practitioner, and were he to be induced to come, the community's medical needs would be well served.

Hartford's physicians had come and gone. Dr. Olmsted had long since left for Norwalk, and for several years no medical service was available. Following the epidemic of 1647, however, the General Court made efforts to provide for medical service and to license physicians, and in the course of the Court's discussions, the magistrates had consulted with Winthrop, who had come to Hartford on occasion to treat a patient or two.

Under Connecticut's licensing law, the General Court, in 1652, appointed Thomas Lord of Hartford as Colony Physician, setting his fees at 12d. for a home call in Hartford, 5s. for Windsor, 6s. for Wethersfield and Farmington, and 8s. for Middletown, plus a stipend of £15 from the colony treasury. In 1655, the Court licensed Daniel Porter, granting him a stipend of £6 and allowing him to charge 6s. for each call. Jasper Gunn was licensed in 1657, although probably with no colony stipend. But none of these men enjoyed a reputation comparable with that of Winthrop.

The first bait was offered in 1651, when Winthrop, probably with his consent, was elected Assistant. Although reelected each year following, he probably did not attend a single session of the General Court until the spring of 1653. Winthrop evidenced little interest in the official business of the colony, but the Hartford leaders persisted, and in 1657 he was actually elected governor. But Winthrop was coy. The General Court offered him the house and lands of the late Governor Haynes, but it was only after two delegations had met with him personally that Winthrop finally accepted, and even then it was with apparent reluctance.

In November of 1657 Winthrop moved his family to Hartford, but the move was not a total break, for Winthrop still maintained his houses in New Haven and New London, as well as his extensive sheep-raising operation on Fisher's Island.

In 1660 the Cromwellian Period came to an end in England, and Charles II was restored to the English throne. Winthrop was then acting as chief executive of his colony, devoting one or two days each week to the practice of medicine, overseeing his various commercial enterprises along the Connecticut shore, and carrying on the extensive scientific correspondence that established him as an authority on mineralogy, geology, mathematics, astronomy, chemistry, alchemy, and the occult "sciences" — a reputation that would result in his election to the Royal Society created by Charles II.

Winthrop had always had doubts regarding the legal status of the colony, particularly since the Fundamental Orders had been a self-entered-into arrangement, not a document emanating from the Crown. Others were of the same persuasion, and in 1662 Winthrop was sent to England to secure a Royal Charter, one, it was hoped, that would provide for a form of government essentially that laid down in the Fundamental Orders. Winthrop's mission was a total success, for the Connecticut Charter of 1662 deviated from the Orders in very few details. Furthermore, the Charter attached the neighboring colony of New Haven to the river towns.

The Charter was read publicly in Hartford on October 9, 1662, in what has been described as an "audience of the Freemen." The document was then given for safekeeping to young Lieutenant John Allyn.

The publication of the Charter fixed Hartford as colony capital. Winthrop stressed that the document implied that Hartford would be the seat of government, but this insistence was hardly necessary, for colony affairs had always centered about Hartford. It had already become the legislative center as the place of meetings of the General Court. When the Court of Assistants (the upper house of the General Court acting in judicial capacity) assumed the functions of a Superior Court, it, too, always met in Hartford. The town's importance as a legal center was fixed in 1666, when the colony was divided into four counties and Hartford was designated as Shire Town, or county seat, of Hartford County.

Hartford would remain the capital of the colony until 1701, when legislative sessions would begin to be shared with New Haven: the April session meeting in Hartford and the October session in New Haven. This arrangement would prevail until 1873, when Hartford would again become the sole capital. Hartford, little Hartford, with a population of a mere 4,000 inhabitants in 1662, thus became the scene of much coming and going and the stage upon which high drama regarding the success or failure of the small Puritan colony was to be played.

In 1662 a Royal Commission, sent by King Charles II to investigate conditions in the several New England colonies, arrived in Hartford. The commission had already been to the Bay Colony, where they had been treated in a most discourteous fashion. In Hartford, however, it was quite different, and John Allyn, their official host, did all that was possible to make their stay pleasant.

Soon thereafter Hartford received several less welcome visitors, Edward Whalley and William Goffe, two of the judges who had condemned Charles I to death, and in search of whom Charles II had sent a party of royal officials. The Regicides had come to Boston immediately upon the restoration of Charles II. When the pursuit became too hot, they moved southward, stopping at several places including Hartford along the way to New Haven, where, joined by another of the judges, John Dixwell, they were concealed, according to legend at least, in a cave on West Rock. The Regicides were never captured. Goffe went to Hatfield, Massachusetts, changed his name, and lived there until his death, although he may have resided for several years in Hartford, using the name of Mr. Cooke.

In 1675 King Philip's War broke out. The intent of Philip, the son of Massasoit, was to unite the North American Indians in the destruction of all English settlements. The war in southern New England lasted for less than two years, but these were busy times in Hartford. Military officers from the New England colonies met on several occasions in First Church Meetinghouse. Major John Talcott, Jr., was in command of Connecticut's several hundred volunteer militiamen, and the Reverend John Whiting served as chaplain.

In 1687 Hartford was visited briefly by a most distinguished and awesome gentleman, Sir Edmund Andros, Governor of the Dominion of New England. During his short stay, Connecticut underwent the most severe crisis in the colony's histo-

Appointed governor of the Dominion of New England, Sir Edmund Andros, under order of King James II, formally assumed control of Connecticut at Hartford on October 31, 1687. Andros demanded that the Connecticut Charter of 1662 be surrendered, and he suffered humiliation after it was "ghosted" away. From Cirker, Dictionary of American Portraits, Dover, 1967

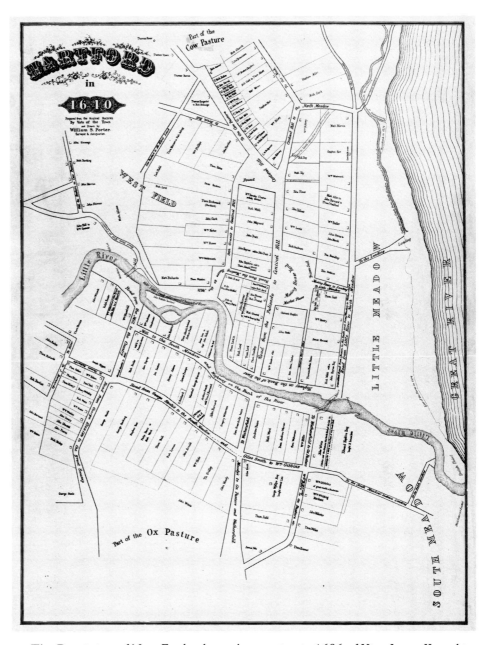

In 1640 spacious lots with surrounding fields and pastures were given to Hartfordites who demonstrated "good moral character." Courtesy, Geer's City Directory

ry. The Dominion of New England was the creation in 1686 of King James II, and its ostensible purpose was to improve trade and provide more adequately for defense. Originally, the Dominion included Massachusetts, Plymouth, Rhode Island, and Connecticut. Two years later, New Jersey and New York were added. Massachusetts had, because of her open persecution of Anglicans and her rough treatment of the several Royal Commissions that had visited that province, lost her charter in 1684; Plymouth was still a "squatter settlement" with no constitutional basis for existence whatever; and now the creation of the Dominion legally voided Connecticut's Charter of 1662 and Rhode Island's Charter of 1663.

Orders were sent to each of the New England colonies declaring that the old colony governments no longer existed, that the elected colony officials were to cease performing their regular duties, and that the provincial general courts were not to function. Instead of the colony assemblies, there would be a Council whose members would be appointed by the Crown and whose function would be to legislate in all matters, including that of taxation, for the entire Dominion. Although this was contrary to both English law and tradition, there was little that Connecticut could do but wait.

The blow came in October, 1687. On the 18th of that month, Andros, then in Boston, received orders to incorporate Connecticut formally into the Dominion. The following day, Andros wrote to Fitz-John Winthrop in New London, ordering the late governor's son to join him in Hartford. Robert Treat of Milford, Connecticut's elected governor, was sent neither an order nor an invitation to be present until three days later.

On October 26, Andros, with a retinue of 75 men, set out from Boston. On the morning of October 31, Andros crossed the Connecticut River on the ferry at Wethersfield. There he was met by a delegation of Connecticut officials, and, escorted by the Hartford County Troop of Horse, all rode to Hartford, where several companies of militiamen presented themselves for review in Meetinghouse Yard. Andros then proceeded to the Assembly Room on the second floor of First Church Meetinghouse.

Upon taking the governor's seat, Andros read the Royal Proclamation. Next he announced the appointment of Fitz-John Winthrop, Robert Treat, and John Allyn to the Dominion Council and proceeded to administer the oath of office, which the three took freely and with no apparent hesitation. Then, several persons who had been at odds with the old government were sworn in as judges, although, as if to soften the blow somewhat, Andros also renewed the commissions of all judges and justices who had been appointed at the last session of the General Assembly.

Finally, Andros demanded that the Charter of 1662 be surrendered. John Allyn, the colony secretary, obligingly placed the Charter on a table in the middle of the room. One by one, the old Connecticut statesmen rose to give their reasons why the Charter should not be returned, and after each plea, Andros, without showing the slightest sign of impatience, gave a lengthy counterargument. The debate continued until long after the early autumn sunset, and candles were brought in and lighted. As Andrew Leete of New Haven, the last speaker for the cause of Connecticut rule, began his argument, he fell into a faint, or feigned a faint, falling upon the table and dashing the candles to the floor.

When the candles were relighted, the Charter was gone. Tradition has it that the document was spirited from the room by Captain Joseph Wadsworth and hidden in the hollow of the huge oak tree that stood on Samuel Wyllys' yard. Perhaps it was placed in Wadsworth's strongbox. But whatever the truth of Hartford's famous legend, no amount of persuading on Andros' part could induce any of those in the room to go out and search for the document. Hence, Mr. Secretary Allyn was obliged to conclude the official account of the day's proceedings with the entry that Andros "took into his hands the Government of this colony." The government, yes: the Charter, no.

Andros returned to Boston, never again to set foot in Hartford, the place of his great humiliation. Nor was Andros long to remain in power. When news of the Glorious Revolution of 1688/9, which overthrew King James II, reached Boston, the authorities there put Andros on the first vessel sailing for England. Thus ended the Dominion of New England.

Connecticut immediately returned to the form of government provided in the Charter, and amazingly there was no retaliation against those who had supported Andros and the Dominion. Robert Treat was reelected governor at the next election, and his successor in that office was none other than Fitz-John Winthrop.

A large mural in the Supreme Court Chamber of the State Library building depicts the men who stood around the Charter (as the story goes) before candles were snuffed out and the document was whisked away and hidden in the hollow trunk of an oak tree. (CHS)

Connecticut's defiance of Sir Edmund Andros was an almost ludicrous incident—considering that the inhabitants of a small colony in a small village on the very edge of European civilization had defied the representative of the English Crown. Another impudent demonstration against royal authority would come during King William's War, an "American sideshow" to the larger European war known as the War of the League of Augsburg.

In this, the first of four "Inter-Colonial Wars," the New England colonies were asked to participate, and participate they most certainly did. Connecticut voted troops for both border defense against the French and the Indians and a proposed expedition against Canada. And, as she would do in each subsequent conflict, Hartford came forth with her full quota of militiamen. In 1689 Hartford troops were sent to reinforce Albany, New York, and in 1693 Hartford men were transported by water to help protect the inhabitants of eastern Massachusetts.

Hartford's participation in King William's War was neither dramatic nor extensive, but from the beginning of hostilities in 1689, every precaution was taken on the home front. Both town and colony authorities designated four strategically located Hartford dwellings as "fortified houses": Bartholomew Barnard's place on Centinel Hill (present Main and Morgan streets), Samuel Wyllys' mansion on Charter Oak Hill, James Steele's place on present Washington Street, and the dwelling of John Olcott on the Windsor Road. Fortunately, refuge never had to be taken in the fortified homes.

Now for the impudent incident. Early in the war, Governor Benjamin Fletcher of New York had been ordered by the Lords of Trade to assume control of the Connecticut Militia and to coordinate the operations of the troops of the two colonies. On October 13, 1693, Fletcher arrived in Hartford, prepared to publish his commission, assume command, and raise troops. The Assembly had already decided against placing all Connecticut militiamen under Fletcher's command, but the olive branch was extended by the Assembly's offering both men and money for the defense of the New York frontier.

The Hartford County Militia Regiment was holding its drill in Meetinghouse Yard, and Fletcher asked the officers to line the troops in formation. The officers complied, and Fletcher ordered an aide to read the official order to the assembled men, whereupon Captain Joseph Wadsworth ordered the drummers to "beat the drum." When the long drumroll had finally ceased, Fletcher again tried to have the order read. Once again the drums drowned out the aide's voice. Fletcher returned to New York, having actually accomplished most of his mission, but he certainly was not a happy man.

King William's War ended in 1697 with the Treaty of Ryswick, but the ensuing period of peace was a brief one, for in 1701 the colonies were called upon to participate in Queen Anne's War, the American phase of the War of the Spanish Succession.

This time the war actually came close to home, for the Indian allies of the French had been sent on the warpath, and there was again concern that Hartford might be attacked. Once more the fortified houses were placed in service, and the town's two "great guns" were put in working order. Hartford County's Council of War met frequently, and on several occasions Hartford hosted meetings of military leaders from neighboring colonies. Hartford men saw service in the guarding of Deerfield, after its burning by the Indians in 1704. Hartford men also participated in expeditions against Montreal, Quebec, and Port Royal on the Acadian Peninsula. This long and tedious conflict ended with the Treaty of Utrecht in 1713.

CHAPTER

III
##

From Puritan to Yankee

~DURING THE 18TH CEN-
TURY HARTFORD CHANGED, GRADUALLY OF COURSE,
FROM A SMALL AGRICULTURAL VILLAGE TO A SMALL
New England city. Hartford would remain small in com-
parison with Boston or Newport, Rhode Island, but it
would become a city nonetheless, and there would be
growing pains. During the century Hartford would
acquire what urban historians have called "the appurtenances of urban living." There would be schools,
taverns, shops, and improved transportation and communication, and the central village—or the "downtown"—would take on much of the appearance, at least,
of a small city.

There had been education in Hartford from the
beginning. Among the earliest women in Hartford were
those who conducted "dame schools." Acting upon the
prevailing English assumption that elementary education
should be provided in the home, they added the
children of others to their own to be taught reading,

writing, and arithmetic. Likewise, the ministers took older boys into their studies to teach them the Latin and Greek needed for admission to Harvard College.

These early teachers were supported entirely by fees paid by the students' parents. In 1642, however, the Town Meeting voted £30 per year "for ever" to be "settled upon the schools." Accordingly, in April of 1643, William Andrews was engaged to "keep the school" with a grant of £16 from the town, in addition to what he would collect in tuition fees, and Andrews and his 16 pupils were ensconced in a small schoolhouse erected on present Sheldon Street. Andrews taught the traditional grammar-school subjects, but in 1650 a Connecticut law required every town having 50 families to maintain an elementary school. In keeping with the law, Andrews added the three R's to his curriculum.

In the 1650s William Gibbons and John Talcott left small bequests (each of £5) toward keeping the school, but much larger encouragement was given by the will of former Governor Edward Hopkins, who died in England in 1657. When the estate was finally settled, Hartford received £400 for the maintenance of a Grammar School, and Hartford trustees accordingly erected a building on what is now Main Street. Here for many years was conducted the Hopkins Grammar School, where both grammar-school and elementary subjects were taught.

The Grammar School was relieved of its lower grades when a Connecticut law of 1690 ordered the setting up of free schools for the teaching of Latin, Greek, reading, writing, and arithmetic. Each school was to be open for at least six months of the year, and the master was to receive a salary of £66 to be paid one-half from colony funds and the remainder from the county. From that time on, elementary education was provided by the town common school and by numerous proprietary operations.

It was perhaps the success of the Grammar School that turned Hartford's leaders to thinking of a college. What was to become Yale University was founded in 1701 as The Collegiate School. It had been opened in Saybrook, and then followed a series of moves and divisions in the student body as the school's trustees tried to find a permanent location. In the spring of 1716, when it seemed that agreement was impossible, the trustees voted to allow the students to "go to other places for instruction, 'til the next Commencement." Under this temporary arrangement, the Hartford trustees, the Reverends Thomas Buckingham and Timothy Woodbridge, attempted to locate the troubled institution in the Hartford area, and their appointment of the young Elisha Williams of Wethersfield as tutor set their plan in motion.

On October 17 the trustees, with Woodbridge and Buckingham dissenting, voted to fix New Haven as the permanent location. Four of the students remained at Saybrook. Ten or so students went to New Haven. Another 14 placed themselves under Elisha Williams at Wethersfield, and among the students who assembled there in late October was Isaac Buckingham, son of the Reverend Thomas Buckingham. The Wethersfield arrangement called for instruction in Williams' home; the students boarded with families in the neighborhood.

On November 20, 1716, the Hartford Town Meeting, prodded by Woodbridge and Buckingham, voted to offer £1,000 to the Collegiate School, should the trustees decide on a Hartford location.

Meanwhile, the "seaside" trustees proceeded to erect a college building in New Haven, but Buckingham and Woodbridge persisted in their obstructionism at every step. When the trustees invited Elisha Williams to move to New Haven as senior tutor, the Hartford ministers persuaded Williams not to accept. And when commencement was held in New Haven on September 17, 1717, and four A.B. degrees were granted there, a lone student, Isaac Burr, was given a diploma at Wethersfield

Jonathan Edwards began the Great Awakening in 1734. From his pulpit in Northampton, Massachusetts, he inspired a new religious fervor throughout much of New England. From Cirker, Dictionary of American Portraits, *Dover, 1967*

29

by Timothy Woodbridge. Also, when all of the students were ordered to meet at New Haven in October, Woodbridge's will again prevailed: the Wethersfield group chose to remain with Williams.

On September 11, 1718, commencement was again held in New Haven, and 10 degrees were awarded. At that same time, the two Hartford trustees were holding their own commencement at Wethersfield, where Woodbridge distributed five diplomas as presiding trustee.

"Yale in Wethersfield" came to an end in June 1719, when the Wethersfield students finally took up residence in New Haven. Woodbridge and Buckingham had been defeated in their efforts to bring Yale to Hartford, but they enjoyed something of a moral victory in 1719 when both were elected as Hartford's representatives to the lower house of the General Assembly. Connecticut law forbade the seating of clergymen, and therefore neither was allowed to serve. Nevertheless, the election indicated that the reverend gentlemen and their efforts had the full support of Hartford's electorate. Another direct result of the college controversy was the vote in 1719 of the General Assembly to build a new State House in Hartford as compensation for the town's loss of the Collegiate School.

During the colonial period of American history, the tavern was the center of the community, much more so than the meetinghouse, for here men from all levels of society gathered to discuss public affairs, transact business, and exchange bits of news. Here were held the ordination balls given at the time of the installation of a new minister, and here, in the earlier days, was held an occasional meeting of the legislature or a court session. Here, also, were entertained such visitors from outside the community as would not be invited to share private entertainment.

The taverns were the scenes of much drinking, but one must remember that our colonial forebears were a drinking folk who could hardly have imagined sitting down to a meal without a pint of beer or cider. The Puritans enjoyed drinking, but they certainly detested drunkenness, which they regarded as the abuse of "God's creature," and here was where problems always arose.

Several of Hartford's earliest settlers had sold spirits to the Indians, and this prompted the General Court, in 1643, to forbid the sale of liquor to white or Indian by any unlicensed person. A law of 1647 forbade drinking more than one-half pint of wine at a sitting and spending more than one-half hour in a tavern. The Connecticut Code of 1650 forbade the playing of shuffleboard in the taverns. A law of 1656 added cards and dice to the proscribed amusements, and to complete the list, an act of 1686 added singing, dancing, and riotous conduct.

In the beginning, liquor was dispensed from private homes, and it was not until 1644 that the first inn was opened in Hartford. The commissioners of the New England Confederation had accepted an invitation to meet in Hartford in December of that year. The commissioners made clear, however, that they did not wish to hold their deliberations in the meetinghouse, nor did they care to accept any sort of private accommodations. On June 3, 1644, the General Court decreed that each town should maintain an inn, and, as to Hartford, during the meeting of the commission, John Steele, Andrew Bacon, and James Boosey would be a committee to secure an appropriate building to function as a public house. That chosen, just east of Meetinghouse Yard, was the home of Thomas Ford. Ford opened his home to the commission and continued to keep an inn until 1660.

Sometime before that date, Jeremy Adams opened a second inn on what is now the Travelers Block on Main Street, and it was here that Governor Andros spent the night of October 31, 1687. Legislative sessions were held here until the completion

Children in colonial Hartford learned their first lessons from a "hornbook" like this one. The paper on which the alphabet and Lord's Prayer had been printed was covered by a sheet of transparent horn to protect it from fingerprints and anything else that might soil or damage it. The wooden frame, with handle, was about four and one-quarter inches long. (CHS)

of the State House in 1720. Adams' place was also the official headquarters on Hartford County Militia training days. When Adams died in 1683, the business was taken over by Zachary Sandford. Members of Sandford's family operated it as the Black Horse Tavern until after the Revolution.

Other inns or taverns in early Hartford were those of Jonathan Gilbert (opened in 1663, "near Meeting House Lane"), Hezekiah Collier (opened in 1760, "just north of the Court House"), Frederick Bull (City Coffee House, successor to Collier's inn), Samuel Pelton (1747, "on the West Side of the square"), David Bull (1757, "The Bunch of Grapes," on the Pelton location), Cotton Murray (the "Globe," also on the west side of Main Street), and Joseph Mygatt (1656, near the present State Capitol). There were also several short-lived operations near the River Landing, as from time to time the ferryman was allowed to operate an inn in his own home.

Most of Hartford's early inns and taverns were eminently respectable. The one exception seems to have been that kept by Disbrow Spencer near the Landing. In defiance of the law, Spencer permitted gambling and even encouraged it, perhaps in the interest of taking a kitty from the players. On October 11, 1703, a brawl resulted from a card-game dispute. Several were injured, and those participants who could be identified were fined. Three years later, Spencer challenged one Henry Merry to a duel, and the two met on the Landing. Someone, however, had alerted the constables, who appeared on the scene and prevented the contest. Both were fined for disturbing the peace.

The existence and continued success of so many places of public accommodation were a reflection of Hartford's growing commercial importance. By the 1720s, what is now Main Street was becoming the center of a considerable market trade, as many new shops were being built. The old home lots were being divided and subdivided, and the newer mercantile buildings were being constructed side by side, usually with party walls separating the one from the other. And as these new structures were transforming the appearance of Hartford's retail center, there was always encroachment upon the public street, as each builder attempted to gain a few feet by pushing the front of his new building farther toward the public thoroughfare. The practice came to an end in 1758, when the Town Meeting ordered all property holders in the central part of the town to provide sidewalks.

But this new regulation did not stop encroachment upon the Ancient Burying Ground, a tract bounded originally by present Main, Pearl, Lewis, and Gold streets. The Burying Ground was "ancient" in that it was laid out in 1640, after several burials had been made in Meetinghouse Yard. At present Main and Gold streets, First Church's third meetinghouse was built in 1739, and after that one business building after another was erected between the meetinghouse and Pearl Street with a total disregard for the graves over which the structures were placed.

By the middle of the 18th century, the neighborhood of Meetinghouse Yard had at least a score of small shops catering to the retail trade, but they were a far cry from the 20th-century supermarket. The equipment was rudimentary. Walls were shelved for the display of small items, bins held grains and powders, and goods shipped in barrels or buckets were merely left in the opened containers. Each shop had a ledger desk that served as the office.

A sampling of ledgers kept by Hartford's 18th-century shopkeepers would reveal sales of nails, gunpowder, flints, cord, wire, brimstone, salt, axes, mohair, drugs, tiles, paper, pots, pans, needles, knives, indigo, logwood, earthenware, thimbles, buckles, buttons, thread, soap, looking glasses, pewter dishes, pepper, molasses, rum, raisins, mace, tea, sugar, flour, various grains and vegetables, lace, gloves, Sile-

John Spencer kept a tavern in Hartford on the road that led north to Windsor. This artifact from his tavern was painted with a facsimile of the Pennsylvania State Seal. (CHS)

sian linen, dimity, dorsetteens, and Italian crape.

These items were supplied from what in the colonial mercantile hierarchy was known as the inland merchant—the wholesaler, of whom there were perhaps a dozen in Hartford. The inland merchant, in turn, bought his goods from the "sedentary" or importing merchant who had direct trade with London or Bristol. Goods passed through the hands of such London exporters as Champion and Hayley, to Boston sedentary merchants like Thomas Hancock and his more famous nephew John, to an inland merchant such as Joseph Pitkin of "east-of-the-river" Hartford, to a shopkeeper "near the Meetinghouse," to Goodwife Smith who lived on the South Side along the road to Wethersfield.

In payment, the shopkeeper, of course, preferred money: Spanish silver dollars, Portuguese gold johnnies, or other French, Spanish, German, or Arabian coins that had come to Connecticut via the West India trade; English shillings, pence, or farthings; stray Massachusetts pine-tree shillings (last minted in 1684); Connecticut coppers (struck at Simsbury early in the century); bills of exchange; or the bills of credit of Connecticut and neighboring colonies. The great difficulty was that money of whatever sort was scarce throughout the colony.

Hartford customers regularly paid the shopkeeper with the products of the farm and forest: hogs, sheep, pork, beef, deerskins, tobacco, firewood, butter, cheeses, birch brooms, feathers, beeswax, grain, turnips, or malt. The shopkeeper passed these items on to the inland merchant, who in turn sent them to the sedentary merchant engaged in the West India or London trade. Customers also could perform such tasks as carting, carpentry, or mason work, and many availed themselves of the opportunity.

But above all, there was credit, and it was, in fact, by a form of credit known as "money-barter" that all 18th-century business was carried on, and all payments in money, goods, or services were merely part of this larger scheme. A bushel of grain was a matter of shillings; a paper of pins was a matter of pence. The goodwife needed her paper of pins on a certain day, and its purchase would not wait until grain had been harvested. Credit made possible the immediate sale. The credit that eased the purchases of the housewife was also enjoyed by the artisans of 18th-century Hartford, and the cabinetmaker, the tailor, or the wheelwright traded with the shopkeeper on the same terms.

Each shopkeeper employed a simple method of bookkeeping in his day-to-day business. An itemized record of purchases and payments was kept in a large ledger. There was a double spread (folio) for each customer. On the left-hand page were recorded sales to the individual, giving the value of the items in terms of pounds, shillings, and pence. Goods were given to customers as they were requested. On the right-hand page credits were entered, as payments were made in money, produce, or services. "Balancings" were made at the end of each year to determine in whose favor the balance stood, but there was still no need for an immediate cash settlement, for with the money-barter system, the process simply was repeated in the next year. Hartford throughout the colonial period never produced a single successful sedentary merchant, although Hartford's external trade was moderately successful in the West India trade and in that with the major ports of Boston and New York.

Few 18th-century Hartfordites cared to invest their capital in shipping. In 1680 Governor William Leete reported to the Lords of Trade that only one vessel listed Hartford as its home port, and Governor Joseph Talcott's report of 1730 was no more encouraging. As late as 1776 only seven Hartford merchants had interests in sailing vessels of any description.

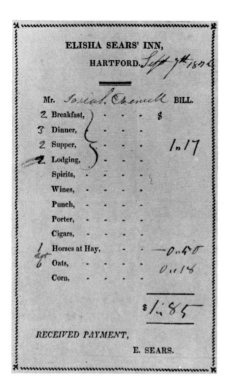

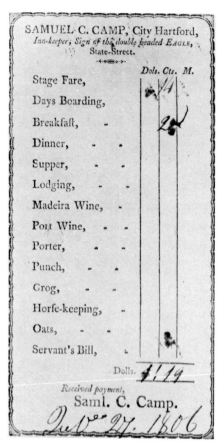

SAMUEL C. CAMP, City Hartford,
Inn-keeper, Sign of the double headed EAGLE,
State-Street.

	Dols. Cts. M.
Stage Fare,	
Days Boarding,	
Breakfast, -	
Dinner, - -	
Supper, - -	
Lodging, - -	
Madeira Wine, -	
Port Wine, - -	
Porter, - -	
Punch, - -	
Grog, - -	
Horse-keeping, -	
Oats, - -	
Servant's Bill, -	
	Dols. 4/19

Received payment,
Saml. C. Camp.

ABOVE AND OPPOSITE:
"Entertainment for Man and
Horse" was provided by
Hartford tavern-keepers, who
rendered itemized statements
listing food, wine, and grog
for the traveler, and hay, oats,
and corn for his horse.
(CHS)

There was, however, something of an exception in the case of vessels built in the small shipyard that had operated on the North Meadows from as early as 1730. The sloops and brigs built there were usually sold to shippers from other ports, although occasionally one would be loaded with Connecticut products and sent directly to an English or Irish port to be sold along with its cargo.

But even though Hartford men preferred to leave the 18th-century shipping business to others, Hartford was becoming quite busy. Improvements at the Landing Place had been begun as early as the 1670s, and as Centinel Hill was cut down, much of it was carted to the riverside, where it was used as landfill. In 1720 Samuel Thornton erected the first wharf, the only one built before the Revolution. Most merchants simply used the common Landing Place, and when vessels were too large to dock at either the wharf or the Landing, business was conducted on deck. Close by the Landing, warehouses were erected in rapid succession, and by mid-century there were 20 or more. Also to be found were smiths, coopers, carters, tavern keepers, and all who catered to the river trade or Hartford's wholesaling enterprises. New streets were opened between the river and Meetinghouse Yard in what a century before had been the Great Meadow, and King Street (present State Street) connected what could be regarded as the retail district with the wholesale district.

Given the nature of Hartford's trade, and perhaps because of Hartford's position as provincial capital, the several 18th-century wars had a profound effect upon the town's prosperity—or lack of it. King William's War (1689-1697) had been a small war, as far as Connecticut was concerned, but Queen Anne's War (1701-1713) was a much larger conflict. Hartford's inland merchants prospered during the war through sales of foodstuffs and other supplies to both the British Army and the colony government, but the most significant economic development during these war years was Connecticut's first issue of colony bills of credit in 1709.

These bills were wallet-size promissory notes issued by the colony in order to pay its debts in advance of the collection of taxes. Although they were a form of government borrowing, these bills of credit performed the function of money as they passed freely from hand to hand before redemption.

The economy took a sharp upward swing in 1741, when Great Britain and France again went to war in what was known in America as King George's War. As had happened during the earlier conflicts, the price of imports from Britain rose by about 30 percent, while locally produced commodities increased at a much slower rate. Hartford's merchants benefited slightly by British Army purchases, which were always paid for in coin, and housewives profited when British troops were billeted in Hartford homes (again for cash) during the winter months. But this hard money did not circulate locally for long, for the Hartford retailers, pressed by the English exporters, "put the squeeze" on every Hartford recipient of British silver.

Hartford's economic hopes rose in 1745, when poorly trained New England militiamen, supported by the British Navy, captured the supposedly impregnable French fortress at Louisbourg on Cape Breton Island, east of Nova Scotia. This almost unbelievable victory sent eager New England merchants to the island in the hope of expanding the Nova Scotia trade. Their hopes were dashed when in 1748 the Treaty of Aix-la-Chapelle returned Cape Breton Island to the French.

Almost a hundred Hartford men participated in the Cape Breton expedition. Hartford was immensely proud of her part in the Louisbourg victory, and news of the event was celebrated on July 8, 1745, with a huge ox roast in Meetinghouse Yard.

The signing of the peace treaty did nothing to end the economic uncertainty, for by the summer of 1748 the price spiral had peaked, and prices began to fall rapid-

The names of the first settlers of Hartford are cut into two of the sides of this obelisk, which stands in the Ancient Burying Ground. (CHS)

ly. Debts could not be collected at any level, and, for the first time in almost 40 years, Boston merchants were reluctant to accept Connecticut bills of credit, which Thomas Hancock declared to be worth little more in Massachusetts than oak leaves. By this time it was obvious to all that although war led to temporary economic prosperity, the long-range effect was one of impoverishment and depression. Connecticut trade was to remain sluggish until the outbreak of the French and Indian War.

Hostilities began on the Monongahela River in present Pennsylvania in the summer of 1754, but it was not until the following spring, with the prospect of large numbers of British regulars being sent to the colonies, that the full economic effect would be felt in Hartford. Beef and pork, two staples produced locally, rose rapidly in price.

Although no battles were fought in Connecticut, Hartford became a strategic center during the French and Indian War. Each spring the General Assembly voted several thousand troops for service in the Lake George region of upper New York. Hartford was the staging point for the march to Albany and the point at which supplies were gathered and sent overland by cart.

The French and Indian War years were years of activity for those who had both influence and capital, for between 1755 and 1758 the imports were double those of 1744-1748, and the increase was due largely to the shipment of military supplies. In 1757 a crop failure in Great Britain and Ireland forced the British to permit the colonists to ship provisions to the British Isles, and beef, pork, wheat, flour, and other commodities sold at higher prices than ever before. But despite the steady flow of army supplies through Hartford during the French and Indian War, no fortunes were made. Even John Ledyard, the leading merchant, engaged in no fewer than eight partnerships for this purpose but was little better off at the close of the war than he had been at the beginning.

European travelers and British officers who had served in America during the war expressed amazement at the "lavish" scale of living in both the seaboard cities and the larger inland towns such as Hartford, and they were quick to note that even those of modest station enjoyed many more creature comforts than their counterparts in England or on the European continent. Certainly the standard of living had advanced far above that of the pioneer stage, and this was reflected in the home. Chairs had long since taken the place of stools and benches, and chinaware had replaced pewter and wood on most tables. The clothing of the people was both comfortable and serviceable, although the fashion was a few years behind what was being worn in England—and perhaps a season or two behind the latest of Boston or New York.

Benjamin Franklin, writing about the British North American colonies in general, noted that an "almost general mediocracy of fortune" prevailed among the people, meaning that there were few individuals with notable wealth and an almost total absence of abject poverty, and he could easily have applied his generalization to the population of Hartford. Students of the colonial period of American history accept the £2,000 estate as the minimum for the well-to-do and the £5,000 figure as representing real wealth. Significantly, during the quarter century before the outbreak of the Revolution, there were in Hartford few of the former and none of the latter. Actually, Hartford was not a particularly wealthy town. The tax list for 1761, for example, gave the entire town's property value at £39,821 11s. 6d., a figure that placed Hartford as number 10 among Connecticut's towns.

The "mediocracy of fortune," however, did not mean that there was a "mediocracy" of status, for 18th-century society was a totally deferential one in

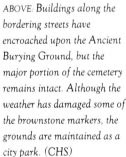

which each person had his place, knew his place, and was usually content with it.

At the top of the 18th-century social structure were what were called the "better sort"—in Connecticut known as "the Standing Order." These individuals, representing from 5 to 10 percent of the Hartford population, included the higher colony officials, the clergy of the Congregationalist establishment, the large landholders, and the more important merchants. It was also the "better sort" who held the judgeships, filled the higher militia ranks, and accepted the necessary, albeit onerous, commissions as justice of the peace. Some of them, although far from all, were members of "proprietary" families: those who, as descendants of early Hartford landholders, still maintained their rights to the common and undivided lands. Among these families were the Allyns, the Bunces, the Goodwins, the Hayneses, the Olmsteds, the Pitkins, the Seymours, and the Wadsworths.

Some 80 percent of Hartford's free, white population fell within what was called the "middling sort"—self-employed shopkeepers, artisans, and small farmers, all property holders or substantial renters, and all the owners of tools of production.

At the bottom of the social scale were those of the "meaner sort," the propertyless workers for wages on the farm or in the shop. This group, which comprised roughly 10 percent of the population, was a fluid one, for in the 18th century, with skilled workmen in great demand and short supply, it was easy for someone who had mastered his craft to start up his own business and thus move into the ranks of "middling sort." Furthermore, many of those working for wages were young, unmarried

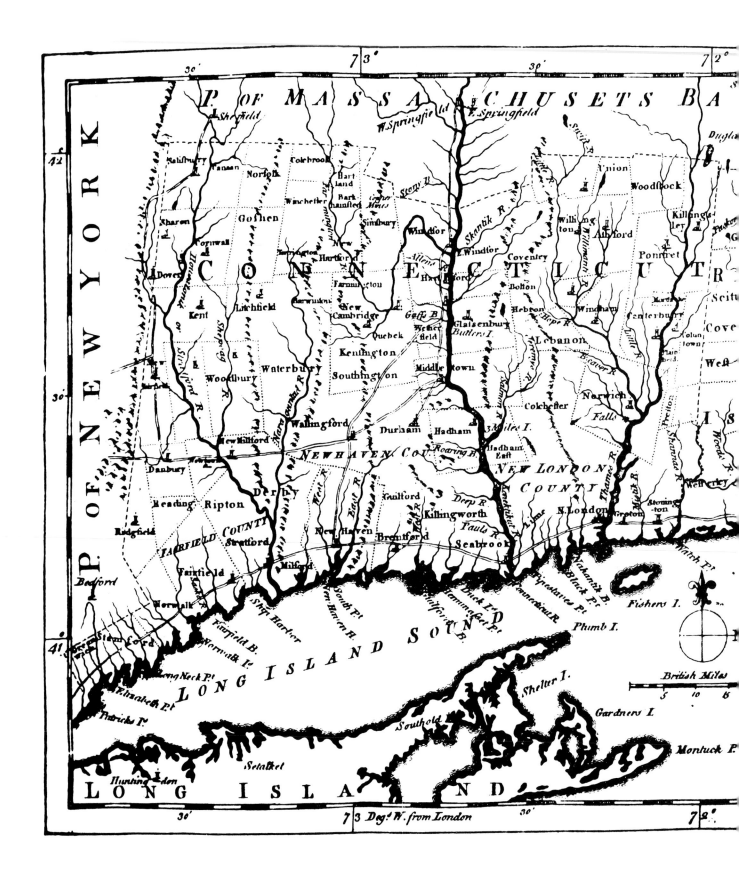

men from families of much higher station than their immediate situation would suggest; and they, too, would leave this lower group as they acquired land or opened shop in competition with a former employer.

Although there was little open snobbery, each individual had constant reminders of his place on the social scale. Only the "better sort" were addressed as "Mister" or "Madam." The "middling sort" were "Goodman" or "Goodwife." Those of the "meaner sort" were simply addressed by their first names. Seating in the meetinghouse was still "according to the dignity of the family," and children in the Grammar School were "placed" in similar fashion.

In the grave and at the ballot box, however, all were equal. On March 3, 1640, the Hartford Town Meeting appointed Thomas Woodford as sexton of the church, with the additional obligation to "attend the making of graves for any corpses deceased . . . [and to receive as compensation] . . . when such graves have been made[,] for the lesser sort, 2s. 6d., for the middle sort, 3s., and for the higher sort, 3s. 6d." The vote, however, had nothing to do with the location of any particular grave. Burials were made in the Burying Ground without distinction as to class or family. The rich were buried beside the poor, and so it was with bond or free, or with white or black. As there were no family plots, graves were dug at random as long as the land held out. When the city block, or what had not already been encroached upon by First Church Meetinghouse, the school, or the shops along the main street, had been filled with graves, bodies were laid one on top of another in several layers for almost two centuries. Although the records are incomplete, it is estimated that there were some 6,000 burials.

In voting, too, there was something of a "mix" as far as social class was concerned, and although political status was somewhat connected with social status and minimal wealth, these were not the only criteria. In 1706 the Connecticut Assembly adopted the qualifications for voting that prevailed until after the Revolution.

To be "admitted" to a town and thus be allowed to vote for local officers, a man had to be of legal age, hold property to the extent of £40, and be acceptable to the ecclesiastical authorities and a majority of the town's voters. To become a freeman, one had to—besides being admitted to the town—give "additional proof of civil conduct and conversation," be approved by the town selectmen, and, finally, be accepted at the annual Open Meeting of the Freemen. The limited available data would suggest that about 63 percent of Hartford's adult males, or about 75 percent of all heads of families, had attained the status of freeman and were thus eligible to vote

This 1758 map shows the division of Connecticut's early counties and townships. From Clark, A History of Connecticut, *1914*

in colony-wide elections and to hold any sort of colony office.

Not all of those living in colonial Hartford could make this transition—or, for that matter, any transition at all. Slavery had been brought to Hartford with the earliest settlers, as Edward Hopkins and others brought blacks with them from Massachusetts, and the Pequot War added the new element of Indian slavery. Virtually all well-to-do families owned a slave or two, although few owned more than three. The exception was the Reverend Timothy Woodbridge, who was noted for the large number of blacks listed among his personal property.

Hartford's slaves seem to have been treated fairly well. Usually they worked side by side with their masters, whether in the field or in the shop. Madam Sarah Knight, who traveled through Connecticut in 1704, although she did not pass through Hartford, noted the familiarity—to her an offensive familiarity—between master and slave, and she was shocked to observe that it was the custom for Connecticut slaves to eat at the same table as their masters.

Slaves were exempted from military duty, but this was a mark of servility, as it was a denial of the right to bear arms. Slaves were permitted to be away from their homes only with the master's permission and were subject to a 9 p.m. curfew. Although slaves were allowed to accumulate small personal property, they were forbidden to sell goods of any sort to whites.

Even the few free blacks were subject to restrictions. All blacks were required to carry identification passes, and free blacks were not allowed to enjoy social contact with slaves. Free blacks, furthermore, could not serve on juries, although they could (and did) testify in court. Blacks were not allowed to hold any sort of public office, nor could they become admitted inhabitants of the town.

A census of 1761 shows that of Hartford's population of 3,938, there were 109 persons listed as black. In 1774, when Hartford's population stood at 4,881, there were 150 blacks, quite a small figure when compared with New London's 552, Stonington's 456, Groton's 360, or even Colchester's 201.

Hartford never had a formal slave market such as those of Boston or Newport, but the slave trade was carried on in Hartford from the earliest days until the Revolution. Eighteenth-century advertisements for the sale of slave babies or teenage blacks more than suggest that Hartford's slaveholders had little regard for the sanctity of slave marriages or the black family. Nor would the repeated advertisements for runaway blacks convince many that Hartford's slaves were content with their lot. Only once, however, did the slaves act in concert and in open revolt, and that incident occurred in 1658, involving both blacks and Indians. Few of the details of the affair are known, but it is certain that several houses were destroyed.

In 1702 a mulatto slave named Abda ran away from his owner, Thomas Richards, and sought the protection of Captain Joseph Wadsworth of Charter Oak fame. When the town constables demanded that Wadsworth surrender the fugitive, the captain refused to turn Abda over, and, with the help of Wadsworth, the slave sued Richards for damages of £20 sterling for being held in bondage. Abda's defense was that his father was a Caucasian, but this was to be his undoing. When Governor Gurdon Saltonstall and the Council heard the case, the governor decreed that because Abda's mother was a black slave, Abda, too, was a slave, as "all persons born to Negro bondswomen" were legally slaves. Abda was returned to Richards. This decision remained for many years the legal foundation of slavery in the Nutmeg State.

About the middle of the century the custom of Negro Election Day, or "'Lection Day," began, when each May Hartford's blacks elected the black "governor."

The Reverend George Whitefield (1714-1770) was the itinerant English evangelist who led the "Great Awakening" in Connecticut. From Cirker, Dictionary of American Portraits, Dover, *1967*

Each slave was fitted out in his master's cast-off finery. The day began at 10 a.m. with a reception, then came the election, and finally the inauguration. The remainder of the day was spent in feasting and the enjoyment of games.

Although Negro Election Day did nothing to mitigate the slaves' rest-of-the-year situation, and although there were those who condemned the practice as having a demoralizing effect upon the participants, the attitude on the part of the masters was not a consciously patronizing one, and the office of black "governor" was a coveted honor for both the master and the slave.

Hartford's white population was almost unbelievably homogeneous. In the summer of 1659 one "David the Jew," and that was how he was known, appeared in Hartford as a small-time peddler. His stay was short, however, as he entered a house while the owners were absent and was fined 20s. and sent out of the community. The Town Meeting used the occasion to pass an ordinance allowing only such transients as should be "concented to" by the Meeting to remain in town. Whether it was by force of this ordinance or merely by chance, Hartford's white population remained almost completely English until long after the Revolution.

Religiously, too, there was a remarkable homogeneity, and Hartford's civil and religious leaders did all in their power to maintain the Congregationalist status quo. During the 1650s and 1660s several Quakers had been driven from the town, and in 1767 one William Edmundson, a professed Quaker, was ejected from First Church Meetinghouse with such force as to injure his arm seriously. John Tiley, a member of First Church, made history in 1745 when he declared himself to be a Baptist and was thereupon excommunicated.

Quakers and Baptists were easy for the established Congregationalists to handle, but with the Anglicans it was different. Anglicanism was the established religion in the Mother Country, and it was, after all, because of the Puritans' differences with England's bishops that the New England colonies had come into being in the first place. Connecticut had always been somewhat timid in taking an open stand against the Church, and the Church of England had come into Connecticut through the back door when the first Anglican mission was organized at Stratford in 1707.

Perhaps hoping to keep in favor with the British authorities, the General Assembly in 1708 passed an "Act of Toleration" that gave immunities to certain non-Congregationalists. Although the law recognized the legal existence of Anglicanism, the Connecticut authorities still collected the ecclesiastical taxes for the support of meetinghouse and minister and embarrassed the Churchmen by causing "public days of humiliation and prayer" to fall upon the great feast days of the Christian Kalender. An act of 1727 permitted the Anglicans to pay the ecclesiastical taxes to the support of their own church, although only such parishes as had a "resident minister" could claim the exemption. As the Anglican missionaries invariably served a number of towns, the parish of the missionary's residence alone seems to have benefited.

Anglicanism was attractive to many Connecticut people. The Great Awakening, the great revival of religion that reached its high point in the winter of 1740-1741, had split the Congregationalists into two mutually hostile factions: the "New Lights," who favored the emotionalism of the revival, and the "Old Lights," who opposed it. It was this division that allowed the Church of England to gain a first foothold in Hartford.

The Great Awakening began in Northampton, Massachusetts, with the revivalistic preaching of Jonathan Edwards in 1734. During the next few years there were revivals of religion throughout central Massachusetts and eastern Connecticut. Several New England ministers, hearing of the evangelistic successes of the Reverend

Pictured here are the signatures of nine generations of Hartford Wadsworths. The Wadsworths were leaders in Hartford's military, religious, economic, and cultural life. From Goucher, Wadsworth *or* The Charter Oak, *1904*

George Whitefield in the middle colonies, invited the famous revivalist to tour New England in the fall of 1740. Whitefield accepted the invitation, and in September he was officially welcomed to Connecticut by Governor Talcott and several of the leading clergy.

Through September and October, Whitefield traversed lower New England, from Newport to Boston, thence to Northampton and down the Connecticut River Valley, preaching to "large and affected congregations." Wherever the evangelist appeared, crowds of hearers, often in the thousands, were entranced by his magnetic personality and astounded by the novelty of extemporaneous preaching. And there were visible signs of "conversion"—cryings out, convulsions, and faintings. Whitefield played the game by his own rules, for into whichever town he went, he decided for himself which of his host pastors were "converted" and which were not. Those of whom he approved, he praised; those of whom he did not, he condemned. For the time, only those who were the objects of Whitefield's censure were unhappy.

Whitefield arrived in Hartford on October 22, 1740, and, despite the fact that the minister, the Reverend Daniel Wadsworth, was notably hostile to Whitefield's methods, preached in Hartford's First Church. Evidently, Whitefield gave an especially heavy dose of hellfire, for he recorded in his journal: "I did not spare them." One must wonder whether Wadsworth was among those not spared.

Whitefield had his imitators, and soon the colony was flooded with itinerant preachers, few of them with more than a modicum of theological learning. These, too, made converts and split congregations.

The colony was in a state of religious turmoil, and in 1741 the Hartford Association of Ministers adopted a resolution questioning the propriety of the emotional conversions. In 1742 the General Assembly passed a law forbidding an itinerant preacher from entering a pulpit except by invitation of the minister.

In May, 1742, the General Assembly tried two of the itinerants, James Davenport and Benjamin Parry, as dangerous to the peace of the colony. During the trial, Davenport addressed a large crowd from the steps of First Church Meetinghouse and almost provoked a riot when his followers attempted to free him and his codefendant. Forty militiamen were called out to keep order. Both defendants were found guilty of the charge, and Davenport was declared to be a madman. Following the verdict, Davenport was marched through files of militiamen to the Landing Place, where he was put on a boat and sent into exile on Long Island.

Whitefield and the others had made converts in Hartford, and these had been admitted to full membership in both First and Second churches. But as has been the case throughout the history of revivalism, many of the converts lapsed, and the long-range effect of the Awakening was a deadening of spirituality in both congregations. Membership fell off rapidly, and by the early 1770s First Church had only 15 male members in full communion.

The Anglicans had offered a peaceable and orderly alternative to the squabbling Congregationalist factions, and parishes were set up in Simsbury (1740), Wallingford (1741), and Middletown (1749). But despite the fact that several of Hartford's newer families had come directly from England and were members of the Church, Hartford's Congregationalist authorities stood firm. In 1761, however, the Reverend Thomas Davies of Litchfield County began holding Prayer Book services in private homes. Davies was soon joined by the Reverends Samuel Peters of Hebron and Jeremiah Leaming of Norwalk, who on one occasion secured use of the State House and attracted a crowd of more than 300, mostly Congregationalists who had come out of curiosity.

The first State House, completed in 1720, replaced Jeremy Adams' inn as the headquarters for legislative meetings. Freemen spent election days defining terms and delineating the functions of city officers. From Hartford, Connecticut, 1889

Benjamin Boardman (1731-1802) served as pastor of the Second (South) Church in Hartford from 1784-1789. (CHS)

Early in 1762 an Anglican parish was organized as Christ Church, and in October of that year land was purchased—just north of present Christ Church Cathedral. Building stones were gathered, but they were soon confiscated by several leading Congregationalists headed by Deacon Samuel Talcott, Jr., of First Church. The Anglicans sued for the recovery of their property, but without success. Soon came the Revolution, and public sentiment turned against the Church of England as being the religion of the enemy. It was not until 1792 that Christ Church, by this time called the Episcopal Church, was able to complete its building. At the time of the cornerstone laying, Prince Brewster, the chief mason and a loyal parishioner, took up his ceremonial trowel and declared: "I lay this stone for the foundation of an Episcopal Church, and Sam Talcott and the gates of Hell shall not prevail against it."

CHAPTER

IV
==

Hartford and the Revolution

~NEWS THAT THE PEACE
OF PARIS OF 1763 HAD BROUGHT THE FRENCH AND
INDIAN WAR TO AN END WAS RECEIVED JOYFULLY IN
Hartford. There were bonfires and fireworks, and the
bell in First Church steeple sounded for an hour. In each
of the meetinghouses sermons appropriate to the occasion were preached, and Almighty God was thanked
most heartily for the victory.

But the Peace of Paris did not mark the beginning of a
new and happier age for the colonials. While it is true that
the French menace to the north had been removed, the
British adopted a new tone in their relations with the colonies. Although the officials at Westminster had no intention of asking the colonies either to help pay for the cost of
the war or to reduce Britain's almost overwhelming
national debt, there was general agreement that the colonists should pay one-third of the support of several regiments of British troops to be stationed in British North
America, ostensibly for the protection of the inhabitants.

In March, 1764, Parliament passed the Sugar Act with the twofold purpose of raising revenue to defend the colonies and of putting an end to the molasses smuggling in which the colonists had long been engaged. The most serious provision, as far as the colonials were concerned, was the reduction of the duty on non-British West Indian molasses from 6d. to 3d. with the understanding that henceforth the duty would actually be collected.

When the British authorities undertook the strict enforcement of the Sugar Act, merchants, distillers, and farmers experienced new misfortunes when it was no longer possible for them to dispose of their agricultural products to those who traded with the West Indies. Nor was it long before the colonists—already short of media of exchange—felt the effects of decreased circulation of specie.

Hartford was not Boston, nor even New London, and given the small amount of the Hartford region's agricultural surpluses involved in the West Indies trade, the Sugar Act might have caused nothing more than a ripple, had not Hartford's first newspaper been started just as the act was going into effect.

On October 29, 1764, Thomas Green printed the first issue of the *Connecticut Courant*, in which he noted:

> ... it behooves the colonies to represent their grievances in the strongest point of light, and to unite in such measures as *will be effectual* to obtain redress. The northern colonists have sense enough, at least the sense of *feeling*; and can tell where the *shoe pinches.*

The *Courant* always would be anti-British—at first, mildly so, and later, vehemently. The *Courant* would soon become one of the largest-circulation newspapers in the colonies, the only paper to be distributed widely in northern Connecticut and western Massachusetts, and as such it would play a significant part in the shaping of public opinion in the back country.

One year after the passage of the Sugar Act, Parliament passed the Stamp Act, which provided that legal instruments drawn up in the colonies were to be executed on paper that bore a stamp of value from 2d. to £6, depending on the importance of the particular instrument, and that all almanacs, calendars, dice, newspapers, pamphlets, and playing cards were to carry the stamp also.

The Stamp Act aroused more opposition than had the Sugar Act, as it operated directly upon a larger—and more articulate—segment of the population. These lawyers, printers, and merchants complained bitterly that there was no silver with which to pay the stamp tax (as required by the act), as the effect of the Sugar Act had been to cause all specie to disappear from circulation.

Once more, the *Courant* spoke out. Publisher Thomas Green took particular delight in reporting in his pages the rough treatment of New Haven's Jared Ingersoll, the Stamp Distributor for Connecticut, as he set out from New Haven for Hartford to advise the governor and Council that he had accepted the position. On September 23, 1765, the *Courant* described Ingersoll's reception in Hartford:

> Last Wednesday Afternoon a large Company of able-bodied Men, came to Town (on Horseback) from the Eastern Part of this Government, and informed those who were willing to join them, that they were on their Way to New Haven to demand the Stamp Officer of this Colony to resign his Office ...
>
> On Thursday Morning, the whole Body, (including a considerable Number from this town) [Hartford] set off, on their intended Expedition, and in about an Hour met Mr. Ingersoll, at the Lower End of Weathersfield, and let him know their Business,—he at first refused to comply, but it was insisted upon, that he should resign his Office of

Stamp Master, so disagreeable to his Countrymen;—after many Proposals, he delivered the Resignation, mentioned below, which he read himself in the Hearing of the whole Company; he was then desired to pronounce the Words, *Liberty and Property*, three Times, which having done, the whole Body gave three Huzza's; Mr. Ingersoll, then went to a Tavern, and dined with several of the Company:

After Dinner, the Company told Mr. Ingersoll, as he was bound to Hartford, they would escort him there, which they did, to the Number of almost Five Hundred Persons on Horseback. After they arrived in Town, Mr. Ingersoll again read his Resignation in Public, when three Huzza's more were given, and the whole Company immediately dispersed without making the least Disturbance.

When the Stamp Act went into effect on November 1, 1765, a special edition of the *Courant* quoted newspapers in New Jersey, New York, Rhode Island, and Massachusetts against the Stamp Act. Then the *Courant* ceased publication for five weeks, ostensibly to avoid the hated tax, but as the stamped paper from England had not yet arrived in the colonies, it must be assumed that Thomas Green was simply making a gesture.

Eastern Connecticut, where the New Lights had dominated for 20 years, was the poorer section of the colony. It was in that radical section of the province that the extralegal organization known as the Sons of Liberty made its first appearance in the summer of 1765. Ingersoll was hanged in effigy in Lebanon, Windham, Norwich, and New London, and it was these Liberty Boys who had led in the humiliation of the Stamp Master in Wethersfield.

Governor Thomas Fitch and the conservatives were appalled by the action of the Sons of Liberty. William Pitkin, Sr., the deputy governor from east-of-the-river Hartford, did not express himself on the matter. Pitkin was not an active "Son," although William Jr. was.

Fitch issued a proclamation that condemned the tumults. The General Assembly voted to send three members to the Stamp Act Congress meeting in New York that fall, and at the same time it adopted a resolution condemning the riots, even though some of the members had themselves taken part.

Under the terms of the Stamp Act, Governor Fitch was required to take an oath to support the act. Fitch was fearful of British action against the colony if he defied the law, and yet he realized that a large portion of Connecticut's population did not believe he should take the oath. In late October the governor came to Hartford and asked the members of the Council to administer the oath. After a long debate, all of the "eastern" Assistants refused to take part in or even to witness the oath-giving ceremony and withdrew from the chamber.

On the day the act was to go into effect, a large crowd gathered at the Hartford State House and buried a copy of the Stamp Act and symbolically buried Governor Fitch with it. The "eastern men," who always had opposed Fitch, now had a winning issue to use against him, and the governor and the four Assistants who had cooperated with him were marked for political death.

On March 15, 1766, a colony-wide Sons of Liberty meeting was held in Hartford. William Pitkin, Jr., the clerk of the meeting, publicized the proceedings in signed notices in the newspapers. People other than Sons of Liberty were allowed to attend the first part of the meeting, which set up a Committee of Correspondence to write to Sons of Liberty in other colonies; but after this business was concluded, all spectators were asked to leave. Some Sons proposed to give the freemen "a lead" in the upcoming election. Even some of the Sons were shocked by this open interference in the election proceedings and answered that the general warning of the

Stamp Act officials were hanged in effigy during the winter of 1765-1766. From Grafton, The American Revolution, *1975*

The Hartford Courant
occupied this building on
State Street in 1880.
Established in 1764, the
Courant *enjoys prominence*
and respect throughout
Connecticut today. From
Hartford, Connecticut,
1889

election was lead enough, and that any other politicking would be "unconstitutional" and "fraught with the worst sorts of mischief." Nevertheless, the Sons endorsed William Pitkin and Jonathan Trumbull for governor and deputy governor.

The last edition of the *Courant* before the May voting day carried the news that the Stamp Act had been repealed by Parliament. Nevertheless, William Pitkin won the election by a landslide, bringing into office with him Jonathan Trumbull as deputy governor and the New Light, radical majority in the Assembly, which would remain in control through the Revolutionary period.

On May 23 Hartford celebrated the repeal of the Stamp Act, but the festivities were marred by an accident that left 6 persons dead and more than 20 injured. As the *Courant* reported the incident on May 26, 1766:

> The morning was ushered in by the ringing of bells; the shipping in the river displayed their colors; at 12 o'clock 21 cannon were discharged and the greatest preparations making for a general illumination.
>
> But sudden was the transition from the height of joy to extreme sorrow. A number of young gentlemen were preparing fireworks for the evening in the chamber of the large brick school house, under which a quantity of powder granted by the assembly for the purposes of the day, was deposited.
>
> Two companies of militia had just received a pound a man, by the delivery of which a train was scattered from the powder cask to the distance of three rods from the

house where a number of boys were collected who, undesignedly and unnoticed, set fire to the scattered powder which soon communicated to that within doors and in an instant reduced the building to a heap of rubbish.

The Stamp Act was dead, but Thomas Green, from his small office above James Mookler's barbershop just north of First Church Meetinghouse, continued to keep the fires of dissatisfaction aglow. Evidently he had hit the right editorial note, for his circulation grew rapidly. What had begun as a one-man operation was expanded in 1767, when Green apprenticed young Ebenezer Watson to the printers' trade. Watson must have been a quick learner, for soon Green took him into partnership, and when, in 1768, Green began a second newspaper in New Haven, Watson became the de facto publisher of the *Courant.* Watson, too, would berate the British on the slightest provocation, and he certainly had the knack of needling his Hartford readers into action by comparing what he regarded as Hartford's inaction with what was going on in other places.

In 1767 Parliament levied the so-called Townshend Acts, which imposed duties on lead, paper, tea, and painters' colors, all articles whose production in the colonies Britain had always discouraged, and the colonists, deferring to British wishes, had never seriously attempted. The colonials regarded this as a low blow, and response from the commercial centers was forthcoming. Boston and New York merchants adopted nonimportation agreements immediately, and in July, 1769, New London, Wethersfield, Norwich, Middletown, and New Haven merchants agreed not to import any English goods until the Townshend Acts were repealed. Oddly, no similar, supposedly binding, written agreement was made in Hartford, despite the "Indignation Meeting" held on October 13, 1770. During the nonimportation period, Hartford retailers were still receiving regular supplies of British tea.

Parliament removed all of the Townshend Duties except that on tea on April 12, 1770. But the repeal was greeted with no enthusiasm in Connecticut, as nonimportation had had a most positive effect on the provincial economy by creating a favorable balance of trade for the New England colonies.

On July 9, 1770, the New York merchants voted to end their nonimportation agreement, and the reaction in Connecticut was immediate, as most of the colony's merchants and farmers had benefited from the favorable balance of trade. Hartford merchants joined their fellows from all parts of the colony in a large gathering held in New Haven on September 13, and at that meeting it was agreed to continue nonimportation in Connecticut and to break off all commercial relations with New York.

But even more important than the effect of the repeal of nonimportation was the effect of the Boston Massacre, which had occurred on March 5, 1770. Bostonians had questioned the necessity of a military presence from the start, and the soldiers became the object of harassment. One such unfortunate incident occurred when small boys began to throw snowballs at the company of British regulars drilling in front of the Boston State House. A trigger-happy sergeant gave the order to fire, and five lives were lost.

Although there was the to-be-expected cry of "brutality," Boston took the "massacre" calmly, and, with John Adams as the lawyer for the defense, a court trial resulted in the acquittal of five of the British soldiers, with two others receiving a penalty of a slight (symbolic) branding on the hand.

Actually, the "massacre" was more of a sensation in Hartford than it was in Boston, for the ever-anti-British Ebenezer Watson burst forth in the March 19 issue of the *Courant* with a tirade that magnified the incident out of all proportion:

The town of Boston affords a recent and melancholy Demonstration of the destructive consequences of quartering Troops among Citizens in a Time of Peace, under a Pretence of supporting the Laws and aiding Civil Authority; every considerate and unprejudic'd Person among us was deeply imprest with the Apprehension of these Consequences when it was known that a Number of Regiments were ordered to this Town under such a Pretext, but in Reality to inforce oppressive Measures; to awe and controul the legislative as well as executive Power of the Province, and to quell a Spirit of Liberty, which however it may have been basely oppos'd and even ridicul'd by some, would do Honour to any Age or Country.

The flare-up over the Boston Massacre died down quickly, as had the indignation over New York's rescinding of her nonimportation agreement. Business went on as usual, and little was heard in Hartford about the alleged enormities of the British, as even Ebenezer Watson took a milder tone. This was a period of calm, but it was also the calm before the storm.

The storm came in 1773. Parliament, hoping to revive the fortunes of the East India Company, which had contributed so much during the recent war and now found itself in serious financial straits, permitted the company under the so-called Tea Act to sell its tea to colonial consignees without having it pass through the hands of middlemen. Although the tax of 3d. per pound was retained, the effect of the Tea Act was not at all what either the company or Parliament had expected. The retail price of tea was actually lower than it had been for many years, and this should have delighted the colonial consumer. But now what was to happen to the tons of tea the Boston merchants had smuggled in from Holland at a greatly inflated price?

Paul Revere's famous engraving of the Boston Massacre shows British soldiers firing on a defenseless group of citizens. From Grafton, The American Revolution, *1975*

The merchants decided to resist, and they turned to the Boston Sons of Liberty and a group of "town toughies," who, disguised as Indians, boarded the ship carrying the first consignment of tea and dumped the cargo into Boston Harbor. The company and Parliament were incensed, and the latter responded quickly with a series of acts known in the colonies as the "Intolerable Acts." The most significant to this account was the one declaring the port of Boston closed until restitution should be made to the East India Company.

Even before the Boston Tea Party of December 16, 1773, the *Courant* was attacking the British again, and Watson, completely distorting the purpose of the act, poetically urged the Bostonians to resist:

> Parliament an Act has made
> That will distress and ruin trade,
> To raise a tax as we are told,
> That will enslave both young and old;
> Look out poor Boston, make a stand,
> Don't suffer any Tea to land.

When news of the Tea Party reached Hartford, the *Courant* applauded the action as that of free-born men against their oppressors. Hartford's Sons of Liberty raised a "liberty tree" in Meetinghouse Yard, and a large crowd attended the ceremony. But there were probably few in Hartford who realized that the Tea Party marked the point of no return in British-Colonial relations. By the British insistence that the destroyed tea be paid for and the Bostonians' insistence that it would not, each side had jockeyed itself into a position from which there was no possible retreat.

Hartfordites were sympathetic with the Bostonians, and upon receiving news of the closing of the port, an informal committee raised several cartloads of foodstuffs to aid what the *Courant* described as the starving Bostonians.

This British cartoon from 1774 shows tea being forced upon a tarred and feathered tax collector. Hartfordites applauded the disregard for Royal authority. From Grafton, The American Revolution, *1975*

The port of Boston was not reopened, but the excitement in Hartford soon abated. Yet Watson's columns continued to put the British in the worst possible light, and the constant barrage of aspersions did much to drive more deeply the wedge between the radicals and the conservatives in Connecticut, something that was reflected in the name of "Whig" being taken by the former and the name of "Tory" being assigned to the latter.

Hartford's small group of Anglicans formed the nucleus of Hartford's Tories, and the Whig Congregationalists did all they could to make life uncomfortable for them. The Reverend Samuel Peters, who came to Hartford to hold Prayer Book services, was often the object of a discourtesy seldom encountered by a man of the cloth. The cleric's brother, Jonathan Peters, fared even worse, for that unfortunate gentleman was sent out of town on a rail, while the delighted Whigs chanted, "A Tory, a Tory, a cursed, damned churchman!" Ebenezer Watson was soon joined in his anti-British propagandizing by the Reverend Nathan Strong, who had become minister of First Church in 1774 and in his sermons preached John Locke's "right of revolution" under the guise of classical Calvinism.

ABOVE RIGHT: These 20 and 40 shilling notes are examples of Connecticut currency from the mid-1770s. By 1781 paper notes were virtually worthless. From Clark, A History of Connecticut, *1914*

On April 18 and 19, 1775, Massachusetts militiamen and British regulars shed the first blood of the American Revolution at Lexington and Concord. Hartford's response was instantaneous, and four companies of militiamen were sent to the Bay Colony as soon as word of the Battle of Lexington had reached Hartford.

On June 30 George Washington passed through Hartford on his way to Cambridge, Massachusetts, to assume command of the New England militiamen, who had been adopted by the Continental Congress as the Congressional Army. During his brief stay Washington was the guest of Colonel Jeremiah Wadsworth. In the summer, companies of volunteers from Virginia, Maryland, and Pennsylvania tarried briefly in Hartford on their way to participate in the siege of Boston. After the British evacuation of that city in March of 1776, many of these same troops passed through Hartford on their way to the defense of New York City.

Hartford was the staging point for the Ticonderoga Expedition when in early May, 1775, General Samuel Holden Parsons gathered men and provisions. And as the scene of military action moved into the province of New York, caravans of as many as 100 ox teams set out from Hartford to Poughkeepsie. In 1778, when Colonel Henry Champion of Colchester gathered his herd of beeves to be driven overland to Valley Forge, many of the animals were obtained in Hartford.

Morale was high in Hartford, and here the clergy did much to help. The Reverend Nathan Strong was in his element, for now he no longer needed to disguise his hatred of Britain and the Church of England. But no less ardent in support of the revolt was the Reverend Nathan Perkins of West Parish (now West Hartford), who, in a sermon preached to a company of volunteers about to leave for Cambridge, declared that "We must resist unto blood ... or be slaves."

BELOW: *The colonies rallied against the British, increasing their resistance after the Boston Tea Party in December 1773. From* Grafton, The American Revolution, *1975*

RIGHT: *It is said that when Washington and the French commander Rochambeau met in Hartford in September*

1780, they planned what became the final, decisive engagement of the Revolutionary War — the Battle of Yorktown. The meeting is memorialized on this plaque affixed to a boulder beside the Old State House. Courtesy, Society of the Descendants of the Founders of Hartford

ABOVE: *Hartford men participated in the capture of Fort Ticonderoga on May 10, 1775. British artillery captured at the fort would later serve the Continental Army well. From Grafton,* The American Revolution, *1975*

When the Continental Congress created Committees of Observation to carry out the policies of the Congress and to see that no British goods be allowed to enter the colonies, such a body was created for Hartford County. There were, at the outbreak of the Revolution, 153 merchants and shopkeepers who advertised the sale of imported goods, and the affairs of each had to be investigated carefully. Hartford's Whigs were quick to accuse, and almost a third of Hartford's merchants and shopkeepers appeared before the committee. Fortunately, most of them were found not to have violated any of the numerous regulations that were in effect.

An early sufferer from the effects of the war was the *Courant.* With the end of all importation from Britain, the printer soon ran out of the high-quality paper the *Courant* had always used, and the August 21, 1775, issue appeared on wrapping paper. The printer urged the women of the community to save linen and cotton rags for papermaking, as a paper mill was already under construction east of the river. The September 11 issue consisted of two pages rather than the usual four, and it contained an apology for the poor quality of newsprint.

Work on the paper mill proceeded slowly, and by the end of the year the *Courant* was forced to suspend publication for a month. Several issues were printed on inferior paper until March, when production at the mill began.

On January 27, 1778, the paper mill was destroyed in a fire that Hartford Whigs insisted had been set by Tories. The Connecticut General Assembly came to the rescue by authorizing a public lottery to raise money for a new mill, and in four months the new plant was in operation.

During the Revolution, Hartford suffered from a severe monetary inflation. In 1775, for example, the *Courant* cost 6s. a year. By 1779 a year's subscription had gone to 30s., which, the printer noted, "our Customers must judge to be very reasonable, especially considering the great Difficulty, Risque and Expense of procuring

Printing Material." Price, however, had no effect upon the *Courant*'s circulation. In 1775 there had been some 700 subscribers, while in 1778 there were about 800.

Ebenezer Watson did not live to enjoy the success of his paper, as he died of smallpox in September of 1777. His widow, Hannah, continued the business without interruption and soon took on as a partner 20-year-old George Goodwin, who had begun working on the *Courant* as a nine-year-old errand boy. On February 11, 1779, the Widow Watson married her next-door neighbor, Barzillai Hudson, a mason by trade and commandant of the county jail at Hartford. The following month the husband became a partner in the firm of Hudson & Goodwin, which published the *Courant*, assumed an interest in a second paper mill, and soon ventured into book publishing. Throughout the Revolution, the *Courant* steadfastly supported the Patriot cause, and its readers were first introduced to some of the more important documents of the times through its pages. Starting on February 19, 1776, the *Courant* devoted most of the space of four issues to a complete serialization of Thomas Paine's *Common Sense*. The *Courant* also reprinted all of the Declaration of Independence, considerable portions of the Articles of Confederation, and much of the Treaty of Paris of 1783.

Because of its inland location, Hartford was a relatively safe place for the incarceration of both Tories (or Loyalists, as they soon came to be called) and prisoners of war. Following the capture of Fort Ticonderoga, more than 50 prisoners were consigned to the Hartford jail. The August 5, 1776, issue of the *Courant* noted the arrival in Hartford of "a motley mess" of 20 or 30 Tories, and the following year prisoners taken at Princeton, New Jersey, also arrived. Of this group, the officers were permitted to go to Middletown each Sunday to attend Anglican services. Two of them were assisted in an attempted escape from Hartford jail by the Reverend Roger Viets, the Anglican rector at Simsbury. The parson was placed under house arrest for the remainder of the war.

Actually, life for the prisoners was reasonably comfortable. Officers were sometimes assigned to private homes rather than to the jail, and usually they were free to walk the streets during daylight hours.

Not all of Hartford's prisoners were so fortunate. On March 19, 1777, Moses Dunbar was hanged for treason, having admitted to accepting a commission in Fanning's King's American Loyalist Regiment. The execution took place on what was then known as Gallows Hill, today the site of Ogilby Hall at Trinity College. On November 10, 1778, David Farnsworth and John Blair were executed for both spying and passing counterfeit money, and on March 21, 1781, Alexander McDowell was hanged for desertion.

Hartford provided no military leaders during the war, but in the more pedestrian line of military supply Hartford excelled. Jeremiah Wadsworth was the leading Hartford merchant during the latter years of the war. He never concealed the fact that the greatest fortune made in Hartford to that time had come from his supplying the French troops, first in Newport and later as they marched toward Yorktown, Virginia, and that he always insisted he be paid for his produce and services in gold.

John Morgan, John Chenevard, and John Caldwell, known as "the three Johns," sometimes operated with Wadsworth and sometimes in competition. Several of the numerous Bull family also had State contracts, and the fact that they operated from Bull's Tavern, the best in town, gave them an advantage. Lesser figures were Ashbel Welles, Amassa King, Hezekiah Merril, and Daniel Olcott. All of these traders were identified at some time and in some way with Wadsworth's activities,

Jeremiah Wadsworth (1743-1804), a prominent Hartford merchant during the Revolution, was sometimes called "Hartford's First Citizen" because of his leadership in banking, insurance, and civic affairs. From Cirker, Dictionary of American Portraits, *Dover, 1967*

BELOW: This mahogany box was made for Jeremiah Wadsworth by Samuel Kneeland of Hartford, circa 1786. It was designed for the safe storage of Wadsworth's Oriental punch bowl. (CHS)

TOP: *The Marquis de Lafayette was among the distinguished military men who met with General Washington and Governor Trumbull in Hartford on September 20, 1780. Courtesy, Library of Congress*

ABOVE: *The Webb House in Wethersfield, where Washington and Rochambeau were entertained at their first meeting in 1781, was known as "Hospitality Hall." From Clark, A History of Connecticut, 1914*

although it is doubtful that they shared fully in the profits. Nevertheless, this was a cadre upon which Wadsworth was to depend later as he advanced bold plans for the improvement of Hartford's economy.

Military supply had brought money into Hartford, and the money circulated freely. But Hartford was also the center of considerable monetary speculation during the war and was referred to by contemporaries as the "Grand Focus" of Continental bills of credit for all of New England. Much money was in circulation, but all of it—except for Wadsworth's gold coins—was depreciated. It has been estimated that Hartford had as many as 70 individuals who were more than nominal security holders.

During the closing years of the war, much occurred in Hartford that would long be remembered. On May 19, 1780, Hartford experienced the "Dark Day," when at about 10 a.m., following a thunderstorm, darkness fell, causing many to think the end of the world was at hand. The General Assembly was in session, and one member, fearing it was indeed the Day of Judgment, moved that the Assembly be adjourned. Another member, old Abraham Davenport of Stamford, took a different view, declaring that either the Day of Judgment was at hand or it was not, and that in either case, nothing could be done about it. Davenport declared that if "the Day" were really at hand, he would prefer to be found by his Creator doing his duty. He therefore moved that candles be lighted and that business go on. The world, as the reader probably knows, did not come to an end, and it was soon learned that the darkness was caused by a forest fire to the west.

The Lord did not make his Second Coming to Hartford, but General Washington did. On September 20, 1780, Washington, along with General Henry Knox, the Marquis de Lafayette, the Comte de Rochambeau, and Admiral de Ternay, met with Governor Jonathan Trumbull at the home of Jeremiah Wadsworth. On March 7, 1781, Washington again passed through Hartford on his way to Newport to confer with the French. Six days later, he stopped briefly in Hartford on his return to Newburgh, New York. But the most significant gathering was that of the Commander in Chief, Governor Trumbull, Wadsworth, Rochambeau, and General le Chevalier de Chasteleux at the home of Joseph Webb in Wethersfield, where the details of the Yorktown campaign were worked out. This time Washington was entertained at a formal reception, highlighted by the firing of 13 cannon.

When the French Army finally moved to join the American troops in Virginia, the main body of troops was kept out of Hartford proper. From June 22 to June 25, 1781, the French camped east of the river. The French officers were entertained in the village, and a French military hospital was opened in Second Meetinghouse. On June 26 the French camped at Farmington, and the following day they moved on to Southington.

Although the enlisted men did not get into town, Hartford people visited the French camps by the hundreds, attracted particularly by the military bands, especially as few Hartfordites had ever in their lives heard concerted instrumental music. Each evening there were dances, and Hartford's young ladies enjoyed a brief social life that might have made Hartford's founders turn over in their graves in the Ancient Burying Ground.

Word of the signing of the Treaty of Paris arrived in Hartford on April 24, 1783. There was a huge celebration, with feasting, fireworks, and military drills. And indeed, there was something of a repeat of the 1766 celebration of the repeal of the Stamp Act, as the fireworks display got out of hand and resulted in the almost total destruction of the State House.

CHAPTER

V

A City of Steady Habits

~Hartford's apparent
wartime prosperity was again superficial.
Merchants had carried on extensive business,
but much of their payment had been in rapidly
depreciating currency, and several of Hartford's businessmen found themselves totally ruined.

As soon as the war ended, Britain began "dumping"
goods upon the American market. The "dumpers" soon
appeared in even the smaller ports, and in the summer
of 1785 the schooner *Peggy* sold English goods in large
quantities while lying at anchor near the Public Landing.

The period between 1783 and 1789 was the poorest
for commerce in American history. In 1784, for example, Britain sent merchandise to America to the value of
£3,700,000 and received only £750,000 in return, with
the difference made up by a severe drain on American
specie. The American merchants were embarrassed by
their rash purchases, as the imports included much of
what might be regarded as luxury goods, and by 1785

the Boston merchants were again pledging not to make any further purchases until the economic situation improved.

Hartford's public leaders saw the root of the new country's economic woes in the weakness of the central government under the Articles of Confederation, and they were outspoken in favor of a stronger national government with power to levy import duties.

Hartford's townspeople, however, felt differently. On September 16, 1783, the Town Meeting went on record as opposing any "encroachment upon the sovereignty and jurisdiction of the states" and urged the Connecticut state government to exercise whatever powers were necessary to regulate commerce and to develop direct foreign trade to such an extent as to relieve Hartford's dependence upon Boston and New York.

It was also at this same time, and in this same mood, that arguments were advanced for the incorporation of Hartford as a city. Within the Hartford mercantile community there were even those who felt that Hartford, despite its temporary depression, showed greater economic potential than New London and New Haven, both still recovering from the losses they had suffered from British attacks during the war. Hartford was just then beginning to develop a flatboat trade on the Connecticut River, and this suggested almost unlimited riches in the transport and marketing of agricultural products from the north. Jeremiah Wadsworth was even suggesting that a canal be cut around Enfield Falls. Noah Webster, of later dictionary fame, was a constant contributor to the *Courant*, always urging incorporation as a means of improving Hartford's economy, insisting that the town government was incapable of regulating "the internal police" and of providing adequate wharves and streets.

Hartford's downtown was becoming increasingly urban, while the outlying sections had undergone little change during the past hundred years. Hartford's compact downtown, with its 250 houses, was occupied by about 1,500 people, or roughly 31 percent of the town's population. East-of-the-River had been set off as a separate ecclesiastical society (Third Church) in 1694, and a meetinghouse had been built in 1699. The "easterners" found their interests becoming increasingly incompatible with those living downtown, and on four occasions—in 1769, 1774, 1780 and 1782—they had petitioned the General Assembly for incorporation as a separate town. West Division (to become West Hartford in 1854) was set off as West Parish in 1711, but there was then no particular interest in a separate town for the "westerners."

Hartford's town government had become quite cumbersome. In 1664 there had been but eight town officers: four selectmen, two constables, and two surveyors. By the eve of the American Revolution, the number had increased to 76! Town Meeting still functioned as the legislative branch of the town government, and the meetings, averaging between four and five a year during the 1770s and early 1780s, were generally orderly. Nevertheless, it was felt by many that the Town Meeting did little more than rubber-stamp action that had already been taken by the selectmen.

That Hartford's town government was inefficient was particularly obvious in the performance of the constabulary. Police protection was virtually nonexistent, as none of the four constables had any training, much energy, or even serious interest in his work, which always was performed part-time. When someone needed services such as those that would now be handled by the police, he simply ignored the constables and did the best he could on his own.

Even old Governor Trumbull soon came to support the idea that several of Connecticut's larger towns should be incorporated as cities, arguing that under city

Had we been sailing upstream on the Connecticut around 1825, we would have seen Hartford just past Wethersfield Cove. Our view of the city would have been very much like what Timothy Cole showed in this engraving. (CHS)

RIGHT: *The notice says "Watchmaker Only," but Thomas Hildrup made fine clocks as well, and he sold molasses, grain, tobacco, pickles, and assorted notions. In 1777 he assumed the duties of Deputy Postmaster, always operating the post office at his place of business. Since Hildrup moved 12 times in 18 years, many people must have wondered where to mail their letters! (CHS)*

ABOVE: *Thomas Hildrup's skill as an engraver is beautifully demonstrated on this watch case from about 1776. (CHS)*

THOMAS HILLDRUP,

WATCH MAKER ONLY,

At the shop for many years occupied by Dr. WILLIAM JEPSON, *a few rods North of the State-House,* HARTFORD,

PROPOSES, if properly encouraged, to open a Repository for buying and selling Watches, on commissions, they being in great demand, and not to be got in the usual way. Therefore, those persons that have any to dispose of, are requested to leave them as soon as possible---a regular book will be kept for the sales, that each party may be convinced of the justice done them. Also continues to repair, in a perfect and durable manner, and warrants them to perform well one year, casualties and very bad ones excepted. Gentlemen in the army, and others at a distance, forwarding their commands by post riders, &c. may depend on fidelity and dispatch. He desires such of his customers as have not an opportunity of applying personally, to be particular in directing their favours, as many have of late been carried elsewhere, to the deception of the parties. For the future, the work will have his name in types within the out side case. Constant attendance will be given from sun to sun, the year round. Every favour gratefully acknowledged, and punctually observed by the public's humble servant to command, THOMAS HILLDRUP.
Hartford, Nov. 15, 1776.
P.S. Four eight day CLOCKS, and a gold WATCH, for sale. Constant employ, and punctual payment to an assistant in the Watch business, who understands finishing. np8 3m

government, land values would "increase in two years sufficient to defray the city-charges of twenty years." To the thrifty Yankees, this was enough. Enough for the downtowners, at least, for as the businessmen became increasingly convinced of the virtue of incorporation, the people at the periphery refused to accept the arguments and strongly opposed incorporation.

But there was a bit of shenaniganism in the process that led to ultimate incorporation, as East-of-the-River was assisted in its fifth appeal for incorporation and was able to hold its first Town Meeting on December 8, 1783, as East Hartford. With the rural vote thus reduced, incorporation received a favorable vote at the Hartford Town Meeting of January 6, 1784. On May 24, 1784, Hartford received a charter as "The Mayor, Aldermen, Common Council and Freemen of the City of Hartford."

The original territory of the City of Hartford was a mere 1,700 acres, roughly equivalent to the settled area of about 1640. It was bounded by the Connecticut River on the east, present Wyllys Street on the south, Washington Street on the west, and Belden Street on the north.

June 28, 1784, was set as election day, and the freemen met at the State House. As there was little understanding of the titles and functions of "city" officers, much of the day was spent in defining terms—to say nothing of politicking. June 29 was something of a repeat of the 28th, but on June 30, a full complement of city officials was selected.

Thomas Seymour was elected mayor, an office he was to hold for 28 years. And, as during the following decades there was to be similar longevity in office noted in the Board of Aldermen and the Common Council, Connecticut's sobriquet, "The Land of Steady Habits," might well be applied to Hartford during these years as "The City of Steady Habits."

The list of aldermen and councilmen reads like a "Who's Who" of Hartford of the time. Aldermen were Samuel Wyllys, Jonathan Bull, Jesse Root, and Samuel

Marsh. Members of the Common Council were John Chenevard, Barnabas Deane, Ralph Pomeroy, James Church, Chauncey Goodrich, Peter Colt, John Olcott, John Caldwell, Zebulon Seymour, Zachariah Pratt, Ashbel Steel, William Nichols, John Trumbull, Barzillai Hudson, William Bull, Caleb Bull, John Morgan, Israel Seymour, Daniel Olcott, and Daniel Hensdale. Jacob Talcott and James Wells were sheriffs, Hezekiah Merril was treasurer, and William Adams was clerk.

Missing from the list was the name of Jeremiah Wadsworth, the most ardent of the pro-city men and one who might properly have been called Hartford's "First Citizen." Wadsworth was then in Europe, having gone to France to collect the last of his French gold *louis d'or,* and he had directed that he be elected to no public office during his absence.

The expectations of those who had promoted incorporation were soon realized to an amazing degree. General Lafayette, who visited Hartford in October of 1784 amid much understandable fanfare, described it as a "rising city blessed with advantages which were the reward of virtuous efforts in the noblest cause." But the rhetoric of the occasion aside, Hartford did indeed prosper, and much of the prosperity may be credited to Jeremiah Wadsworth, who, from the time of his return from France, served as either alderman or councilman until his death in 1804.

The city fathers availed themselves of every opportunity to present Hartford as an inland commercial center, and inspectors were appointed to see that all goods sent out from Hartford were of the finest quality. New streets laid out on the flats along the river extended the commercial district. Prospect Street became the site of fashionable residences. A fire engine was purchased in 1785, and an informal company, "The Proprieters of the Hartford Aqueduct," attempted to set up a public water system, even progressing as far as to lay several hundred feet of wooden pipes. Although no conventional sewers were to be installed before 1843, regulations adopted late in the 18th century clearly suggest that public sanitation was a serious concern. Soap factories, tanneries, and slaughterhouses, some of them located quite near some of Hartford's most pretentious dwellings, were constantly being ordered to clean up or close up.

But Hartford's hoped-for trade with foreign ports was not realized. Most of Hartford's trade was simply river trade, although it was a profitable one, with the towns along the Connecticut River in Vermont and New Hampshire.

In 1783 Hartford became a major stop on a regular stage line between New York City and Boston. Postal service, too, was much improved by the Congress during the war, and for many years thereafter Thomas Hildrup, the Hartford jeweler, gave first-rate service as postmaster. The "ultimate" in intercity communication was the reasonably travelable New Haven and Hartford Turnpike, completed in 1799.

All these busy activities stimulated trade and even manufacture. A rum distillery, a large one for the time, was established on the bank of the Little River by Wadsworth and Barnabas Deane. A pottery was opened in 1787 by Archibald Welles, Jr., close by, giving name to Potter Street. William and George Bull opened a shop for the sale of the fuel-saving Franklin stove, and Frederick Bull greatly enlarged his shop for the sale of general hardware. Commerce Street was laid out between Front Street and the Connecticut River, and, as it attracted small shopkeepers who specialized in less-than-quality merchandise, the section was known for a while as "Cheapside." In this vicinity, Caleb Bull opened a retail store, and Aaron Bradley operated a blacksmith shop advertised as "at the sign of the Horseshoe, No. 3, Cheapside, Jones Street."

On Main Street and State Street (as King Street had been renamed) were

An 1810 ad for children's books with titles like The History of Nancy Truelove *and* Whittington and His Cat *was certain to attract customers to the Peter B. Gleason and Company bookstore. (CHS)*

various shops that reflected the new prosperity and perhaps something of a new urbanity. In 1775 one Mary Gabriel had appeared out of nowhere and advertised herself as a "mantua-maker and miliner from Paris." After that, retail shopping in Hartford was never quite the same. Postmaster Hildrup received stiff competition from James Tiley, a silversmith, goldsmith, and jeweler on State Street, and from Jacob Sargent, a watchmaker, who in 1795 opened shop "at the Sign of the Golden Watch." By about 1800 pewterware was being produced in several small Hartford shops, and by 1843 there were 23 jewelers and silversmiths operating in the city.

In 1788 Hartford fell just a bit short of taking a large step in the American industrial revolution, when Jeremiah Wadsworth organized the Hartford Woolen Company. Wadsworth was the largest subscriber to the capital stock of £1,250, and among the other 30 investors were Hartford merchants Peter Colt, John Caldwell, and Nehemiah Hubbard. A mill was erected along the Little River, and an Englishman was brought in to supervise the operation. Workmen with the requisite skills were almost impossible to find, but at its peak the mill was producing about 5,000 yards of broadcloth a year. President Washington wore a suit made of the material at his first inauguration, and members of the Connecticut Congressional delegation were similarly attired. Although the "manufactory," as it was called locally, sold its product as far away as New York City, success was not to come its way. The Connecticut General Assembly exempted the building from taxation and in 1794 awarded a bounty on the mill's production. Even a lottery in 1790, authorized for the purchase of additional machinery, could not sustain an industry whose managers were totally ignorant of the methods of industrial production, and in 1797 the plant was closed.

Wadsworth attributed the failure of the Hartford Woolen Company to the lack of adequate capital, and in 1791 he proposed a corporation of much larger proportion than the Woolen Company. Here he hoped to attract New York capital, and in his initial attempt he secured the promise of some $19,000. Unfortunately, the New Jersey Society for Establishing Useful Manufactures was being organized under the leadership of Alexander Hamilton, and the funds first promised to Wadsworth went to the New Jersey project instead.

But Wadsworth was eminently successful in other areas, particularly in banking, for here he had more experience than any other person in Connecticut. Wadsworth was one of the founders of the Bank of North America, president of the Bank of New York from 1785 to 1786, and one of the directors of the First Bank of the United States. Late in 1791 Wadsworth had his clerk, Peleg Sanford, sound out the Hartford business community as to interest in setting up a local bank and the possible extent of the participation of each. The response was favorable, and Wadsworth and a few close associates from the wartime years—Oliver Phelps, Barnabas Deane, and James Watson—began drawing up the plans. Every effort was made to make the bank a local affair and to keep out speculators. On May 14, 1792, capital of $100,000 was raised by shares of $40 each. The entire amount was subscribed immediately, most of it by men who had a connection with Wadsworth's wartime military supply business. Wadsworth was elected first president of the bank, but he declined, allowing John Caldwell to serve in his stead. The Hartford Bank opened for business on August 8, 1792.

Although the founders of the Hartford Bank were conservative men, it was the first bank in the United States to set aside the old system of keeping accounts in terms of pounds, shillings, and pence. Congress had declared the Spanish silver dollar to be the monetary unit for the country by the Currency Act of April 2, 1792, just as the Hartford Bank was being created. Thus, unhampered by previous records kept in

Ten Dollars Reward! RAN away from the Subscriber, on the night of the 15th instant, a Negro Boy, named *Cæsar*, 18 years old, nearly 6 feet high, stout and well made, walks pretty erect, speaks fluently: He wore away a light colored sailor jacket, a mixed green and black swansdown vest, a pair of blue overalls, a Holland shirt, a pair of gray socks, a pair of thick shoes, a brown homemade great coat, and a large old Hat; has a small scar on his left cheek. He has lately been guilty of theft, and made his escape through fear of punishment. Whoever will return said Negro, or secure him so that his master may get him again, shall receive the above reward, and all reasonable charges.--- All persons are forbid harboring, trusting or employing said Negro, on penalty of the Law. SAMUEL M'CLELLAN. *Woodstock*, Connecticut, May 16, 1803.

A runaway slave was not an uncommon occurrence. Although this young lad escaped in May 1803 from northeastern Connecticut, his master advertised for him in Hartford's Connecticut Courant, offering a generous reward for his apprehension. (CHS)

the old fashion, the Hartford Bank began business with all accounting in terms of dollars and cents, and on June 15, 1792, it began issuing its first bank notes in dollars.

It would be almost half a century later that Hartford would come to be known as "The Insurance City," but there was already, in the 1790s, some inkling of future preeminence. That there was simply "insurance" in Hartford at this time was nothing at all remarkable, for insuring began as soon as small vessels sailed from Hartford in the 1630s, and never did a sailing vessel leave a colonial port without insurance that the vessel and cargo would arrive at the destined port. Individuals acted as brokers in receiving promises from persons who would be willing to compensate the insured in the event of a disastrous voyage. During the 1790s this was still the conventional way of working maritime insurance. Likewise, similar arrangements were often made to compensate for loss of buildings and/or their contents. During the early 1790s, however, an informal—and unincorporated—group that called itself

After the 1720 State House was severely damaged in 1783, Jeremiah Wadsworth campaigned for a new building. Located at Meetinghouse Square, the new State House was completed in 1796 and built of brick with brownstone trimmings. From Hartford, Connecticut, *1889*

FACING PAGE, BOTTOM: *In the 17th and 18th centuries each householder kept two or more leather buckets handy in case of fire. Family, neighbors, and passers-by would bring more buckets and form a line from a source of water to the person nearest the fire, who would then throw water on the flames. The State House had a shelf or so of fire buckets, each marked for identification with the State seal.* (CHS)

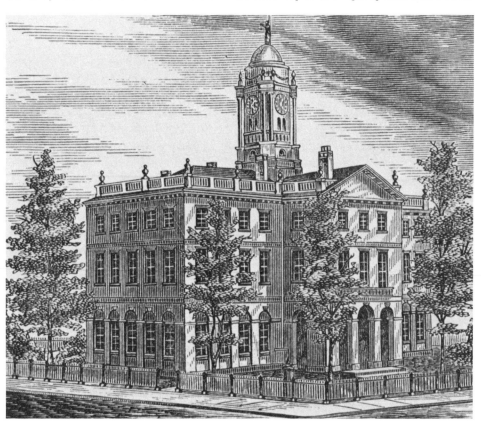

the Hartford Insurance Company became so formalized that it used printed policy forms, the earliest extant of which is dated February 8, 1794, for "insurance on the dwelling and its contents of William Imlay." Of particular interest are the seals of Peleg Sanford and Jeremiah Wadsworth as insurers. The later chartered company of that name did not come into existence until 1810, but it might be noted that those who participated in the organization of the later company were members of the earlier venture—as well as stockholders in the Hartford Bank.

Marine insurance, too, was formalized with the chartering of the Marine Insurance Company in 1803. By more than mere coincidence, John Caldwell, the first president of the Hartford Bank, was also the first president of Marine Insurance. This company was later absorbed by the Protection Insurance Company, which went out of business in 1854.

The Aetna (Fire) Insurance Company of Hartford was incorporated in 1819. Again, there was something of an overlapping of directorate with the Hartford Bank, but despite the fact that these early insurance companies were investors in the Hartford Bank, much of the capital consisted of personal notes of the stockholders who pledged the company to provide cash when it was needed to pay a claim. By 1881 the Aetna was the largest insurance company in the United States.

Hartfordites seem always to have had a penchant when it came to buildings, to tear down the old. Only one architectural vestige of this post-Revolutionary period of Hartford's history remains—what is known locally as the Old State House.

The 1720 State House had suffered severe damage in 1783, and repair had been both hasty and inadequate. Jeremiah Wadsworth, who quite properly regarded Hartford as "his" city, felt that the new state in the new nation deserved better of the new city, and he began a campaign to replace the old eyesore with a more

BELOW: Funds to build the State House of 1796 were raised by selling lottery tickets at five dollars apiece. Prizes ranged from $10 to $8,000 and the possibility of winning a prize was almost one in three. (CHS)

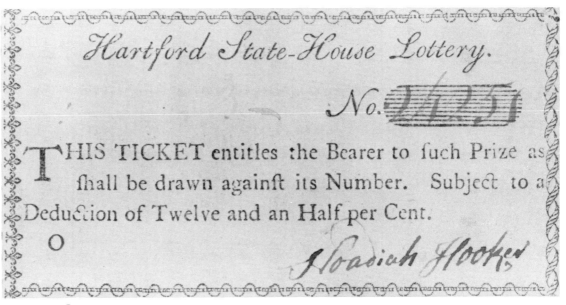

appropriate building to be located on Meetinghouse Square.

Wadsworth began with a $500 contribution, and 51 others contributed a total of $3,600. An appropriation by the General Assembly raised the available fund to $13,600, but even this was not sufficient to erect the building according to the plan of Boston architect Charles Bulfinch, and funds sufficient to the purpose had to be raised by a lottery. When the building was completed in 1796, the 1720 State House was moved to Church Street, near Christ Episcopal Church.

Few buildings in America have been subject to greater misunderstanding and historical misinterpretation than Hartford's Old State House has been. Since the restoration of the building in the 1970s, the zealous have made the claim that Hartford's Old State House is the oldest in the nation, but this is patently untrue. The Maryland State House at Annapolis was completed in 1779 and has been used as such ever since. Delaware's present State House in Dover has been in continuous use since 1792. In Rhode Island, Newport's "Old Colony House," built in 1739, was used as the State Capitol until 1900. Boston's "Old State House" was built in 1713 and served as Colony/State Capitol until 1795. Finally, in case the foregoing is not enough, the left wing of the *really* old "Old State House" in Newcastle, Delaware, built some time before 1664, was both Provincial and State Capitol until 1777, and for over a century thereafter was used as a city hall!

"In the Midst of Dissenters"

~As the two national political parties—the Federalists under Alexander Hamilton and the Republicans under Thomas Jefferson—lined up, there was little doubt that the Federalists would make the greater appeal in Hartford. Hamilton's policies of strong central government, sound national credit, easily circulating currency, and encouragement of industry naturally appealed to the Standing Order, and Jefferson's vaguely stated, quasi-agnostic religious attitudes guaranteed that he and his party could receive no support from the Congregationalists.

Hartford's civic leaders had long been on record as favoring a strong central government, and great was their rejoicing when on January 3, 1788, the convention to vote on ratification of the Federal Constitution of 1787 opened in the State House. The day was extremely cold, and the convention was adjourned to First Meetinghouse, which had recently installed a stove. The debate itself was not without its unpleasant moments, but it was the general public in the gallery that punctuated the proceedings with foot-tapping, foot-shuffling, whispering, coughing, and spitting. The vote on ratification was taken on January 9, with 128 delegates voting "for" and 40 delegates voting "against." Hartford's two delegates cast their votes for ratification.

President Washington undertook a ceremonial tour of the New England states in 1789 "to cement the bonds of the Union," as he put it. Washington at once made clear that the journey was being made at his own expense, and this news was especially pleasing to thrifty Hartfordites.

On October 19, Washington arrived in Hartford, where he was greeted by the Governor's Troop of Horse in full uniform and a large number of gentlemen on horseback. Washington spent the night at Bull's Tavern. The following day he visited the Woolen Manufactory, and the next morning he set out for Springfield. On the return trip, the President stayed once more with Mr. Bull, although this time there was no ceremony.

Washington made diary entries for each of the visits. Regarding the Woolen Manufactory, he noted that the product was "good," although not of finest quality. He also observed that Hartford was "more compactly built than Middletown," and he was surprised to learn that there was still no Episcopal Church.

Hartford's Federalists were fully supportive of the administrations of both Washington and John Adams. Jay's Treaty, negotiated in 1794 by Federalist John Jay, was immensely popular in Hartford, especially as the treaty opened the British West Indies to the smaller sailing craft that were engaged in exporting the Hartford region's agricultural surpluses.

When Britain and France became involved in the French Revolutionary and the Napoleonic wars, Hartford Federalists came out firmly on the side of the British. The Republicans, whose strength was largely in the South, chose the other side, and even Jefferson became blinded to the cruelties and bloodshed of the Reign of Terror, offering the excuse that a little bloodletting now and then is healthful to a nation.

During Jefferson's administration, the Hartford people, as did most New Englanders, turned even more against the second President from Virginia. Both the Embargo and the Non-Intercourse Act had a devastating effect upon New England's economy, as crops, for want of a market, were allowed to rot in the field, and ships decayed at dockside.

When Congress declared war against Britain in what Americans call the War of 1812, New Englanders were more sympathetic with Britain than they were with the American side. After all, the declaration of war had been along strict party lines. The Republicans, led by the "Warhawks," a group of young Western and Southern congressmen with territorial designs on both Canada and Florida, voted for the war, and the Federalists voted solidly against it.

New Englanders called this conflict "Mr. Madison's War," and they determined to let President Madison and his party fight it on their own. New England governors refused to permit the nationalization of the state militia, and New Englanders refused to invest in the government bonds sold to finance the war. The Hartford Bank would not purchase government securities, the Hartford Common Council passed an ordinance forbidding federal recruiting within the city, and the Courant took sadistic pleasure in reporting American military defeats.

The antiwar spirit reached a climax when prominent Massachusetts Federalists called a meeting at the Hartford State House for December 15, 1814, to discuss an antiwar resolution presented to the Massachusetts General Court by Harrison Gray

Otis. The convention consisted of 12 delegates from Massachusetts, 7 from Connecticut, 4 from Rhode Island, 3 from New Hampshire, and one (unofficial) from Vermont. Hartford had been chosen because of its pronounced Federalist tone, but there were already enough Republicans in the community to cause embarrassment. Pressure was put upon the clergy to see that none would offer an opening prayer, and, as the delegates went into their closed session, crowds gathered outside the State House to protest the proceedings. Someone lowered the American flag to half-staff, and a band of musicians paraded around State House Square playing funeral dirges. Even some Hartford Federalists felt that the holding of such a potentially treasonous convention was going too far.

The convention adopted a series of resolutions reflecting both New England sectional interests and Federalist partisan principles, and these were published following adjournment on January 5, 1815. There were resolutions against military conscription and the nationalization of state militia. There were also proposals to amend the Constitution so as to limit embargoes to 60 days, to require a two-thirds vote of both Houses of Congress to declare war, and to limit Presidential tenure to a single four-year term. No vote was taken on secession, but there is strong evidence that the delegates had resolved that if the convention's recommendations were not received favorably by Congress, New England would secede from the Union and make a separate peace with Britain.

Almost immediately, the serious matters discussed at the Hartford Convention became academic. On January 8 Andrew Jackson won the only American land victory in the Battle of New Orleans, and within two weeks of the convention's adjournment came news that the Treaty of Ghent had been signed on Christmas Eve of 1814. The terms of the treaty were *status quo ante bellum*, and all Americans could rejoice that although the United States had lost the war, the new republic had certainly won the peace.

Political Federalism was virtually defunct on the national scale, and from then on Federalist power in Connecticut would decline rapidly. The Hartford Convention has sometimes been called "Federalism's last gasp," but already there had been signs in Hartford that the Federalist Party had become a hollow shell.

One of these portents was the competition offered to the *Courant*. That noble old paper had seen its first rival in *The Freeman's Chronicle or the American Advertiser*, which, although it was to last only from September of 1783 until the following July, was to be followed immediately by the *American Mercury*, which was begun by Joel Barlow and Elisha Babcock and survived until 1835.

The *Mercury* began as a conservative paper, usually taking an editorial position not unlike that of the *Courant*. As the political parties took shape, however, the *Mercury* came out solidly in support of Jeffersonian Republicanism, taking a leading part in the agitation for a new state constitution.

As the *Mercury* moved into the Jeffersonian camp, the Federalists received new support from the *Connecticut Mirror*, founded in 1809 by Theodore Dwight. This paper was never a financial success, and in 1833 it merged with the *Mercury*, ironically, by that time staunchly Jacksonian Democrat!

The next step in the development of the newspapers came in 1817, when the Hartford *Times* was founded by John M. Niles, then a leading Hartford Republican, later a founder of the Democratic Party in Connecticut, and ultimately United States Senator. Niles made clear at the beginning that his paper would be anti-Federalist, but during the entire lifetime of the *Times*, it would always be "anti"—anti-Federalist, anti-Whig, and anti-Republican—until its demise in 1976.

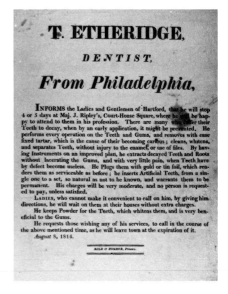

Philadelphia dentist T. Etheridge ran this 1814 advertisement in the Connecticut Courant informing "the Ladies and Gentlemen of Hartford that he will stop 4 or 5 days at Major J. Ripley's, Court-House Square, where he will be happy to attend to them in his profession." His services included plugging teeth "with gold or tin foil," or extracting them and making replacements "so natural as not to be known." (CHS)

HAVING received a confirmation of the diſtreſſing intelligence of the DEATH of the great, the highly beloved

WASHINGTON,

THE Inhabitants of the town of Hartford, deſirous of teſtifying their reverence and affection for the memory of " the man, firſt in war, firſt in peace, and firſt in the hearts of his countrymen," propoſe to attend Divine Service at the *North Meeting-Houſe*, on FRIDAY next. At half paſt one o'clock in the afternoon, a proceſſion will be formed at the State-Houſe, at which the Citizens of this, and the neighbouring towns, are requeſted to attend. Each perſon who joins the proceſſion, will wear a BLACK CRAPE on his left arm ; and the Committee reſt ſatisfied that no perſon will join the proceſſion, without this badge of mourning. The propriety of wearing Crape on their left arms, on the melancholy occaſion, is reſpectfully ſubmitted to the Citizens at large. The Proceſſion will move preciſely at two ; the people are therefore requeſted to be punctual in their attendance. It is deſired of the Citizens, THAT THE SHOPS AND STORES MAY BE SHUT THRO' THE WHOLE OF FRIDAY, that the Day may be devoted to this ſolemn Funeral occaſion.

JOHN CALDWELL,
THOMAS Y. SEYMOUR,
ENOCH PERKINS, } COMMITTEE.
THEODORE DWIGHT,
WILLIAM BROWN,

Hartford, Dec. 24, 1799.

ABOVE LEFT: *When the news of George Washington's death reached Hartford, the following Friday was set aside for a solemn procession. Each citizen was asked to wear a mourning band of "black crepe" on the left arm, and shops were to remain closed "thro' the whole of Friday."* (CHS)

ABOVE: *George Goodwin & Sons got into the business of bookselling, printing, and publishing in 1815. The Connecticut Courant was probably their largest client. This paper label was a handsome example of the Goodwins' work.* (CHS)

But the journalistic opposition notwithstanding, and in spite of the not-too-successful attempts of the Republicans to gain at least an electoral foothold, during the first 15 years of the 19th century the Federalists continued to act as if their day would never end. All local offices were still held by Federalists, and all civil and civic honors went to those of the Establishment. Much of the Federalist power—and indeed the glory—was symbolized in the elaborate ritual of Election Day, the opening of the May session of the General Assembly.

Early in the morning, the Governor's Foot Guard, resplendent in scarlet-and-buff uniforms of the design of the Coldstream Guards, paraded in front of the State House. At 11 a.m. the governor led the short procession of Foot Guard, state officeholders, and about 100 clergy (Congregational, of course) to the First Church Meetinghouse. Four ministers participated: one offered the opening prayer, another preached the "election sermon" (a "State of the Church" message), a third gave the concluding prayer, and a fourth pronounced a benediction. Then the procession reformed and proceeded to the State House, where the Governor's Guards, as His Excellency passed, presented arms. Dinner followed, and at 2 p.m. the Assembly convened. The votes were counted, the results announced, and the victors installed. The ceremonies ended at about 6 p.m. with a salute from the Foot Guard. The next few days were filled with parliamentary debate and much social entertaining, and at each Hartford Federalist's open house the gustatory delight was "election cake," a uniquely Connecticut delicacy served by tradition only at functions incidental to Election Day. On the second day of the legislative session came the Election Ball, always held in one of the larger taverns.

America's first literary school—the Hartford Wits—found their common bond in their defense of the Standing Order. Most of the Wits were Yale graduates, none was a native of Hartford, and the members represented a wide range of professions. John Trumbull was a lawyer. Lemuel Hopkins was a physician. Richard Alsop of Middletown was part owner of a Hartford bookstore. Joel Barlow and Elisha Babcock were the publishers of the *American Mercury*. Theodore Dwight was a Hartford lawyer, editor of the *Mirror*, secretary of the Hartford Convention, and a brother of Timothy Dwight, president of Yale College. David Humphreys was a gentleman farmer from Derby. Jeremiah Wadsworth, although not himself a poet, was both friend and patron of the Wits, and it was Wadsworth who usually picked up the tab at the Wits' early informal meetings at the Bunch of Grapes or the Black Horse Tavern.

Although the Wits began writing even before the end of the Revolution, their works are characterized by an intense patriotic devotion to the new nation and, in their later writings, to the Federalist cause. John Trumbull's *M'Fingal*, written in 1775 and revised extensively in 1782, was an amusing satire on the Tories. Dwight's magnum opus was a 10,000-line mock epic entitled *The Conquest of Canaan*. Barlow published *The Vision of Columbus* in 1787 and revised and expanded it in 1807 as *The Columbiad*, in each edition shocking his readers with forecasts of such improbable events as the construction of a canal across the Isthmus of Panama and the elimination of the study of Greek and Latin in American schools. *The Anarchiad* (1786), a collaborative work in which most of the Wits had a hand, was a well-reasoned plea in verse for a stronger central government.

The verse of the Wits usually appeared first in the *Courant*, the *Mercury*, or the *Mirror* before it was published in book form, and, as there was then no copyright protection, there were frequent reprintings in other American papers. Collectively, the Wits were the most widely read Americans in their day, not solely because of their literary skills, which were considerable, but also because they were able to put into verse the intense nationalistic feeling of the American people.

But it was their political Federalism that spelled their doom as a literary movement. As Federalism declined, so did their literary output and their popularity. Joel Barlow continued to write, but he soon disassociated himself from the coterie and the Federalist Party and converted to the political views of the Jeffersonian Republicans.

The theater made its first appearance in Hartford during the days of the Hartford Wits. Before the Revolution, few in Hartford would have considered the theater as desirable, or even acceptable. But at Yale College, the academic nursery of the Wits, rudimentary forms of drama had appeared during their own undergraduate years, as Yalies were sneaking out in the evenings in defiance of college rules to participate in amateur dramatics at taverns in nearby Amity and Milford.

Having been brought up on such fare, it would seem reasonable that the Wits would have had some interest in serious theater in Hartford. Unfortunately, however, in 1773 the Connecticut General Assembly had passed "an Act for the Suppression of Mountebanks," sometimes called the "Circus Law," which was sufficiently broad to preclude professional (or traveling) performances of any kind.

It was something vaguely resembling a circus that first appeared in Hartford in defiance of the law. In June, 1787, Thomas Pool of New London put on an "equestrian show" in Hartford. The show consisted of feats of trick riding and a clown act, but Pool was not molested by the authorities.

Something approaching real theater came in the summer of 1788, when the *American Mercury* advertised:

By Permission.
Entertainment.
Mr. Smith respectfully informs the Ladies & Gentlemen of the Place, that on this, and Wednesday and Friday evenings next, at Mr. Frederick Bull's will be delivered a series of elegant
Dramatic Speaking,
ALSO a variety of Songs and Musical Dialogues, a copy of which may be seen at Mr. Bull's.

During the winter of 1788-1789, Bull's Tavern was the scene of both classical drama and parts of Royall Tyler's popular five-act comedy, *The Contrast.* In the early 1790s traveling companies presented several plays, including *She Stoops to Conquer,* and in 1795 an English company that had been dividing its time among Philadelphia, Boston, New York, and Providence offered to play regularly in Hartford if a proper building could be provided. Ephraim Root erected a small theater on what is now Temple Street, and in this enterprise he was assisted by 57 Hartford gentlemen including Jeremiah Wadsworth, John Morgan, Timothy Burr, Jesse Root, Barzillai Hudson, William Imlay, Peleg Sanford, Daniel Wadsworth, and Samuel Trumbull. These names, as well as others, represented Hartford's oldest families, but also to be noted is that several of them were Episcopalians, and that not one of the Wits participated. Of even greater interest is that one woman, Mrs. Francis Hodgkinson, an actress from New York, was "cut in" for a one-sixtieth share. Both this lady and her husband performed there occasionally, and Mr. Hodgkinson functioned for a while as manager.

Over the next few years there were visiting performances, usually sold out, by the Old American Company on tour and by the Hodgkinsons' resident company. The end of this worthy enterprise came in May, 1800, when the General Assembly passed "An Act to Prevent Theatrical Shows and Exhibitions," which provided for a fine of $50 for every performance in defiance of the law. Nor was the cause of music in Hartford advanced when in 1815 the Common Council passed an ordinance forbidding the playing of any wind or percussion instrument within the city limits between sunset and sunrise except by militiamen under command of their officers.

But the dramatic stage, even in its brief decades, could not hold its own against the "exhibition," and performances of this sort became increasingly frequent. In 1789 two "Arabian camels" were shown at Mr. Bull's, the exhibit being "highly praised" by President Ezra Stiles of Yale College. The next year a "Mr. Bennett" performed on the slack wire at the schoolhouse. And in August of 1795 the first real circus, Ricketts Equestrian Circus, "with riders, dancers, and a clown," came to Hartford. Mr. Franklin's Circus, with riders, clowns, and freaks, performed on South Green in 1799. By 1813 the circus had become such a popular form of entertainment in Hartford that Eleazer Potter made a large addition to the rear of his tavern "to be occupied as a circus." Potter was host to various traveling shows, and their popularity brought the operation to the attention of the General Assembly.

Meanwhile, two attempts were being made at permanent exhibitions. When the State House was completed in 1796, Joseph Steward rented a third-story room as painter's studio and exhibition room, or "Museum," as Steward always called it. Here he did portraits of local worthies from life, and of such persons as Benjamin Franklin from the popular steel engravings of the time. When the state government found need for the space, the museum was moved in 1808 to a location on Main Street opposite the Episcopal Church. In 1824 Steward's curiosities were taken to the

South Church, the second meetinghouse of Hartford's Second Church, stands on Main Street at the corner of Buckingham. Built in 1827, the church has since been restored with white trim and red brick. (CHS)

fourth floor of the building on the corner of Main Street and Central Row, at which location they were soon forgotten and eventually disappeared — except for a few pictures that became the property of The Connecticut Historical Society.

On February 15, 1795, Reuben Moulthrop, the New Haven portrait painter, moved to "Mr. Jane's" the wax museum that he had been showing in New Haven for three years. Among Moulthrop's 15 figures were the King of France, President Stiles, and "The Drunken Sailor." Moulthrop's exhibition was enhanced, as the *Courant* announced, by "several beautiful airs by Master Salter (a boy of 9 years of age) on the Piano Forte, accompanied on the Violin by Mr. Salter — with sundry pieces on the Piano Forte, performances to be seen at any half hour each day" — admission 25 cents.

These changes in the pattern of life for early 19th-century Hartfordites were paralleled by profound changes in the city's religious life. Just as Federalist political power was on the decline, so, too, was the Congregationalist Establishment. First and Second churches had survived the Revolution — but barely. Membership was at a low ebb, and both meetinghouses had fallen into disrepair.

When Francisco de Miranda, the Venezuelan revolutionary hero, visited Hartford in August of 1784, he found First Church Meetinghouse to be "dirty and in bad taste," and the singing, as well as the manners and the attire of both the men and women, to be "quite inferior" to that of Wethersfield, where he had been just a week before. Second Church had been without a settled minister from 1777 until 1784, when Benjamin Boardman began a series of short pastorates. In the latter year, Second Church had a membership of only 27, or four fewer than it had at the time of its organization in 1670.

When the *Report of the Census of 1790* was published in 1792, one statistical figure shocked Congregationalist Hartford: the American population having any formal connection with organized religion was five percent! But if the national figure was cause for alarm, what about Hartford, where the percentage was even lower?

Ecclesiastical historians agree it was this disturbing data that set into motion the Second Great Awakening that had its origin in the Connecticut Valley of Connecticut and Massachusetts, when, in the mid-1790s, a group of Congregationalist ministers known as the Neo-Edwardsians attempted to rekindle the enthusiasm with which Jonathan Edwards had begun the First Great Awakening of 50 years before. The effects of this new Awakening would be felt in Hartford for years.

The successive pastors of Second Church conducted "revivals of religion" regularly, but with only modest success. Not so at First Church, for there Nathan Strong led large-scale revivals in 1798, 1800, 1808, 1813, and 1815; and Strong's successor, the Reverend Joel Hawes, continued the practice.

Both congregations built new meetinghouses, First Church in 1807 and Second Church in 1827, and both of these elegant structures are still in use. But even the new meetinghouse soon was not large enough to accommodate the congregation that had been gathered at First Church by the Second Great Awakening. In 1824 North Church was built on Main and Morgan streets for no other apparent reason. (This congregation would become Park Church in 1866.) Fourth Church was begun in 1832 by extreme revivalists who thought that First Church had not gone far enough in that direction. The Pearl Street Church, the Asylum Hill Church, the Windsor Street Church (officially known as the Pavillion Congregationalist Society), and the Wethersfield Avenue Church were all geographic accommodations to the town's later physical spread, but they were also convincing evidence that while post-Revolutionary Hartford Congregationalism was ailing, it was not beyond resuscitation.

This engraving is from a portrait of the Reverend Joel Hawes, minister of the First Church in Hartford from 1818 to 1864, and minister emeritus until he died three years later. (CHS)

RIGHT: *The fourth meetinghouse of Hartford's First Church (built on the site of the third) was painted cream color. It is pictured circa 1875. (CHS)*

ABOVE: *This engraving shows the North Church, built in 1824, which stood on Main Street at the corner of Morgan. (CHS)*

It was during the low period of the Congregational Establishment that other religious groups gained a foothold in the community. The Quakers had infiltrated quietly, and in 1788 they organized the Hartford Society of Friends. The Baptists were almost as unobtrusive, although they soon grew in considerable numbers. John Bolles, "the Father of the Baptist Church in Hartford," began holding services in his home before the first Baptist congregation of 16 members was formally organized in 1790. The first Baptist meetinghouse was located at Market and Temple streets in 1794, and according to tradition, the structure had originally belonged to a Methodist congregation upriver and had been washed downstream by a spring flood. In 1831 the congregation built a new house of worship on the site of the present Cheney Building on Main Street, only to move on to a still larger building at Main and Talcott streets. As early membership increased, a split-off group in 1834 built a meetinghouse—South Baptist Church—on the site of the present Federal Building. Both congregations were brought together in 1922 as Central Baptist Church, and the present structure at Main Street and Linden Place was begun in 1925.

During the late 1790s several Methodist preachers visited Hartford but found few hearers. On July 14, 1791, Francis Asbury preached in First Congregational Church and recorded in his diary that he could "scarcely find a breathing of living, holy spiritual religion here except amongst a few women in East Hartford."

Nevertheless, Methodist preachers continued to visit Hartford, although much of their thunder was stolen by the Congregationalist ministers as the Second Great Awakening got into full swing. In 1820, however, a small Methodist congregation was organized. The following year the *old* Old State House, which had been moved from the square to the rear of Christ Church, and which had already served as tenement house, school, and printing shop, was refurbished as the Methodist meetinghouse. Here the Methodists worshiped until a new church building was erected on Asylum Street in 1860. An offshoot of this church was South Park Church, which began in 1850. The 1720 State House, incidentally, was used, after the Methodists moved out, as the carriage factory of Force and Goodnow. Later it was moved to the rear of 185-187 Pearl Street, where it again housed a printing shop until 1910, when it was torn down to make room for the Telephone Company's new building.

ABOVE: *After studying diseases affecting the brain and nervous systems, Dr. Eli Todd (1768-1833) became aware of the need for an institution for the mentally disturbed. He was largely responsible for establishing Hartford's Retreat for the Insane, which opened in 1824. (CHS)*

ABOVE RIGHT: *From the corner of State Street we gaze down Main Street to the south. Church spires (from left to right) are: St. John's (Episcopal), South (Congregational), South (Baptist), and Center (Congregational). (CHS)*

During their early years in Hartford both Methodists and Baptists were frowned upon by the Congregationalists. The preachers of these denominations had little training in theology, and their sermons were offensive to orthodox Calvinists, who could not accept the idea of extemporaneous preaching—even though they themselves were insistent upon the use of extemporaneous prayers. The outdoor baptisms performed by the Baptists in the Little River were thought to be "publicly offensive." Gradually, however, the public came to feel that the members of these sects, although mostly from the more humble levels of society, were upright in their private lives and had as high a regard for the general well-being of society as had their critics. The Congregationalists also came to realize that the Methodists and Baptists differed little in doctrine and worship practices from themselves, and as the century progressed, the original differences came to be less and less important.

The Episcopalians, meanwhile, had been going their own not-so-silent way. Christ Church's membership grew rapidly, and there were converts from Hartford's oldest families. The parish rolls were soon graced with such old Hartford names as Adams, Bull, Burr, Goodwin, Imlay, and Wadsworth, and such new but equally important names as Bradley, Cutler, Morgan, Ogden, and Sigourney. Although Christ Church had had no settled rector until the arrival of the Reverend Menzies Raynor in 1801, the consecration of the parish's fourth rector, Thomas Church

Brownell, as Bishop of Connecticut in 1819, made Hartford the center of diocesan activity.

Hartford Episcopalians represented something of a crosscut of the local social spectrum, but most of Christ Church's leaders were responsible members of the business community, individuals of more-than-average formal education and with cultivated tastes somewhat beyond the commonality of the small city. Whatever may have been their cultural attainment, though, or even their social suavity, Hartford's Episcopalians were being excluded from the nascent banking and insurance operations. As they were recovering slowly from their complete discrediting in the eyes of the Establishment as Tories during the American Revolution, many of them felt that only with a college under their own control could they enter the ranks of first-class citizens.

In 1813 a number of well-to-do Hartford Episcopalians worked out a plan whereby both their own economic ends and the cause of higher education in Connecticut could be served, and the plan involved, of all things, a bank.

The Phoenix Bank was founded in Hartford in May, 1814, by Episcopal laymen. In their petition to the General Assembly for a charter, the promoters offered

to the State of Connecticut a "bonus" of $50,000 to be divided among Yale College, the Bishop's Fund, and "any purpose whatever, which to your Honours may seem best," the "purpose" being an Episcopal college.

The capital stock of the Phoenix Bank was to be $1,000,000, although it is said that the response was so great and so immediate that it could have been set at $7,000,000. The directors of the Hartford Bank even proposed raising the capitalization of their own institution to $1,000,000, but the suggestion came too late, and the Phoenix Bank opened on schedule. As shares were purchased, payments to a total of $50,000 were made to the State, and immediately the Yale Corporation and the trustees of the Bishop's Fund applied for financial grants. The Assembly promptly voted $20,000 to Yale. The Bishop's Fund received nothing, and the Episcopalians found that this elaborate scheme of legislative bribery had been futile.

The outcome was a violent newspaper controversy carried on through late 1815 and early 1816. The Episcopalians made clear that to deny the Bishop's Fund its share of the Phoenix Bank "bonus" was a flagrant disregard of the Episcopalian minority in favor of Congregationalist Yale. The Congregationalists vigorously defended the religious test, insisting that no Episcopalian should object, despite the fact that the test, actually a subscription to Congregationalist orthodoxy, kept Episcopalians from the Yale faculty.

This picture from the eastern shore looks toward Hartford from above the covered bridge, circa 1855. The sloop at right has a hinged mast so that it can be towed under the bridge. (CHS)

The ramifications of the bonus controversy were soon felt in Connecticut politics. Traditionally, the Episcopalians—representing a conservative element in Connecticut society—had supported the Federalist Party, and it was the Episcopal vote that had enabled the Federalists to remain dominant in the state long after Federalism had disappeared elsewhere. The failure of the Episcopalians to receive the Bishop's Bonus, however, turned them from their former Federalist support to a fusion of Republicans and Protestant sectarians known as the Tolerationist Party. By 1816 the party was well organized. The Republican minority provided the working organization, Episcopalians supplied the leadership, and Methodists and Baptists gave voting strength. So effective was the new alliance that in the September election the Tolerationists won 87 seats in the Assembly to the Federalists' 114.

The Tolerationist victory at the polls in 1816 frightened the Federalists, and the legislature adopted a conciliatory policy and passed "an Act for the Support of Literature and Religion," which appropriated the $14,500 due Connecticut from the federal government for Connecticut's minimal services during the War of 1812. Through the fund's disbursement among the religious interests and Yale College, the Congregational societies in the state received one-third; the trustees of the Bishop's Fund, one-seventh; the Baptists, one-eighth; the Methodists, one-twelfth; Yale, one-sixth; and the remainder was to stay in the treasury. Obviously, this was an attempt by the much reduced Federalist majority to salve the wound of the loss of the Phoenix Bank bonus. Yale was the only party to be satisfied. The Congregationalists thought that their share was too small, the Episcopalians regarded their $2,070 as poor compensation for the Phoenix loss, and the Baptists and Methodists regarded their small share as an insult. The whole bonus plan accentuated sectarian bickerings and hastened the ultimate Federalist downfall. In the state election of 1817, all religious elements outside the Congregational Establishment united forces, and the Tolerationists won both the governorship and a large majority in the Assembly. A year later the Council, too, passed into Tolerationist control.

By then, the chartering of an Episcopal college should have been an easy matter, especially as the new State Constitution of 1818 completed the internal revolution in the state and once and for all disestablished the Congregational churches.

A few days before Christmas 1822, Bishop Brownell met with 18 clergymen to draw up a petition to the General Assembly for a college charter, asking that it be located in either Hartford, Middletown, New Haven, or New London, and that final selection be left to the discretion of the trustees, with the act of incorporation to take effect as soon as $30,000 should be raised.

Bishop Brownell and his associates planned well. The suggestion that the college be named for Bishop Samuel Seabury was passed over, and the name "Washington" was chosen instead. Care was taken to include non-Episcopalians among the original incorporators, and among them was the Reverend Elisha Cushman, pastor of the Baptist Society in Hartford.

A charter was granted on May 16, 1823, an event hailed as a victory for Connecticut Episcopalians, the city of Hartford, and the friends of religious liberty throughout the country. Hartford dwellings and places of business were decorated with bunting, and in the evening cannons were fired and bonfires were lighted.

Washington College had been placed under a self-perpetuating board of trustees, and the charter made no mention whatsoever of the Episcopal Church. The charter forbade the "making of religious tenets of any person a condition of admission to any privilege in said college."

On Tuesday, July 8, 1823, at the first meeting of the trustees, a committee to

TOP: John Warner Barber's detailed panorama of Hartford was drawn in 1832 from the opposite bank of the Connecticut. Each steeple and tower is correctly in place, and considerable shipping activity is evident along the riverfront. (CHS)

ABOVE: The east lawn of the State House was set apart from the routine of the marketplace by a fence. (CHS)

procure funds for the institution was appointed. Subscription papers were made out in two forms: one (the particular subscription) for pledges to be made upon condition of the selection of a particular location for the college, and the other (the general subscription) for pledges to be made without regard to location. The committee was not confident that the entire $30,000 could be raised within the diocese, and it therefore appointed the Reverend Nathaniel Wheaton, rector of Hartford's Christ Church, to go to England to solicit donations.

In September, 1823, Wheaton sailed from New York, armed with a letter signed by Bishop Brownell and addressed "To the Bishops, Clergy, and Laity of the Church of England." The letter emphasized the difficult position of the Church in Connecticut, "Planted in the midst of Dissenters ... and opposed by many prejudices." Also mentioned was the common bond of religion uniting England and America: *"The best friends which Great Britain has in America, will be found among the members of the Episcopal Church; and ... every thing which conduces to the extension of this church, will be found to strengthen the bonds of relationship and amity which connect the two countries."*

The trustees, of course, had no idea that this letter would be circulated in Connecticut. Even if they had, there would have been little that could have been changed if the statement of the case were still to be clear to the English Church. Copies of the letter fell into unfriendly hands and were printed in the *Courant* of March 2, 1824. The inevitable consequence was a heated debate in the Hartford newspapers. With the Episcopalians seeking to strengthen "bonds of relationship," the Standing Order had full reason to believe that their earlier suspicions of Episcopal political loyalty had been justified. Likewise, the Congregationalists, who had enjoyed legal Establishment until only five years before, resented the Episcopalians' reference to themselves as members of *The* Church and to all others as Dissenters (both correct in English usage); and this could not help but revive the old fear of Prelacy.

Wheaton returned to Hartford in November, 1824, with a mere $946.67, with which, in accordance with his instructions, he purchased scientific apparatus and books for the college library.

By March, 1824, a "general subscription" of only $10,000 had been raised. Another $20,000 had to be secured, and the location of the college would depend upon the result of the "particular" subscription. Hartford's pledges in money amounted to $10,865. But what had not been anticipated was the response from the artisans, laborers, and shopkeepers of Hartford, many of them not members of the Episcopal Church. Goods and services, translated into monetary value for the subscription list, were pledged in excess of $4,000, and this must have convinced everyone that Washington College was to be truly a community enterprise. On April 20, 1824, Hartford Town Meeting voted $5,000 for the purchase of land for the college. This brought the Hartford pledge to almost $20,000. On May 6, 1824, the trustees voted that whereas the sum of $30,000 had been raised, the college would be established in Hartford. The trustees purchased a splendid tract at West and Buckingham streets about 100 rods west of the South Meetinghouse.

Classes were scheduled to begin on September 23, 1824, but the college buildings had scarcely been started by that date, and instruction for the first nine students began in the basement of the Baptist meetinghouse.

The two buildings were ready for occupancy at the opening of the fall term in mid-September, 1825. The brownstone structures were imposing. According to later description, they followed "the Ionic order of architecture, [were] well proportioned,

The Dexter *was one of a fleet of small upriver steamboats that shuttled between Hartford and Springfield. The boats were designed low, to slip under the fixed bridges along the way, and narrow, to fit into the canal at Windsor Locks. Courtesy, Connecticut Printers*

and well adapted to the purposes for which they were designed."

Washington College, more than anything else, brought Hartford's Episcopalians into full participation in community activities. Hartford was proud of her own institution of higher learning, and during the early years of the college's existence, Town and Gown relations were pleasant. The Washington Archers, a uniformed student marching group, were usually on hand to parade on national holidays, and on several occasions members of the faculty delivered the town's Fourth of July oration. When Hartford held her Centennial Celebration in 1835, the college took a prominent part. When The Connecticut Historical Society was organized in 1825, the entire faculty enrolled as charter members. What was certainly the most obvious example of Congregationalist forgiveness of the Episcopalians for their disturbance of the status quo was that First Church allowed the college to hold its commencement exercises in its meetinghouse until the completion of the present Christ Church. Episcopalianism had done much to make Hartford a brighter, livelier, and even more "intellectual" place, but nothing would be of more significance than the Episcopalians' effort to repeal the "Circus Law" that had kept Hartford in the aesthetic backwater.

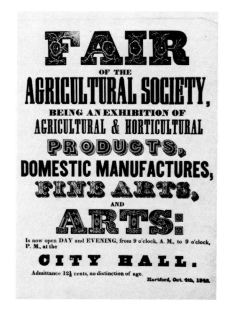

The Hartford public had always enjoyed the circus-act type of entertainment that had been disguised as "educational exhibitions," but even here there had been occasional drivings-out-of-town. And quite early the townspeople had exhibited a fondness for music, although, again, most of what was offered was passed off as "devotional."

There were exceptions, of course, as, for example, when in 1805 George K. Jackson, an Englishman, presented a series of concerts featuring selections from Handel's oratorios in the several churches. There were also occasional instrumental performances of a secular nature given in conjunction with the "dancing assemblies" held during the 1820s in the public rooms of the Exchange Coffee House or Gilman's Saloon. The new City Hall, a beautiful Greek Revival structure erected in 1829 on Market Street, boasted a large public hall on its third floor, and here, on occasion, a musical performance would be given. The legitimate theater had been dead since the first attempts in the 1790s. By the 1830s, certainly a consequence of the Great Awakening's reviving the prohibition of "frivolities," musical entertainment had degenerated to the point where it consisted solely of "sacred concerts" given by visiting groups whose offerings were chiefly subjective, revivalist hymns.

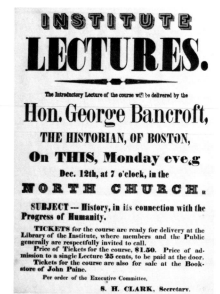

Bishop Brownell could never reconcile himself with third-rate entertainment being performed illegally and a music-starved populace being deprived of anything better because of an antiquated law. In 1837 the bishop was joined by Judge William Hamersley in circulating a petition demanding the repeal of both the Circus Law and the Theater Law of 1800. When 1,000 signatures, most of them from Hartford, had been obtained, Brownell personally presented the petition to the General Assembly, declaring that Connecticut was the only state in the Union and the only part of the civilized world in which the entertainment covered by the existing laws was forbidden. The "Brownell Petition" stirred up a hornet's nest, and the Assembly was soon flooded with defenses of the existing laws as essential to the preservation of common decency.

For more than 150 years Hartford has been on the "lecture circuit." The earliest city directories listed several public halls. Hartfordites could hear a prominent political figure or learn how people lived in distant lands. (CHS)

The General Assembly turned down Brownell's request, and, as if to make a further point, it added billiards and ninepins to the list of forbidden pleasures. In 1852, however, the Assembly relented to the extent of allowing each town or city to decide for itself whether the theater should be permitted locally. In 1853 the Hartford Common Council announced its willingness to license theaters and circuses.

Bishop Brownell had lost his case before the General Assembly, but he, too, was able to make his point—in Hartford, at least. Although the Congregationalists would still maintain an official position against "frivolities," and the Methodist and Baptist preachers would thunder out sermons against "worldly pleasure," Hartford's attitude toward concerts and other forms of entertainment changed immediately, and almost beyond belief.

By the mid-1850s, Hartford social and aesthetic life had changed amazingly. During the social season, numerous dances were held by the "leading families." Among these the most fashionable were the Cotillion Parties—or "harmonical soirees"—held in Gilman's Saloon and the balls held by Blackford's Brass Band, the Hartford Quadrille Band, and the Hartford Brass Band. Music lovers enjoyed the annual visits of the Germania Society (a 40-piece symphonic orchestra) and Monsieur Paul Jullien's Ensemble (the principal competitor to the Germania Society).

FACING PAGE ABOVE: City Hall was used for an agricultural exhibition in October 1842. Admission was 12-1/2 cents. (CHS)

There were also concerts by Ole Bull, Adelina Patti (who appeared in Hartford in 1853 as an eight-year-old prodigy), Jenny Lind (whose one recital in Hartford was broken up by the booing victims of a ticket scalper), Louis Moreau Gottschalk, and the Pyne and Harrison English Opera Troupe. Those whose tastes had not matured beyond those of earlier decades enjoyed the appearances of the Baker Family, the "Ballad Concerts" of Mr. and Mrs. L. V. H. Crosby, the Welch Family, the Campbell Minstrels, and Davis' Ethiopian Serenaders.

The Young Mens Institute (later to become the Hartford Public Library) and the Hartford Arts Union sponsored lectures by such notables as Ralph Waldo Emerson, Oliver Wendell Holmes, and Wendell Phillips. Fanny Kemble gave Shakespearean readings, and Lola Montez, erstwhile mistress of King Ludwig I of Bavaria, lectured on "European Women." In the summer months there were almost nightly concerts by the city's bands, which had come into existence on the crest of the new enthusiasm for music. In the fall there were the Hartford County Fair (sponsored by the Hartford County Agricultural Society, organized in 1817) and the horse races at the Trotting Park in the South Meadows. Sometimes there were traveling panoramas: "The Burning of Moscow," "The City of Paris," and the ever-popular "Holy Land" and "Solomon's Temple." Not bad for a city that had once outlawed almost all performances!

Gleason's Pictorial Drawing Room Companion carried this engraving of Hartford's Main Street, circa 1845. The view looks south from the corner of State Street. The military group was probably a detachment of the Governor's Foot Guard. (CHS)

VII

The Great Age of Enterprise

~**A** FACTORY, BY DEFINI-
TION, IS A PLACE WHERE A NUMBER OF PEOPLE WORK
WITH MACHINERY IN THE PRODUCTION OF GOODS. IN A
way, the early water-powered gristmills along the Little
River would fit the description, but these small operations seldom involved more than the miller himself, a
journeyman or two, and perhaps an apprentice. The
Hartford Woolen Manufactory more precisely met the
definition, for here there were a score of workers who
used water-powered looms, and perhaps the short-lived
carding mill built on Main Street late in the 18th century and utilizing the treadmill power of dogs might also
qualify—if one cared to stretch the point a bit.

The craft-shop type of production had won Hartford
artisans a good reputation in such lines as furniture,
leather goods, and pewterware. Hartford silversmiths
were respected widely, and one of them, William
Rogers, in partnership with his brothers, Asa and
Simeon, opened a shop on State Street in 1825. Rogers

sold out in 1862 to Horace Wilcox of Meriden in the first of a long series of absorptions that would result in the International Silver Company.

In printing and publishing, too, Hartford had made a name. Hudson and Goodwin of the *Courant* took pride in having published the book version of Barlow's *Vision of Columbus* and Trumbull's *M'Fingal*, and they made a large profit from their 1780 edition of the *New England Primer* and Noah Webster's *Speller*. During the 1820s and 1830s Hartford was the textbook-publishing center of the United States, with more than 30 small firms engaged in the business.

Hartford's real publishing fame came in "subscription publishing," which was launched about 1820 by Silas Andrus. Here was a variation of the "Yankee Pedlar" operation, as agents would be sent out into the countryside with a blank-page, bound dummy of a yet-to-be-published book. Orders, accompanied by a small down payment, would be taken, and the number of copies to be printed would be determined by the number of advance subscriptions. Andrus was soon followed in this business by O.D. Cooke and Sons and Thomas Belknap.

Then came the series of quickly changing partnerships that finally became Case, Lockwood & Co., by the 1880s the largest printing house in the United States. Hartford was without question the major center for subscription publishing, and if one might wonder why Samuel L. Clemens (Mark Twain) moved to Hartford in 1871, the answer is simple: his publisher was there.

In 1819 William S. Marsh, one of Hartford's smaller printers, published John C. Pease and John M. Niles' A *Gazetteer of the States of Connecticut & Rhode Island*, a volume that has been regarded as a statistical gold mine ever since. In their description of Hartford, the compilers noted that blacksmiths and cabinetmakers were plentiful and that there were a cotton mill, 2 woolen mills, a linseed-oil mill, 6 tanneries, 5 potteries, a button-making shop, 2 tin shops, a Britannia-ware shop, a bell foundry, 15 shoe shops, 6 book binderies, 8 distilleries, a machine-card factory with a production worth $10,000 a year, a buggy-whip factory with a similar value of annual production, 2 hat factories (one employing 36 workmen), 2 looking-glass factories whose combined production amounted to $30,000 a year, and 4 coppersmiths, two of them "large scale" and the larger of the two employing some 20 men.

Hartford industry took a new turn in 1821 when the Alpheus & Truman Hanks Company, usually called the Hartford Iron Foundry, opened on Commerce Street. Production was at first limited to cast-iron plows, but a small machine shop was added in 1830. Samuel Woodruff joined the partnership in 1830, and H.B. Beach came in 1845. Eight years later the firm was reorganized as the Woodruff and Beach Iron Works. This company was the first in Hartford to become involved with steam technology, and during the 1840s and 1850s it was the largest producer of steam engines, boilers, and heavy machinery in New England. During the Civil War the plant turned out marine engines for use by the Union Navy. Despite the high reputation of the firm, Woodruff and Beach went out of business in 1871.

A similar operation was the Phoenix Iron Works, founded in 1834 by Levi Lincoln, the prolific Yankee inventor. The Phoenix first specialized in the ornamental ironwork that was an essential architectural element of the "Italian villa" style of the more pretentious Hartford residences in the decades preceding the Civil War. Phoenix later turned to the production of machinists' tools, including the widely used Lincoln milling machine, and thus was set another industrial trend that would make Hartford famous. The Phoenix Iron Works would become Taylor & Fenn.

These early industrial operations were scattered throughout the city. Those that produced chiefly for local sale and that did not depend upon water power were

One of the many manufacturing plants to congregate along the Little River was the Jewell Belting Company, established in 1845 by Pliny Jewell, Sr. Descended from a line of tanners, Jewell conceived the concept of substituting leather belting for gears in the running of machinery. At the outbreak of the Civil War, the firm, now known as P. Jewell & Sons, was the leading manufacturer of industrial leather belting. From Hartford, Connecticut, 1889

located on such retail streets as Main or State. Those that utilized water power were, of course, located along the Little River, and here, from that stream's confluence with the Connecticut westward for over a mile, most of the larger establishments were located. Such operations as tanning demanded proximity to flowing water, and it was in what is now Bushnell Park (the river has long since been put underground) that tanning, slaughtering, and brickmaking were carried on. And it was in the vicinity of these foul-smelling businesses that those who worked there for wages came to live in equally foul-smelling tenements.

By the 1830s Hartford's working class had already been set off, both socially and geographically, from the rest of the community. Hartford's more prosperous merchants and most of the rising industrial capitalists had homes on Morgan, Temple, Front, and Grove streets and on Lord's Hill beyond the present railroad station. Those who worked in the factories and larger shops lived in a slumlike narrow band that extended from the wharves on the Connecticut River, westward on the north side of the Little River, across Main Street at the present Wadsworth Atheneum and City Hall, and down Gold Street (then called Hotel Alley) to the warren of hovels that surrounded the tanneries.

Wages for these people were low. Skilled hands were paid $12 to $20 a month, and young men entered their lives of drudgery at between $6 and $8. For this, all worked a 12-hour day, 6 days a week—and there were no vacations.

This stage in Hartford's industrialization coincided with the rise of Jacksonian democracy, and the *Times,* staunchly Jacksonian, became the champion of the workingman, urging the "Workies" to unite in support of a 10-hour day and the Democratic Party. Perhaps because of the *Times'* encouragement, organizations made up of masters, journeymen, and apprentices were formed, but these were not labor unions in the modern sense, but, rather, self-improvement and charitable societies.

In 1836, however, something more like a modern labor union appeared as the "Journeymen Carpenters and Joiners Society." Whatever may have been the goals of the society, they were never put to the test, for in 1837 came the Great Panic, which resulted in severe unemployment. As workers were laid off, those who had been involved in any phase of the workingmen's movement were the first to be discharged. The effect of the Panic of 1837 was to set the labor movement back at least two decades.

But the efforts were not entirely in vain, as in 1855 the 10-hour day became law in Connecticut—except where both employer and employees should agree upon a longer day.

The railroad came to Hartford in 1839, and this new facility would have a profound effect upon both Hartford industry and Hartford society. The Hartford and New Haven Railroad had been chartered in 1833, and the capital of $1,500,000 had been raised in both New York and Connecticut. The early history of this line was a stormy one, for there was much opposition from both the stagecoach lines and the steamship companies. Nevertheless, Hartford soon became an important railroad center, as the line was extended to Springfield in 1844 and to New York City in 1849. During the 1850s a network of tracks connected Hartford with Manchester, Willimantic, Putnam, Norwich, and New London.

It was during the construction of the Hartford and New Haven Railroad that Hartford saw her first influx of non-English immigrants, the Irish. The first Irishmen had come to the Hartford area in the mid-1820s, when some 400 laborers from Galway and Cork worked on the series of canal locks built around the Enfield Falls on the Connecticut River about 15 miles north of Hartford. During the late 1820s and

ABOVE: *From 1824 on, there was a regular overnight steamboat service between Hartford and New York. The Hartford and New Haven Railroad advertised a quicker route in 1842. (CHS)*

early 1830s, a contingent of Irish laborers had found employment in the construction of the Farmington Canal. As the completion of the canal coincided with the beginning of the railroad, most of the Irish workmen crossed Talcott Mountain to share in the backbreaking tasks of grading and laying tracks. As the Hartford and New Haven went into operation, it was usually possible for these men to stay on as members of the maintenance crews that worked out of Hartford.

The first of these new arrivals were single young men who shared rooms in the cheaper boardinghouses near the tanneries. Then came young married couples who took small quarters in the tenements. Perhaps no subsequent immigrant group was less welcome in Hartford than were these Irish. Most of them were illiterate, and none had any sort of vocational skill. Furthermore, these men had worked on the canal and the railroad for 75 cents a day and had adjusted their scale of living accordingly. Thus, they were unpopular with the resident workers, who saw a threat to their own jobs. But even the employers, who seemingly might have profited from their presence, gave no encouragement. In fact, for many years it was common to see the words "No Irish need apply" at the employment door of most Hartford factories. Nor did Hartford's black population welcome the Irishmen, for it was in the heavy lifting, loading, and digging sort of job that the newcomer was forced to compete with the black.

Only from the leaders of the Democratic Party did the Irishman receive a welcome, and even this was a qualified one. The Irishman was helped with his naturalization, for each new citizen meant a new Democratic vote, and although the politicians had little respect for the Irishman as an individual and would never have even dreamed of allowing him to run for public office, he was useful.

The arrival of the Irish saw the beginnings of the Roman Catholic Church in Hartford. As early as 1823 there had been occasional services according to the Roman liturgy in private houses and the State House, but it was not until 1828 that the Right Reverend Benedict J. Fenwick, Bishop of Boston, sent the Reverend R.D. Woodley to Hartford to organize a parish. Fenwick immediately purchased a lot on Wells Street, in the area where the Irish population had begun to congregate, but he soon learned that as the new Christ Episcopal Church was nearing completion, the Episcopalians' old structure could be purchased at a very reasonable price. Fenwick bought the building, moved it to a Talcott Street location several blocks away, and on June 17, 1830, consecrated it as the Church of the Most Holy Trinity. The Reverend James Fitton was installed as pastor.

Hartford Episcopalians had been particularly encouraging in the early efforts to further Roman Catholicism in the city, and it had been through the good offices of two Episcopal laymen, James Ward and Samuel Tudor, that Bishop John B. Cheverus had been permitted to say Mass in the State House. But an amusing incident occurred as the two bishops closed the deal on the old Christ Church building. Just before the papers were signed, Brownell said, "Well, Bishop Fenwick, as we have a fine new church building, we will let you have the old one," to which Fenwick replied, "Yes, and you have a fine new religion, and we will keep the old one." Touche!

The Roman Catholic Church prospered in Hartford, and its membership grew in proportion to the rapidly increasing Irish immigration. One of Father Fitton's first projects was to open a parochial school in the church basement. In 1839 a small burial ground was purchased at the western end of North Cemetery. Church-sponsored benevolent societies were organized to meet the economic and social needs of the Irish immigrants. By 1849 the membership had grown to such an extent that a second parish, St. Patrick's, was created, and in 1851 a beautiful Gothic St. Patrick's

ABOVE: Steamers did not attract overnight travelers only; often they were chartered for special holiday excursions and outings. In 1859 L. Boardman offered this trip to the mouth of the Connecticut River, connecting with "the cars" for New London or the boat to Long Island. (CHS)

Church was completed at the corner of Church and Ann streets. During the 1830s layman Alfred Tally published the *Catholic Press*, a weekly paper, in the basement of Holy Trinity.

The new immigration, the coming of the railroad, and a general acceptance by Hartford's business community of the idea of making Hartford an important manufacturing city infused a new spirit into the community. Population grew rapidly. From 6,901 inhabitants in 1820, the figure grew to 9,787 in 1830, to 12,793 in 1840, to 13,552 in 1850, and to 29,152 in 1860.

The railroad had done much to reduce freight costs, and Hartford's newer industries found it desirable to locate where they could use water power and also be near the railroad and use the new facility to carry raw materials and finished products. Hence, railroad spurs and sidings were extended westward along the Park River, by this time known popularly as the "Hog River" because of the pollution caused by the dumping of industrial wastes into the small stream. Also, each sizable factory attempted to provide living accommodations for the workingmen's families by building company-owned houses in proximity to the plant. These trends led to a territorial expansion of the city, as the city fathers annexed all contiguous, populated areas. In 1853 the city limits were extended both northward and southward, and in 1859 most of the Park (or Hog) River industrial sections were added. The southern line was extended to the Wethersfield town line in 1873, and additions of 1881 brought the city to its present geographical extent.

Among the largest of the new plants was the Jewell Belting Company (1845), later known as P. Jewell & Sons, which opened in the old tannery section. By the outbreak of the Civil War it was the leading industrial-belting producer in the world. Bidwell, Pitkin & Co. (1849), later Pitkin Brothers & Co., manufactured boilers, steam engines, feed-water heaters, and building-heating equipment. Sharps Rifle Manufacturing Co. (1850) purchased a 25-acre tract, then repaired the dirt road running along the river and renamed it Rifle Street (now Capitol Avenue). Sharps rifles soon earned a wide reputation. By 1860 nearly 450 men were employed, and the yearly output was 30,000 units. During the Civil War Sharps produced 140,000 rifles for the Union Army.

The largest pre-Civil War industrial operation was the Colt Patent Firearms Manufacturing Company. Although reared in Ware, Massachusetts, Samuel Colt was the son of Christopher Colt and the grandson of John Caldwell, both leaders in the Hartford business community at the turn of the 19th century. Colt (born in 1814) had little use for formal education, but by the time he was 21 he had invented the revolver, on which he secured patents in Great Britain, France, and the United States. In 1836 he opened a plant for the manufacture of revolvers in Paterson, New Jersey, with capital of $300,000 that he had raised among several New York investors. Despite government contracts for the new weapon, the company failed. Undaunted, Colt accepted more Army contracts and had the revolvers produced at the Whitney Arms Factory in Hamden, Connecticut, until 1847, when he began production in small rented quarters in Hartford, first on Pearl Street and later on Grove Street.

But Sam Colt had his eye on bigger things, and he soon began buying up land on South Meadows. On this tract Colt erected in 1855 what was probably the largest individually owned factory in the world. Along the bank of the Connecticut River, Colt constructed a huge flood dike, 15 feet high and 60 feet wide at its top, the largest flood-control project then undertaken east of the Mississippi.

Colt also built a workingmen's village of three-story buildings south and east of

Although he received little formal education, Samuel Colt became one of the most successful and flamboyant businessmen of his time. His accomplishments are many and include: the invention of the modern revolver, the creation of the massive Colt Patent Firearms Manufacturing Company, and the establishment of the Hartford Gas Company, but he is perhaps best known for his humane and fair treatment of his workers. From Clark, A History of Connecticut, *1914*

his huge H-shaped factory. In addition to providing comfortable homes at reasonable rentals, Colt opened a community house and library, offered an educational program, and encouraged his workers and their families to participate in sports. Colt had an extraordinary fondness for music, and this was reflected in his sponsoring Colt's Band, one of the better wind ensembles in the state and one that furnished music for the frequent summertime concerts and the many parades held in Hartford. For many years Colt's Band led the Connecticut contingent at the United States presidential inaugural parades and provided music for the commencements at Trinity College. The band was not a professional organization in the regular sense, and the members received no direct remuneration. They did, however, receive a full day's pay for any appearance in uniform. On Colt's frequent trips to Europe, he scouted for talent, looking for young men who could both play a musical instrument and work at a lathe.

Sam Colt's dike was soon grown over with willow trees, and the flamboyant industrialist came to have an odd reversion to thrifty-Yankee type. Deciding to put the willow shoots to practical use, Colt opened a factory for the production of willow furniture. When he learned that the world's best willow workers were to be found in a small village near Potsdam, Germany, Colt tried to induce a few of them to come to Hartford. None would come as individuals, but Colt offered good pay, and the entire village was induced to migrate, asking only that there be good German beer and some leisure time to enjoy music. To make the German willow worker feel completely at home, Colt built a small group of German-style homes, several of which still stand and are known as Potsdam Village.

Samuel Colt died in 1862, and the business, by this time incorporated, continued under a series of successful general managers and superintendents. His widow, Elizabeth H. Jarvis Colt, from her splendid Italian-villa-style Armsmear (now a home for widows and daughters of Episcopal clergy), presided as the *grande dame* of Hartford society until her death in 1905. In 1869 she built the Episcopal Church of the Good Shepherd, midway between the Armory and Armsmear, as a memorial to

The result of many years of hard work on the part of owner Samuel Colt, the Colt Patent Firearms Manufacturing Company grew from its meager rented headquarters on Pearl Street in 1847 to become the largest individually-owned factory in the world by 1855. From Asher & Adams, Pictorial Album of American Industry, *1876*

her husband and their three children who died in infancy, and a few years later she built the Caldwell Colt Memorial Parish House of the Church of the Good Shepherd as a memorial to her son. Upon Mrs. Colt's death, the entire 140-acre tract to the southeast of Armsmear became the property of the City of Hartford as Colt Park.

Sam Colt was a capitalist, and nothing seems to have pleased him more than making money. He also was a showman, and one of his greatest pleasures was Colt's Band with its flashy military-style uniform. Colt was a social climber as well, and one of the highlights of his adventure-filled life was his presence at the coronation of Czar Alexander II. Certainly Colt was a civic-minded person, and although it might be said that having ample utilities was essential to his own industrial operations, he was one of the leading forces in setting up the Hartford Gas Company in 1849 and the Hartford Water Works in 1853. But in his own day he was best known for the humane way in which he treated his workers. Although Colt paid the highest dollar in wages and always wanted the most work for the dollar, he regarded each worker as an individual, and he never ceased trying to find ways to make his men happy and more productive.

The same could not be said for all Hartford employers of the time. Steam technology had been perfected to the point where any small plant able to supply water and fuel could be mechanized. Steam equipment was dangerous. Users of steam knew that it was dangerous, and they soon came to accept an occasional boiler explosion as one of the facts of industrial life. By the mid-1850s boiler accidents were occurring throughout the United States at the rate of one every four days, and factory owners simply regarded them as "acts of God."

On Tuesday, March 2, 1854, at 2:10 p.m., the steam boiler at the Fales and Gray Car Works on Potter Street exploded. Nine persons were killed outright, 12 died later, and more than 50 others were seriously injured.

A coroner's jury concluded that the cause of the Fales and Gray explosion was "an excessive accumulation of steam ... [and] that excessiveness of steam in said boiler was owing to the carelessness and inattention of the engineer." The jurors also offered a series of recommendations intended to prevent the recurrence of similar catastrophies: 1) regulations should be devised to prevent careless or irresponsible persons from being placed in charge of boilers; 2) regular safety inspections should be made by municipal or state authorities; 3) boilers should be placed *outside* the factories for which power is being provided; 4) employers using steam as power should pay close attention to the safety of workers; and 5) some measure should be adopted to prevent steam boilers from being rated for carrying more steam pressure than would be consistent with safety.

Each of the recommendations eventually came to be adopted by public agencies. Twelve days after the Fales and Gray explosion, the Hartford City Council appointed a committee to study steam-boiler safety, and in 1864 the Connecticut State Legislature passed a boiler-inspection law, under which all unsafe boilers would be "retired" until defects had been corrected.

Hartford's citizenry was appalled at the city's inadequate facilities for caring for a large number of injured people. Two months to the day after the explosion, a public meeting voted in favor of a public hospital, and before the end of the month the Hartford Hospital was organized. This institution soon became recognized as one of the best in Connecticut. In 1866 Hartford Hospital accepted its first intern, and in 1877 it introduced a two-year school of nursing. Readers may feel they were born a century too late when they learn that all medical and surgical services were free of charge until 1892.

ABOVE: *Francis Ashbury Pratt worked as a foreman at Colt Patent Firearms Manufacturing Company. Pratt was best known as an inventor and mechanic.* Courtesy, Pratt & Whitney Co., Inc. From Cirker, Dictionary of American Portraits, Dover, 1967

Another consequence of the Fales and Gray explosion was the organization in 1857 of the Polytechnic Club by a group of younger Hartford men associated with industries or institutions that used steam power. Elisha King Root was then superintendent of Colt's Armory, of which he later became president. Francis Ashbury Pratt was a foreman at Colt's, and Amos W. Whitney was employed in a similar capacity at the Phoenix Iron Works. These two would soon establish the Pratt and Whitney Machine Company. Edward M. Reed was superintendent of the Hartford and New Haven Railroad. Charles Brinkerhoff Richards, also of Colt's, was later to achieve international renown as an inventor of industrial machinery. Charles F. Howard was an Asylum Street merchant. Jared M. Ayres was a teacher in East Hartford. Jeremiah Merwin Allen was the steward at the American School for the Deaf, sometimes called "America's Pioneer Institution for the Handicapped," which had been founded in 1817.

Although the Polytechnic Club's stated purpose was that of "discussing matters of science in relation to everyday life," by the 1850s steam power had come to be such a part of American everyday life that it was the club's favorite topic of discussion. The members of the club reasoned that if the cause of a phenomenon were known, a remedy could be found. Steam boilers were material objects, the creation of human hands and entrusted to human hands for operation. Thus, good materials in construction, fine workmanship, careful operation, and periodic inspection to detect deterioration would virtually preclude boiler explosions.

When the Polytechnic Club learned that many of these principles had been arrived at independently in England, and that several companies had been created there for the purposes of inspecting and insuring boilers, they came to the conclusion that an inspection and insurance company on the English pattern would be both desirable and feasible. Unfortunately, the coming of the Civil War turned their attention to the immediate task of war production. In 1866, however, the Polytechnic men joined other Hartford businessmen in establishing the Hartford Steam Boiler Inspection and Insurance Company, an organization that was able to bring all the Polytechnic principles to reality.

These industrial developments did nothing really to help the labor situation in Hartford, and on the matter of the immigrants things went from bad to worse. Such large construction projects as Colt's Armory called for bringing in additional laborers, but once the factory buildings had been completed, there was no use for them inside. The wives and daughters of the Irishmen were able to find work as domestics, but the husbands were still unable to move upward on the wage ladder. Colt had brought in Englishmen and Germans, but these people had mechanical skills. There were even occasional physical clashes between the Irish and the other working people.

The immigrant question soon entered local politics. As the Whig Party declined, a new party, the American Party, sometimes called the "Native Americans" or "Know-Nothings," appeared on the scene. This organization was intensely patriotic, "nativist," and particularly opposed to Roman Catholicism. The party and its supporters were soon to be found in Hartford, and, although it could never be proved, when the Church of the Most Holy Trinity was burned in 1853, most Hartfordites agreed that the arson had been the work of the Know-Nothings.

In November, 1854, Thomas M. Day, a leading member of the American Party, purchased the *Courant*, and the paper's orientation immediately switched from Whig to Know-Nothing. Connecticut became ardently Know-Nothing and in 1855 elected William T. Minor of Stamford governor and William Field of Pomfret lieutenant governor. A year later Albert Day, a Hartford Know-Nothing, became lieute-

Amos W. Whitney co-founded the Pratt and Whitney Machine Company with Francis Ashbury Pratt in 1869. Whitney previously worked as a foreman at the Phoenix Iron Works and was known for his inventive skill in improving production methods. From Cirker, Dictionary of American Portraits, 1967

FACING PAGE, BOTTOM: The Pratt & Whitney Company was incorporated in July 1869. Located on the north bank of the Park River, the factory was known for producing "intrinsically excellent tools of undeniable accuracy of working parts" such as the lathe pictured here. From Asher & Adams, Pictorial Album of American Industry, 1876

nant governor. Connecticut Know-Nothings also sent William W. Welch of Norfolk and John Woodruff of New Haven to the United States House of Representatives. The party soon gained control of the Legislature, which, under Governor Minor's prodding, revised the state's constitution so as to make literacy a prerequisite for voting. Fortunately, the Know-Nothing Party was short-lived, for after the Presidential election of 1856 it disintegrated quickly. The newly founded Republican Party came forward as the political heir to the virtually defunct Whigs.

When the Civil War broke out in 1861, there was a complete reversal of attitude toward the Irish. The draft laws permitted the hiring of substitutes for those whose names had been drawn. "Substitute brokers" brought over thousands of young Irishmen, and the Hartford papers carried full-page advertisements of their availability. The Connecticut Legislature even repealed Connecticut's Prohibition law, arguing that the federal government needed the tax revenue from the sale of whiskey, but also feeling that it had made a deserved concession to the drinking preference of the Irish.

On Saturday, April 12, 1861, the Hartford telegraph office received news that the first guns of the Civil War had been fired against Fort Sumter. On the following day Hartford's churches were crowded, and each congregation, as a newspaper account read, "with heavy hearts but exultant patriotism ... sang 'My Country, 'Tis of Thee.'" In the afternoon a huge crowd gathered in State House Square, where the flag was raised and, with tears streaming down the cheeks of many, "My Country" was sung once more.

On April 15 President Lincoln, declaring that a "state of insurrection" existed, called for 75,000 three-month volunteers. Enlistments were prompt, and the Hartford Volunteer Rifles was one of the first companies to be accepted by the federal

BELOW LEFT: *One of the initial enterprises in the education of the deaf began in 1816 as the Deaf and Dumb Asylum on Asylum Avenue. As enrollment grew, additional wings and porches were added. The enlarged institution is shown circa 1910. In 1920 the school moved to West Hartford and is now known as the American School for the Deaf. (CHS)*

BOTTOM LEFT: *Elaborate ads, complete with pictures and fancy type, helped 1861 Hartford businesses reach prospective buyers and customers. From Geer's City Directory, 1861*

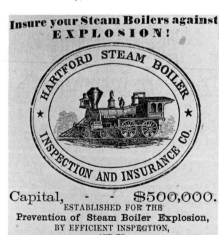

government. The Third Regiment was soon mustered into service in Hartford, and on May 10 and May 18 tearful crowds saw the men off to war at the Hartford Railroad Station.

Throughout the war years Hartford seemed most supportive of the war effort. Parades were held each time a new contingent of troops left for the South. Colt's and Sharps were working full steam. Irishmen volunteered for service in the Connecticut Irish Regiment (the Ninth), and scores enlisted in the two black regiments. Hartford insurance companies insured without premium all medical supplies, food, and blankets collected in Hartford and shipped to the Army by the Hartford and New Haven Steamboat Company. The *Courant,* now safely in Republican hands, and the Hartford *Evening Press* never missed an opportunity to praise the actions of President Lincoln and the Union Army. For a while it seemed that all of Hartford was working to preserve the Union. More than 4,000 Hartford men served in the Union Army and Navy, and almost 400 of them died in the service.

But that support was on the surface. Underneath, there was a pro-Southern spirit—"Copperheadism," as it was called—and it was the *Times* that kept the spirit alive. The *Times* had been pro-Democratic since the days of Andrew Jackson, and it had never deviated from that strict party line, even to the extent of openly defending the institution of slavery. On the Kansas and Nebraska question, the *Times* boldly sided with the slavocracy, and for the infamous Dred Scott Decision it had nothing but praise. Pro-Unionists were appalled that there was so much Anti-Union sentiment, and the Reverend Horace Bushnell, distressed by the active Copperhead spirit in Hartford, justified President Lincoln's suppression of habeas corpus as a legitimate perversion of the Constitution in the interest of preserving the Union.

In 1862 the Democrats, styling themselves "Peace Democrats," tried to unseat staunchly pro-Union Republican Governor William A. Buckingham of Norwich. The Democratic candidate was Thomas Hart Seymour of Hartford, Governor of Connecticut from 1850 to 1853, a veteran of the Mexican War, and U.S. Representative in Congress from 1843 until 1845. Seymour's platform was little short of treasonous, as he declared that should he be elected, federal conscription laws would not be enforced in Connecticut.

Buckingham won reelection, but Seymour was to make a second bid in 1864. That was a "Presidential year," and Lincoln's Democratic opponent was General George Brinton McClellan, the recently ousted Commander of the Army of the Potomac. McClellan had a rather strong following in Hartford. During the election campaign there were huge McClellan rallies, held in competition with the "Wide-Awake" parades of the Republicans.

News of Lee's surrender reached Hartford on April 9, 1865. A procession formed spontaneously, and the Hartford citizenry marched down Main Street headed by Christy's Minstrel Band, carriages, and fire steamers. That night almost every dwelling and commercial building in Hartford was illuminated.

In 1869 Gideon Welles returned to Connecticut after serving as Secretary of the Navy in the cabinets of Abraham Lincoln and Andrew Johnson. After an absence of eight years, he recorded in his diary:

> Hartford ... has greatly altered— I might say improved, for it has been beautified and adorned by many magnificent buildings, and the population has increased. ... A new and different people seem to move in the streets. Few, comparatively, are known to me.

These changes, and subsequent ones, will be the subject of the chapters that follow.

FACING PAGE, RIGHT:
Established in 1866 for the prevention of steam boiler explosions, the Hartford Steam Boiler Inspection & Insurance Company offered businesses protection against explosion through proper boiler inspection. From Geer's City Directory, 1867-1868

Passersby can't miss the little stove Mr. Phillips has placed on the sidewalk next to a hitching post in front of his store. Mr. Hills probably preferred to display his products indoors. (CHS)

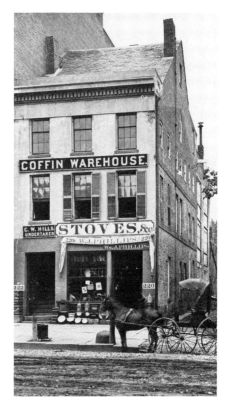

Insurance City

~BOTH THE HARTFORD
BANK AND THE PHOENIX BANK HAD BEEN EMINENTLY
SUCCESSFUL, AS EACH SERVED A PARTICULAR CLIEN-
tele: the Hartford's depositors and borrowers were largely Congregationalist and Federalist, and the Phoenix's
were predominantly Episcopalian and Tolerationist. In
1824 the Connecticut River Company was chartered to
improve navigation on the Connecticut River, and
shortly thereafter the Connecticut River Banking Company was created as an adjunct to perform the normal
functions of commercial banking. Because the primary
company was regarded as performing an exceptional
public service, the CRBC stock was to be exempted
forever from taxation.

Also in 1824 the Connecticut Branch of the Second
Bank of the United States was moved from Middletown
to Hartford, and this brought an additional bank
capitalization of $300,000 to the city. Although the
Bank of the United States was the bank of deposit for

the federal government, the Hartford Branch seems to have had little to do with the day-to-day financial affairs of the community. Nevertheless, it was the destruction of the bank upon the expiration on March 4, 1836, of the charter (which President Jackson refused to renew) that brought on the disastrous Panic of 1837. Furthermore, Jackson's infamous "Specie Circular," which required payment in gold or silver for all lands purchased from the federal domain in the West, prompted the Hartford banks to suspend specie payment. Fortunately, they survived the crisis.

Meanwhile, acting upon the assumption of the impending destruction of the Bank of the United States, a group of Hartford financiers had founded the Farmers' and Mechanics' Bank in 1833. It was this institution that after 1836 became the depository of federal funds for Connecticut. Obviously, the Farmers' and Mechanics' Bank was pro-Jackson. Another bank founded in the next year, the Exchange Bank, was definitely anti-Jackson, and in their petition for a charter of incorporation the Exchange promoters predicted, with amazing foresight, the Panic that would follow the coming destruction of the Bank of the United States.

The Phoenix Bank had paid a "bonus" to the State of Connecticut in return for its charter, but the matter of a bonus had been overlooked in the issuance of the charter of the Farmers' and Mechanics', thanks largely to Democratic Governor Henry W. Edwards and his legislative friends. For the Exchange Bank, however, a bonus *was* demanded, and a sizable bonus it was. On a capitalization of a mere $500,000, a payment of $15,000 was made to the State of Connecticut for the benefit of the Connecticut Silk Manufacturing Company, plus $8,000 for an iron railing around the Hartford State House.

The number of banks in Hartford and their obvious political preferences had little to do with the city's economic health, which was described frequently in the local press as "prostrated." The Whig victory in the election of 1840 brought encouragement, even to those of the Jacksonian persuasion, and the decade of the 1840s was one of growth and prosperity for banking in Hartford—so much so that a new series of banking institutions came into being as the country slowly recovered from the lingering effects of the Panic of 1837. The State Bank of Hartford was organized in 1848, and the City Bank followed three years later.

In 1852 the Connecticut State Legislature passed the Free Banking Act, which opened banking to virtually all those who chose to engage in it, and under this "easy incorporation" act were organized the Bank of Hartford County (later American National) in 1852, the Charter Oak Bank in 1853, and the Mercantile Bank in 1854. The act was repealed in 1855, but the multiplication of banks continued, and in 1857 both the Aetna and the Merchants' and Manufacturers' Bank (later the First National) were chartered.

These new ventures appeared at a most unfortunate time, for hardly had they begun operation when the nation's economy was struck by the Panic of 1857. The long period of expansion and speculation had reversed. Railroad stock, in which the banks had invested heavily, fell rapidly in value, and financial exchanges with the South and the West were seriously impeded. Money was scarce, and specie seemed to disappear.

The older Hartford banks weathered the Panic of 1857 fairly well, but the newer ones—the Bank of Hartford County, the Charter Oak, the Exchange, and the Mercantile—all went into temporary receivership, and the Bank of Hartford County was forced to reduce its capital.

The coming of the Civil War revitalized banking in Hartford, as each bank subscribed generously to the 20-year loans offered by the federal government. Also,

The Phoenix Mutual Life Insurance Company was on Pearl Street in 1897, on Elm Street in 1921, and now it occupies this striking structure on American Row. Courtesy, Phoenix Mutual Life Insurance Company

under the National Currency Act of 1865 all Hartford banks except the State Bank and the Connecticut River Banking Company became "national" banks.

A new dimension was added to Hartford banking when the Hartford Trust Company was chartered in 1867. The following year, the Charter Oak Trust Company also came into existence, although, probably to avoid confusion, its name was soon changed to Security Trust. This institution would soon consolidate with the Fidelity Trust Company and eventually merge with others to become the Hartford National Bank and Trust Company, which by 1900 would be the largest banking institution in Connecticut. A similar process occurred as the Hartford Trust Company consolidated with the Connecticut Trust and Safe Deposit Company to become the Hartford-Connecticut Trust Company, which would come to serve the largest number of trust accounts in the state.

It is perhaps the savings bank that has, because of its "provident" function, been something of a link between banking and insurance operations. In 1819 Society for Savings was founded as the first mutual savings bank in the state. Its objectives were, as the bylaws read: "to aid the industrious, economical and worthy; to protect them from the extravagances of the profligate, the snares of the vicious and to bless them with competency, respectability and happiness."

Society for Savings was created by 41 public-spirited Hartford men, none of whom would have any intention of making the small, regular deposits at compound interest upon which the savings-bank idea was based. Hartford's working people quickly recognized the opportunity afforded them, and during the first six months of Society's operation, deposits, mostly in amounts of less than a dollar, amounted to $4,352.77. As the number of depositors increased, the money on deposit was lent on thousands of mortgages, and Society's resources helped start many a small business or even expand larger ones. At the time of Society for Savings' 150th anniversary in 1969, there were 248,687 accounts to the amount of $1,499,685,073. Later Hartford savings banks, all of them successful and serving a most useful function, were the State Bank for Savings, the Mechanics, and the Dime.

It is sometimes said that no Hartford bank has ever failed. The same, unfortunately, cannot be said of the city's insurance companies, but it might be noted that as Hartford's insurance people have been highly innovative, it was the unworkable innovation that on several occasions brought ruin to the investors.

Hartford's good name in fire insurance came largely from the several Hartford companies' handling of difficult problems in a most dramatic way. In December, 1834, fire swept the lower end of Manhattan Island and destroyed property valued at over $20,000,000. Most of the New York insurance companies immediately declared bankruptcy, and those that did not take this course made no immediate effort to compensate their insured. The Hartford Fire Insurance Company had relatively few accounts in New York City, but the company's losses amounted to over $60,000, a trifle compared with the total damages but still a large sum for a comparatively small Hartford company. Hartford Fire's president, Eliphalet Terry, took immediate action, and whether it was from a sense of Puritan conscience or Yankee cunning, Terry went to the Hartford Bank and offered his own sizable personal fortune in return for the bank's promise that it would honor all drafts he would make on behalf of Hartford Fire.

Upon his arrival in New York City, after a sleigh ride the entire way in sub-zero temperature, Terry announced that the Hartford would honor each and every claim made against the company. From a temporary office he wrote bank drafts to compensate the insured, and at the same time he wrote new policies for literally hundreds of

In 1899 the First National Bank constructed this building on the east end of the United States Hotel block. Ernest Flagg, who designed the chapel and the principal halls of the U.S. Naval Academy in Annapolis, was the architect. (CHS)

those who had been insured with companies that were unwilling or unable to pay. It was this incident, perhaps more than any other, that spread the good word of Hartford as the center for good insurance.

In 1845 fire again swept a portion of lower Manhattan. This time Thomas K. Brace, the president of Aetna, set up a table amid the smoldering ruins. The Hartford Steam Boiler Inspection and Insurance Company also followed this practice, as it invariably set up a table at the site of every insured building destroyed by boiler explosion, and the agents on the spot wrote policies for many times the amount paid out in damages.

When the Great Chicago Fire of 1871 virtually destroyed that metropolis, Hartford's insurance companies attempted to repeat the New York heroics. Aetna, Hartford, and Phoenix came through almost unscathed, but less fortunate were the Connecticut and the Merchants, and although the latter was rebuilt as the National, and the Connecticut met claims partially and then greatly reduced its capital, an early historian of Hartford insurance made the obviously exaggerated statement that suffering in Hartford was "second only to that of Chicago itself." After the Chicago fire, only four companies—Hartford, Aetna, National, and Phoenix—remained as licensed insurers.

But for those Hartford carriers that withstood the Chicago fire, it was their day of glory! Governor Marshall Jewell, a director and large stockholder of the Phoenix, happened to be in Detroit at the time. The Phoenix president, Henry Kellogg, sent the governor a telegram asking him to go to Chicago to assure the Phoenix's insured that all claims would be met. Jewell rushed to Chicago, where, standing on a packing crate among the still-smoldering ruins, he announced that Phoenix would pay in full all claims certified by the company's Chicago agent. It is said that the crowd was so heartened by the news that it "cheered, cried, and laughed by turns."

Still another trial of the Hartford fire-insurance business came with the San Francisco earthquake and fire of April 18, 1906, and again the companies came off remarkably well. As of January 1, 1901, there were six companies operating in the city—Aetna, Connecticut, Hartford, National, Orient, and Phoenix—to which soon were added the Automobile, Mechanics and Traders, Standard, Travelers Fire, World Fire and Marine, and the American office of the Rossia, the largest insurance company in Czarist Russia. The list could be extended by adding such smaller "mutual" companies as the Hartford County Fire Insurance Company, Connecticut Valley Mutual, and Hartford Tobacco Growers, all of which had headquarters in Hartford.

Despite Hartford's achieving preeminence in the fire-insurance line, life insurance was quite late in making its appearance. Although most Yankees had no scruples against insuring their material property against "acts of God," to insure one's life seemed to many Congregationalists to be a substitution of a human commercial agency for trust in Divine Providence. But while members of Hartford's Protestant clergy were denouncing life insurance as both impious and immoral, life-insurance companies were being set up in neighboring states, and Hartfordites began paying premiums on policies on their lives—premiums that added nothing to the Hartford economy.

Finally, in 1846, the Connecticut Legislature incorporated the Connecticut Mutual Life Insurance Company of Hartford. Other companies followed, and some of them had peculiar twists. In 1848 the Connecticut Health Insurance Company began business along lines suggested by its name, but as it had been organized without its founders' having any real understanding of projected risks and losses, it soon changed both its name and function to Hartford Life Insurance Company. This company experimented with a sort of "group insurance," whereby policies were issued for the insurance (as property) of black slaves. This phase of the business was protested angrily by Harriet Beecher Stowe and her Abolitionist friends, who staged a sit-down demonstration on the company's steps. The company stopped writing such policies, and whether from this or other concerns, it soon collapsed.

The Charter Oak Life Insurance Company (1850) met a similar fate because most of its small capital was in the form of stockholders' notes—few of which could be collected. Hardly more successful was the Continental Life Insurance Company, which, during its brief existence from 1862 until 1887, was the victim of bad management.

In 1851, at the peak of the Humanitarian Reform Movement, the American Temperance Life Insurance Company was founded to insure only those who would sign a pledge to abstain totally from alcohol. As there were just not enough nondrinkers in the area to work up an effective clientele, the company dropped its original name in favor of Phoenix Mutual Life Insurance Company and eliminated the pledge. In 1866 Connecticut General was formed to insure, at a markedly higher rate, the lives of those whom the regular life-insurance companies regarded as bad risks. The plan was abandoned after a two-year trial, and Connecticut General became a standard company.

Meanwhile, several of the fire-insurance companies had either added life insurance to their services or created subsidiary companies to pursue the business. Of these, Aetna first entered the line in 1850.

The Travelers Insurance Company began in 1863 almost as the result of a joke. James Goodwin Batterson, the Hartford architect and builder, while in England on an extended business trip, was amazed to learn that accident insurance was a popular form of protection in the British Isles. Thinking that such an insurance company

BELOW: In this view to the north along Main Street, a portion of the fence enclosing the State House grounds is visible in the right foreground. On the opposite side of the street is the Phoenix Bank. Jaywalking was discouraged by placing crosswalks of granite slabs; these slabs provided the only routes for pedestrians when the unpaved street was muddy. (CHS)

BELOW RIGHT: The design and decoration of the Exchange Bank, built in 1834 on State Street, suggests that it was a little bank with big ideas. Thirty years later this little bank became the National Exchange Bank. (CHS)

RIGHT: Phoenix Mutual Life Insurance Company, organized in 1851, advertised $11 million in assets with 30,000 policy holders. After the Chicago fire, the company held firm and paid all certified claims in full. From Asher & Adams, Pictorial Album of American Industry, 1876

could be created in Hartford, Batterson tried to interest his friends. All were skeptical. One day at noon, Batterson had been having a heated argument on the subject with James Bolton, president of the Hartford Bank. Hoping to test Batterson's sincerity on the matter of accident insurance, Bolton asked Batterson how much he would charge him for $5,000 in insurance against accidental death on his way home to noonday dinner and back to the bank. "Two cents," said Batterson, and Bolton handed him the desired sum. Bolton returned to his office safely, and Batterson retained the two cents.

Batterson made his point, a charter was received, and the Travelers Insurance Company began doing business as the first accident-coverage company in the United States. Despite the corporate name, Travelers began to write life insurance on a non-participating plan in 1865. Within a few years Travelers had entered virtually every type of insurance, becoming the first real multiple-line company in America. By 1980 the Travelers Group (the parent company and six subsidiaries) had an annual premium income of over $1,500,000,000 and ranked among the 25 largest corporations in the country.

During its earlier years the Travelers had many imitators. One of these was the Hartford Accident Company (1866), which in 1868 became a regular life-insurance company under the name of Hartford Life and Annuity Company, differing from the others only in that it made use of a "safety fund" whereby it carried its original insured according to the annuity plan until 1934.

Somewhere along the line, Hartford had become "The Insurance City." By 1981, 39 companies had their home offices in the Greater Hartford area. Combined, these companies had worldwide assets of $46,000,000,000. It was then estimated that each business day of the year saw $39,000,000 coming into the city and its immediate environs as premiums and that each year $13,000,000,000 was being paid out in claims.

BELOW: In 1931 the Aetna Life Insurance Company moved to Farmington Avenue. Since then, new buildings and extensions have created this "campus." Courtesy, Aetna Life Insurance Company

BELOW LEFT: The Travelers Insurance Company was located on Prospect Street in 1873. Travelers was the first accident insurance company in the U.S. (CHS)

BOTTOM: Incorporated in 1819, Aetna Insurance Company, "The leading American insurance company," insured against losses by fire or navigational hazards. The company added life insurance to its coverages in 1850. From Geer's City Directory, 1863-1864

The "New Yankees":
Hartford's Minorities

~HARTFORD'S EARLIEST
BLACKS HAD ALL BEEN SLAVES WHO LIVED WITH THEIR
MASTERS, EITHER IN THEIR OWNER'S DWELLING OR IN A
small servants' building to the rear of the main house. As
Connecticut's "gradual emancipation" laws went into
effect, however, there was no longer any room for the
freed blacks at their former quarters.

Most of them, having little vocational skill and receiving little encouragement to acquire the means of obtaining a better life, found cheap rentals in scattered areas of
the city, usually a block or so on an east-side industrial
street or near the tanneries, sections known by such
names as "Hardscrabble," "New Guinea," and "Sinking
Fund." These were cheerless and unhealthy ghettos,
overcrowded and with a total lack of sanitary facilities
and pure water.

The relatively more prosperous blacks were concentrated, by the 1820s, in the Talcott Street section and on
South Green. In 1820 William Saunders opened a tailor

shop at 10 Talcott Street, a business that was to be carried on by his descendants until 1921. During the early 1820s Jeremiah Jacobs opened a cobbler's shop on South Green. Others followed, and by the 1850s there were scores of small, black-operated businesses in both of these sections. Many of them prospered, but there was considerable segregation. Hartford city directories, for example, had separate listings for blacks and whites. Black businessmen in the Talcott Street area, although they almost invariably lived at the same address as their place of business, had their residence listed among the blacks and their business listed among the whites.

The situation of the pre-Civil War blacks, as well as the attitude of those blacks who had some education and enjoyed modest financial success, may be illustrated by the case of Augustus Washington, a well-known Hartford daguerreotypist. Washington felt that there was considerable prejudice against his race in Hartford, and he found it incongruous that as a businessman he was obliged to pay taxes even though he was not allowed to vote. Washington's proposed solution to the problem was that all blacks should migrate to the new country of Liberia. Washington also observed, and probably correctly, that although blacks were treated with respect in their day-to-day business relations with whites, they were still precluded, as he put it, "from every avenue to wealth and respectability" and could neither secure employment in the government nor receive an education beyond the most rudimentary level. Washington ultimately moved to Liberia.

Traditionally, the blacks had attended white churches, where they had been seated either in the rear or in the balcony. In the early 1820s Hartford blacks began an interdenominational effort that resulted in the Talcott Street Church. One of the founders of this congregation was Jeremiah Asher, a Baptist, and when the formerly independent congregation became Congregationalist in 1833, Asher returned to the Baptist Church on Main Street, where he led a successful campaign against "Negro seating."

The Talcott Street Church's fourth minister, the Reverend James W.C. Pennington, was an escaped slave, who, thanks to Connecticut friends, received a good education and was assisted in making a trip to Europe. While in Germany, Pennington received an honorary doctorate from the University of Heidelberg. In 1850 Congress passed the Fugitive Slave Act, which ordered all United States marshals to assist in the return of runaway slaves. When Pennington's Maryland master took steps to recover his slave property, John Hooker of Hartford, a direct descendant of Thomas Hooker and a brother-in-law of Harriet Beecher Stowe, purchased Pennington from the owner for $150. Hooker held the bill of sale for two days before turning it over to Pennington, claiming that he wanted to know what it felt like to be the owner of a Doctor of Divinity.

Hartford schools, too, were segregated, but the impetus came from the blacks themselves. In the earlier years, such blacks as received any education at all were enrolled in the city's common schools. In 1830, however, the black community requested separate schools for children of their own race, and in 1833 two black schools were set up as part of the public school system. One school was at the Talcott Street Church, and the other was at the Zion Methodist Church, which had been organized on Elm Street a few years earlier. Neither of these schools offered instruction equal to that of the others within the system. The black schools were closed in 1868, and the entire public school system became integrated.

From the time of the American Revolution on, there had been considerable antislavery sentiment in Hartford. One of the earliest to speak out against slavery was Noah Webster, and it was perhaps Webster's widely circulated pronouncements that led to the organization in 1790 of the Connecticut Anti-Slavery Society. By the 1820s this society faded out, as the American Colonization Society, largely Southern in membership, grew in strength.

The American Colonization Society was not immediately concerned with the freeing of slaves, since its primary interest, an almost selfish one, was that of sending free blacks to Africa, particularly to Liberia. Although some blacks, such as Augustus Washington, were taken in by the idea, most preferred to remain in America and improve their lot here. Bishop Thomas Church Brownell, although not sympathetic with the spirit of the American Colonization Society, was concerned for the spiritual well-being of those blacks who chose to migrate. Under the bishop's direction, the African Mission School was begun at Christ Church in 1830 to train clergy for service in Liberia. The project received much publicity but little support, although three blacks who had completed the one-year program were ordained priests in the Episcopal Church. Two went to Liberia, and one served the first all-black Episcopal parish in New Haven.

In 1837 J.S. Bullock of Georgia came to Hartford to place his children in one of Hartford's private schools. In the Bullock household was a female slave, Nancy Jackson. When Bullock returned to Georgia, the children were left in Nancy's care. The black governess immediately sued for her freedom under Connecticut law, and the court decided in her favor.

As Abolitionism gained momentum in New England, Hartford blacks supported the movement with enthusiasm. August 1 became "Black Independence Day," as it celebrated the emancipation of the slaves in the British West Indies in 1827. Blacks and whites published antislavery newspapers. The *Christian Freeman* was published in Hartford for several years after 1835, and the *Charter Oak*, another Abolitionist paper, was begun in 1838. Within a year the *Charter Oak* boasted a circulation of 3,000. During the 1840s the Reverend James Pennington edited his own Abolitionist paper, the *Northern Star and Clarksonian*. William Saunders was the Hartford agent for William Lloyd Garrison's *Liberator*, although it had few subscribers in the city.

But Garrison himself was not especially popular in Hartford. On one of his few appearances in Hartford, actually at an anti-Bible rally (as the famous Abolitionist condemned the Bible because of its sanction of slavery), the meeting was broken up by the booing and jeering of Trinity College students.

Perhaps Hartford was not much given to rallies, choosing to work in a less spectacular way. As the Underground Railroad developed, Hartford became an important stop. A "Mr. Foster," who has never been identified and who may have been several persons using the name, was particularly active. It might be added, however, that those Hartford whites who were most active in the movement to free the slaves took a somewhat cynical attitude toward the freed. The Underground Railroad ran through Hartford, but the city was not the terminal. Runaway slaves were assisted on their way to Canada—not invited to remain in Hartford.

The question of slavery even entered local politics, when the Fugitive Slave Law was endorsed by a committee of Hartford Democrats. On the other hand, the Beechers, Hookers, Stowes, and others violated many a state and federal law in sending guns and ammunition to Kansas as the antislavery forces tried forcibly—even murderously—to keep slavery from the territory.

By the 1860s Hartford's blacks had developed a social life of their own. Although public lectures and entertainment were open to persons of all races, the blacks formed a social calendar around the two black churches and the Prince Hall

TOP: The Reverend James Pennington was known internationally for his eloquent preaching and convincing commentaries, and for his part in the successful operation of the Underground Railroad by which escaped slaves made their way north to freedom. Courtesy, Connecticut Historical Commission

ABOVE: Pictured here is the Harriet Beecher Stowe house, on Forest Street, after its restoration in 1905. (CHS)

Masonic Lodge. Balls were popular, and masquerades were especially so. In 1869 Hartford blacks organized a uniformed military company, the Cambridge Guard, along the lines of the Governor's Foot Guard.

After emancipation, Black Independence Day took on new meaning. In 1866 the celebration was advertised as a Grand Union Jubilee. Admission was 25 cents per person, the price including a picnic dinner with all the fixings. The day ended with a grand ball at Gilman's.

Perhaps the proudest day for Hartford blacks was the return of Connecticut's Twenty-Ninth Regiment at the end of the war. The regiment had been created in 1863, had fought in several battles, and was one of the first Union regiments to enter Richmond at the fall of the Confederate capital. The regiment's return to Hartford was a day of rejoicing, with a parade, a reception in City Hall, and a splendid banquet. On the following day, the regiment was given breakfast, paid, and dismissed. As one woman wrote: "Colored people for once can say that they have had the city."

The post-Civil War decades brought significant changes to Hartford's black community. In 1860 the reliable estimate was that only four percent of the city's blacks had come from the South. By 1870 Southern-born blacks constituted 25 percent of the black population, and by 1900 blacks who were descended from New England pre-Revolutionary families composed a very small proportion.

Having obtained the franchise, Hartford's blacks became loyal Republicans, making much of the fact that the Republican Party was "the Party of Lincoln." Although they never were encouraged, or even permitted, to run for public office, the Republican loyalty was to last for almost three-quarters of a century.

ABOVE: Pastors of the First (Center) and Second (South) Congregational churches officiated at the dedication of this little church in 1833, which at the time had just seven members. Over the years, membership in the Talcott Street Congregational Church grew and included many prominent blacks, including Deacon Holdridge Primus and, for several years, James Pennington as its minister. Courtesy, Connecticut Historical Commission

93

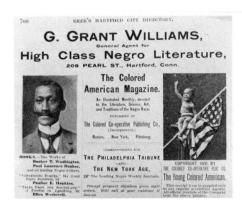

TOP: An advertisement in
Geer's Hartford City
Directory in 1900 featured
"G. Grant Williams, General
Agent for High Class Negro
Literature." Mr. Williams
was officially accredited as an
agent for the magazine, The
Young Colored American.
Courtesy, Connecticut
Historical Commission

ABOVE: For a number of
years evening English classes
aided the integration of
immigrants into the Hartford
community. (CHS)

Relations between Hartford Yankee whites and the blacks fell somewhere between "cool" and "cordial." With the Irish, however, it was another matter, because they competed with the blacks in the job market. During the mid-1830s there had been open clashes between Irish and blacks, and in July, 1834, there was what amounted to a three-day race riot.

This conflict was reflected in Hartford's political life, and the lineups that resulted in the post-Civil War decades became permanent. The Republicans had come through the war as the party of Union and respectability, while the Democrats were branded as the party of division and treason. Most Yankee Democrats switched their allegiance to the new party, and this left the Irish-Americans, who before the war had not been regarded as more than "voting fodder," in complete control, a position from which they were never to be dislodged. What few Yankee Democrats had remained were completely alienated by the party's nomination of William Jennings Bryan as the Presidential candidate in 1896. Thus, by the turn of the century, the Democratic Party had become, as one of the Hartford newspapers put it, "the party of the outs, the immigrants, the [Roman] Catholics, and the poor."

The Republicans, the Yankee party almost by default, made little effort to win the votes of most of the later immigrant groups—particularly the Poles and the Eastern European Jews. But there was a natural affinity between the Republican political leaders and the Italian-American voters. Although the alliance never went so far in Hartford as it did in New Haven —where the Democratic Party became the party of the Irish-Americans and the blacks, and the Republican Party became that of the Yankees and the Italian-Americans— it was a natural one. With the Irish control of the Democratic Party, there was little hope for Italian-American advancement with the Democrats. Also, as many of the recently arrived Italians were grocers, tailors, and shoemakers, as small businessmen they felt a kinship with the larger businessmen whose influence in Republican politics was impressive. A small business was a small business, but it was a business nevertheless.

The United States census of 1870 listed 10,644 of Hartford's population of 37,743 as "foreign born." Of these, 20 were listed as Austrian, one as Belgian, 396 as Canadian, 13 as Danish, 789 as English, 92 as French, 1,458 as German, 2 as Greek, 7,438 as Irish, 23 as Italian, 17 as Polish, 5 as Russian, 359 as Scottish, and 16 as Swedish. Ten years later (1880) the foreign born totaled 10,389 out of 42,551, with each immigrant proportion roughly that of 1870. Although to most Hartford Yankees these immigrants were still little more than "faces in a crowd," each group was making its cultural adjustment, albeit in the "halfway house" of the ethnic neighborhood. These ethnic enclaves would multiply and expand as the number of members of the respective groups increased.

The old slum by the tanneries had long since disappeared, for in the 1850s Hartford, prodded by the Reverend Horace Bushnell, had undertaken one of America's first projects in urban renewal in razing the shanties and creating Bushnell Park. The park project took almost two decades to complete, and the result was one of the most impressive municipal parks in America. But the park's greatest significance to this part of Hartford history is that it reshaped the ethnic contours of the city. South of the park, new and elegant townhouses were built along Elm Street, and newly rich manufacturers and merchants built imposing Italianate mansions on Washington Street. Blacks moved from the shanties to the "North End," which extended from Talcott Street northward along Main and Windsor streets. Irish families moved southward to the Barry Square area and the Franklin Avenue section, as developers opened one cross street after another and built three-story flats.

ABOVE: *Charles Street was a cheerful minor artery of "Little Italy." Pictured here are some of the children of that community.* (CHS)

BELOW: *With cooperation from younger siblings, these two girls actively competed in a baby-washing contest at the Brown School Playground.* (CHS)

Still-newer ethnic groups tended to concentrate in "colonies" of their own. The recently arrived Germans lived in the Park Street section. Poles located just south of the Park River between Main Street and Colt's. Lithuanians settled between Bushnell Park and Main Street. French Canadians, who began arriving at the turn of the century and by 1930 numbered 3,739 foreign born, located in the Park and Broad Street section. The Italians concentrated on the East Side along Front Street.

Each of these communities preserved some of the flavor of its old culture, and as most of the people were Roman Catholics, parish organization came to be along ethnic lines. Of these groups it was the Italians who preserved the greatest portion of their national heritage, so much so that the East Side was known as Little Italy. Here, in an area of some 10 or 12 city blocks, were Italian markets, small Italian restaurants (several ranked among the finest in town), and the shops of numerous barbers, tailors, and cobblers. Little Italy was the scene of many a colorful religious festival held by St. Anthony's Roman Catholic Church or the small Episcopal Church of St. Paul.

Hartford's Chinatown consisted, early in the 20th century, of about 20 Chinese business establishments on the south side of State Street between the Old State House and Front Street. Here were several small Chinese restaurants and Chinese import stores. The back rooms of some of these places functioned as opium dens.

Hartford's Jewish population was late in concentrating geographically. Jews were never strangers to Hartford following the unfortunate encounters with the law of "David the Jew" in 1659, for as early as 1661 several Jews were living in the home of John Marsh, and the town and city records suggest that a Jewish presence was constant from that point on. These were Sephardic Jews, originally from Spain or Portugal. Several were horse traders, while others were peddlers who worked out of Hartford selling small housewares in the back country.

These early Jews were quite inconspicuous. After all, the early Congregationalists have been described as "Old Testament" Christians, and the affinity between the two religions (especially the "thou shalt nots" and Sabbath observances) is obvious. The Connecticut Constitution of 1818, however, did not give freedom of religion to non-Christians, and it was not until 1843 that Jews were allowed to worship publicly. By that year there were enough Jews in Hartford to organize the first congregation (Reform), Beth Israel, with about 200 members. Beth Israel took over the former Baptist Church on Main Street, renamed the building Touro Hall, and used it as both a religious and social center until a handsome synagogue was built on Charter Oak Avenue in the 1870s. Beth Israel's first rabbi, Isaac Mayer, served as drama critic for the Hartford *Times.*

The German Jews were accepted easily into Hartford's city life, and by 1860 two members of this faith, Alexander Rothschild and Marcus Herlitscheck, were elected to the city council. German Jews soon became active in the legal and medical professions.

A second wave of Jewish immigration came late in the 19th century, when persecution was intensified in Russia, Poland, Lithuania, Hungary, and Rumania. These Eastern European Jews were largely Conservative, often less skilled vocationally than the earlier Germans (although some were expert furriers, cabinetmakers, and metalworkers), and much more inclined to live in ethnic areas. These newer arrivals formed neighborhoods along Main Street and Albany Avenue. By 1910 some 80 percent of Hartford's Jews were of Eastern European origin.

Immigration has had varied social effects upon American cities, but the immigrant has been blamed for creating conditions of which he had no part and in

TOP: *After almost 30 years of holding services at the old First Baptist Church on Main Street, the Congregation Beth Israel purchased land on Charter Oak Avenue and erected this synagogue in 1876. (CHS)*

ABOVE: *In one area of the marketplace, a rabbi dispatches a chicken in accordance with prescribed Jewish ritual. (CHS)*

which he was the victim rather than the cause. The immigrant, for example, did not make the slum; the slum already existed when the immigrant arrived, and, as he was usually poor at the time of his arrival, he was obliged to take whatever housing he could afford. Regarding Hartford, it may safely be said that the coming of the immigrant reduced the total area of slum districts rather than expanding it. Each of the ethnic neighborhoods had a pride that encouraged both landlords and renters to do their best to present the most favorable image of the groups.

By the 1890s one really decrepit slum remained, Gold Street, which bordered on the south side of the Ancient Burying Ground and what was left after the greater part of the poorest section of town had been taken over by Bushnell Park. Gold Street was then a dirty, narrow alley, the city's "red light district," and the habitat of the poorest of Hartford's poor.

Emily F.G. Holcombe, the wife of John M. Holcombe, president of Phoenix Mutual Life Insurance Company, decided that the Gold Street slum would have to go. Enlisting the support of the pastor of First Church, the Reverend George L. Walker, "The Gold Street Woman," as the crusader had come to be known, persuaded the city authorities that Gold Street would have to be rehabilitated. The worst of the buildings were torn down, and others were rebuilt. The street was widened, and the space between the street and First Church was planted in grass and shrubs. The passing of the last of Hartford's old slums was celebrated on April 21, 1899, when speeches were made by clergy and civic leaders, and Colt's Band led the assembled crowd in singing *Praise God, From Whom All Blessings Flow.*

Continued immigration to a city always has the effect of what sociologists call "cushioning." Each new group takes the low-paid, menial jobs at the bottom of the work force, and the arrival of each new group pushes the older group up a notch on the vocational scale. This was certainly true in Hartford, for by the end of the century, the Irish, who had been present for three-quarters of a century, had moved to a position of dominance in city politics, the police force, and the fire department and enjoyed considerable success in business and the professions.

Only once since the Civil War did Hartford's Irish become suspect. That was in the 1890s, when statewide Protestant clergy and laymen organized the American Protection Association. The APA began in New Britain in 1893, and within the year a local "chapter" appeared in Hartford. The APA was something of a throwback to the Know-Nothing movement of the 1850s, as it denounced the Irish Roman Catholics as being more loyal to Ireland and the Roman Catholic Church than they were to the United States. The Bridgeport *Independent Leader* was the APA propaganda outlet, but it found its opposition in Hartford's *Connecticut Catholic,* the predecessor of the *Catholic Transcript.* A significant piece of symbolism was effected by the new Bishop of Hartford, the Right Reverend Michael Tierney, who chose Washington's Birthday, 1894, as the day of his consecration in the new (1892) Cathedral of St. Joseph on Farmington Avenue. Although the bishop made his point in his sermon for the occasion that the Irish were just as good and loyal Americans as were the Yankees, the sermon temporarily suspended one of Harford's most colorful traditions, the St. Patrick's Day Parade. Both the bishop and the *Connecticut Catholic* took the position that the parade had outlived its usefulness and that Ireland's patron saint should be honored with banquets and "intellectual exercises." Fortunately, the American Protection Association soon thereafter passed out of the picture, but so, too—unfortunately—did the St. Patrick's Day Parade.

Certainly it was the constant immigration that swelled Hartford's population, which by 1900 had reached 79,850, of whom 23,219 were foreign born. Ten years

ABOVE: *From the 1860s to the 1890s, horse cars offered Hartford folk reliable public transportation. From the Melvin Collection (CHS)*

BELOW: *It was easier to lay rails than to pave streets in 1862, when the Hartford and Wethersfield Horse Railway Company was organized. Its name pretty much described its route—along Main Street and Wethersfield Avenue, from Spring Grove Cemetery to the center of Wethersfield, which was a distance of about 4.5 miles. (CHS)*

later, when Hartford's population stood at 98,915, immigrants and the children of immigrants composed 67 percent, a proportion just below that of New Haven (69 percent), Bridgeport (72 percent), Meriden (72 percent), and Waterbury (74 percent).

The increase in population was reflected in the geographic spread of the city, and from the time of the Civil War it was no longer possible for the workers of a particular business or factory—Colt's excepted—to live within walking distance of the work place. Also, as wealth increased, those who prospered were no longer satisfied to live in the older residential sections of the city. The Nook Farm colony to the west and Washington Street to the south provided examples of locations that combined some of the advantages of country living with urban proximity. No longer was Hartford a "walking city," the term applied by urbanists to one with a radius of less than a mile.

All these shifts were dependent upon transportation, and it was the horsecar that had made them possible. Since 1863 the Horse Car line had operated between State House Square and the Wethersfield Green. Lines were soon extended in several directions. One followed Retreat Avenue to Vernon Street, and from there by Broad Street back to the center of the city. Another ran from Park Street to Central Row, then down State Street to the Connecticut River. A third line ran the length of Albany Avenue. In 1884 service was extended north on Main Street to Capen Street, and in 1885 a line was constructed across the bridge to East Hartford Center. By the mid-1880s the horsecar line represented the ultimate in intraurban transportation, although the unpaved streets of the time were described as a mixture of mud and manure. Riding in such conveyances was far from comfortable—bad odors in the summer and insufferable cold in the winter—but the possession of a horsecar line was one of the features that distinguished the city from the town.

The Capital of Connecticut

~I<small>N</small> 1870 HARTFORD BE-
CAME INVOLVED IN A CONTEST WITH NEW HAVEN AS
TO WHICH CITY SHOULD BECOME THE SOLE CAPITAL OF
Connecticut. The Charter of 1818 had retained the
arrangement whereby alternate legislative sessions were
held in New Haven and Hartford, but in the late 1860s
there was considerable agitation for a single capital,
especially since the state government had expanded its
functions through the creation of bureaus and commissions that were much in need of office space. Furthermore, the State Houses in Hartford and New Haven
were both in need of repair. Hartford seized the initiative and offered the state $500,000 toward the erection
of a new capitol, and Hartford officials proceeded at
once to take steps to acquire the Trinity College campus
for its location.

A public meeting was held in Hartford on March 11,
1872, to sound out public opinion as to how high a price
might be offered. Although Hartford's municipal debt

then stood at $3,000,000, the sense of the meeting seemed to be in favor of purchase, even if the offer should reach $600,000. The Board of Aldermen consequently voted to purchase the Trinity Campus for $600,000, and on March 21, 1872, the college trustees accepted the offer.

Although the trustees were uncertain as to where the college would relocate, they sent President Abner Jackson to England to engage an architect for a complete, new campus and authorized him to commission a preliminary plan from any architect he might select.

Jackson engaged the services of London architect William Burges, and in September, 1873, he returned to Hartford with the most elaborate plan yet designed for an American college campus. Had the plan been completed, it would have been, as one Hartford paper boasted, "next to the Capitol at Washington, the most imposing edifice in the United States." In both spirit and detail, the Burges plan was executed in what would now be called "Victorian Gothic."

On October 12, 1872, the trustees decided in favor of a Vernon Street site and agreed to pay $225,000 for it. The trustees also voted to begin construction in April, 1874. To be completed in the first stage of development were a portion of the chapel sufficient to accommodate the current student body, the library, the dining hall, one block of lecture rooms, and two sections of dormitories. To superintend the actual building, the trustees engaged the eminent Hartford architect F.H. Kimball, who had recently been in charge of the construction of the Connecticut Mutual and the Charter Oak Life Insurance Company buildings.

On Commencement Day, July 1, 1875, Bishop John Williams turned the first sod, and excavation began immediately thereafter. During the winter of 1877-1878 the final touches were put on the new buildings, and on Friday, May 17, 1878, instruction was begun on the new campus. During the summer of 1878 the old buildings were demolished quickly.

The Trinity College part of the story had a happy ending, but the same could hardly be said of the new State Capitol. This was a story of bureaucratic bungling, naive aesthetic taste, and, of course, waste. In 1871 a commission was appointed by the legislature to solicit architectural plans and to make an appropriate selection. Five designs were submitted, but the committee could not agree, and the members resigned in 1873. A new commission was appointed, and this time 11 plans were offered. But again what made the selection process a particularly difficult one was the matter of basic architectural style.

The state capitols that had been erected from the Jeffersonian era on had all been executed in the Classical Revival style, whether Greek or Roman or a combination of the two. By the 1870s, however, "Gothic Revival" had become the vogue, as evidenced by the plans for Trinity College then being drawn by Burges, and "Gothic," or some variation thereof, was a popular choice for dwellings and such buildings as city halls or public libraries. The trouble was that state capitols had never been built in "Gothic." It just wasn't done. But the commission would have it no other way. A "Gothic" capitol it would be, and the design selected was that of Richard Upjohn, an architect who had wide experience in academic and ecclesiastical buildings but who never in his life had designed a state capitol, or, for that matter, any sort of government structure.

The original plan was for a Gothic, somewhat churchlike building with a steeple, but capitols did not have steeples, and there was immediate public opposition to the idea. Upjohn next proposed a clock tower, but again public pressure convinced both the architect and the commission that all capitols have domes—not clock

towers—so, a dome it would be, regardless of the incongruity of a gold-leaf Roman dome on a Gothic, quasi-ecclesiastical edifice. Although the result was garishly handsome, Frank Lloyd Wright, the renowned American architect, described it as the most ridiculous building he ever had seen.

But the problems were not only with the design, for at all stages of construction there were also technical difficulties. When the masons had halfway completed the tower over the Grand Court, everything gave way, and the partially completed dome tower came down in a great mass of rubble. Work had to start all over again. Other less spectacular disasters slowed down the speed of construction and greatly increased the cost. The original estimate for the entire building was $900,000. When it was finally finished in 1880, the total amount spent was just short of $3,000,000.

Whatever its aesthetic deficiencies may have been, the new Capitol stood as the symbol of Hartford as The Capital City. Hartford's city fathers, as well as the citizenry, acquired a new civic pride, and one of its first manifestations was the largest gathering yet held in Hartford, and this even before the new Capitol had been completely finished.

September 17, 1879, the anniversary of the Civil War Battle of Antietam, had been designated by the Connecticut Legislature as Battle Flag Day. The principal event of the celebration was a mammoth parade in which the Civil War battle flags were carried from the old Hartford Arsenal to the State Capitol, where they were placed in permanent display cases. Following the parade there were addresses by visiting dignitaries, and then followed a sumptuous dinner, at which, in tents pitched in Bushnell Park, thousands of veterans and their friends consumed literally tons of food. At 7 p.m. began a "grand illumination," and it was estimated that of the 100,000 persons who witnessed the parade, some 30,000 remained in Bushnell Park for the evening display.

The "illumination" was the brainchild of Morgan G. Bulkeley, the president of Aetna Insurance, and there were those who attributed Bulkeley's election in 1880 as mayor of Hartford to the success of this event. From the Willimantic Linen Company's plant were brought the six arc lights that were placed strategically about the

State Capitol. Power was provided by a small engine borrowed from the Colt factory. On the roof of the Plimpton Building on Jewel Street was placed a 3,000-candlepower searchlight, equipped with colored-glass lenses that could transform the beam into green, red, blue, or purple, and so mounted that its light could be directed at random about Bushnell Park and the lower part of the city.

From 7 o'clock until 10, the amazed and delighted spectators, seated upon blankets on the park's grassy slopes, watched the searchlight play on the Ford Street Bridge, the Capitol, the decorated arches, the fountain, and at random about the park. "Now and then," as the *Courant* reported, "the light would strike some unexpected spot, and there would be a slight scream and a lively scramble as some affectionate couple who had been seated near together on the river bank would find themselves in daylight and beat a retreat."

The following day the lights were returned to Willimantic and the engine to the Colt factory. For most of those who had witnessed the electrical display, the evening of September 17 had been one of entertainment, splendid entertainment, but nothing more. For those interested in the economic potentiality of electricity, however, a new age had begun. Hartford would soon demand public electrical service. The city was ready for the new Electrical Age.

Hartford at that time was thriving as an important banking, industrial, insurance, and wholesale-distribution center. During the year 1880, more than 500 steam vessels and 270 barges had dumped thousands of tons of coal, lumber, salt, iron, fertilizer, dyewoods, potatoes, cement, lime, and other commodities on the river docks of Hartford, certainly a significant volume for a minor, inland river port.

Geographically, the city was still confined to a radius of two miles from the Old State House, which had just then become Hartford's City Hall. The commercial area extended some eight city blocks from the Connecticut River westward to the railroad depot at the foot of Asylum Hill, and from Sheldon Street on the south to Belden Street to the north. Residential areas had sprawled in each direction along the main traffic arteries toward Wethersfield, New Britain, Farmington, and Windsor.

Transportation was well provided for. Regular steam-packet lines ran between Hartford and New York, and connecting lines provided accommodation to Boston, New London, or Providence. Railroads also offered service to Boston, New York, Providence, and Springfield. For intraurban travel, there were horsecar routes serving the outlying sections. Public hacks served short-term travel needs, and 21 livery stables offered horse-drawn vehicles for hire. Visitors were accommodated at the 21 hotels, which ranged from the palatial Allyn House to flophouses, and there were 144 saloons.

Police protection was insured by a force of 45 patrolmen, and the fire department employed almost 100 men. Sanitary engineering was a science then in its infancy, and the inadequacies of the sewerage system were a constant vexation to householders. The water system was much more satisfactory; from six reservoirs, a daily average of 6,000,000 gallons flowed through 70 miles of underground pipes to 4,962 homes, business houses, and industrial concerns.

Hartford streets were, for the time, well lighted. Since 1821, when a few feeble oil lamps had first been installed at public expense, the City had accepted responsibility for providing street illumination, and since the incorporation of the Hartford City Gas Light Company in 1849, the number of gaslights had risen steadily until 1880, when more than 1,000 jets gave off their yellow glow along 80 miles of city streets.

There was a splendid school system, culminating in Hartford Public High, and there were several proprietary academic operations that offered training in the "commercial branches." There were also the Theological Institute of Connecticut—chartered in 1854 and soon to become the Hartford Theological Seminary—and Trinity College. Fifty-two churches and synagogues ministered to those of almost every religious persuasion. Local and world news was provided in 11 weekly or daily papers. Magazines directed toward religious, vocational, and educational interest were also published in Hartford, and the city was, with its 24 printing houses, enjoying the last glow of her golden day as an important publishing center. Telegraph service had been available since the early 1850s, and the first telephones had been installed in 1878.

Several of the city's industries were nationally known. Colt's Patent Fire Arms Manufacturing Company, the Weed Sewing Machine Company, Hill's Archimedean Lawn Mower Company, and the National Stove Company were among the major manufacturing plants. Altogether there were 800 factories of all sizes and descriptions—foundries, breweries, tanneries, machine-tool works, and woodworking shops, to name but a few—and in 1880 they paid wages of $8,457,000 to 20,951 employees.

Hartford had entered the Electrical Age with Battle Flag Day, and it was assumed that electricity would soon be available commercially. The question was who would provide it.

Hartford investors soon became eager participants in starting the American Electric Company, formed in New Britain late in 1880, but this company was involved in producing electrical systems, not in supplying electrical service from a central power station. Consequently, a power struggle began for investor support and legislative favor between the older-type utilities and the promoters of yet-unborn companies to be created for the specific purpose of supplying electrical service.

Hartford's oldest utility was the Hartford City Gas Light Company, and, as it was assumed that much of the city's electricity consumption would be in street lighting, the gas company regarded itself as the logical producer of electricity. The company had supplied street illumination as well for more than 30 years, and it had pro-

TOP: In 1889 Sage, Allen and Company began at the corner of Main and Pratt streets. Later, the company moved into larger quarters on the other side of Main. Today, it is one of Hartford's finest department stores, with branches in several Connecticut towns and shopping malls. (CHS)

ABOVE: The new Union Station in 1889 with its elevated tracks alleviated the hazardous traffic situation at the foot of the Asylum Street hill. (CHS)

vided much of Hartford's indoor illumination as well. In 1880 it also had some 800 cooking stoves connected to its lines. In March 1881 the gas company petitioned the Connecticut Legislature for a charter amendment to permit it to produce and distribute electricity within its gas-franchise territory.

Hartford's second utility company was a newcomer. The Hartford Steam Heating Company had been chartered on March 25, 1879, to furnish steam through underground pipes for heating and power. Pipes were laid through the principal business streets during the summer of 1880, and the system was put into operation that fall. Leakage of steam accounted for both bad service and costly operation, and by the spring of 1881 there was reason to believe that the $500,000 business venture had been a failure. The steam company nevertheless felt that its Pearl Street plant could be utilized in the generation of electricity, and in the spring of 1881 it, too, petitioned for a charter amendment to permit the sale of electricity as a sideline.

There were those in Hartford who felt that the best interests of the city would be served by an electric company operating independently of both the City Gas Light Company and the Steam Heating Company. One of them was Mayor Bulkeley, who began making plans for an independent company. Bulkeley persuaded both of the utility companies to abandon their plans, and on April 12, 1881, the Hartford Electric Light Company was incorporated by act of the Connecticut State Legislature. In June of 1881 American Electric installed a lighting system in the Allyn House. Shortly thereafter, the American Theater on Market Street installed a single outside arc light. The theater's newspaper advertisements always read, "Look for the Electric Light"—a light that provided enough illumination for the theater's pit band to read music in the short sidewalk concert that preceded each evening performance.

Bulkeley's position as mayor of Hartford raised the question of conflict of interest, and the Hartford Electric Light Company got off to a late start. Nevertheless, when the company's subscription books were opened on January 12, 1882, there were sales of 200 shares, at $100 each, totaling $20,000, hardly a working capital for even the most miniscule corporate undertaking. Only 20 percent of this amount was to be put up immediately, and even this was not paid in cash but was represented by real estate or secured notes. On February 6, 1882, the directors held their first session and elected A. C. Dunham as president and Sylvester C. Dunham as secretary.

In late May, 1882, an agreement was made whereby the Light Company would have steam supplied by the Steam Heating Company's boilers. By the evening of Saturday, April 7, 1883, all was ready, and at sundown lights were turned on at the depot, at Rathbun's Pharmacy, Marwick's Drug Store, Goerz Brothers' Saloon, Conrad's Bakery, and Mansuy's Carriage Shop at 17 Elm Street. On Pearl Street, a single streetlamp was exhibited in front of the company's plant. It was not an imposing exhibition, but the Hartford Electric Light Company was at least in business.

The Hartford newspapers commented most favorably on the inauguration of service, and Hartford businessmen, too, evidenced their support of the new enterprise, as in rapid succession lights were installed in Brown-Thomson's "One Price Clothing Store," Cadden's Clothiers, Heublein's Saloon, and Smith, White & Co.'s furnishings store. In less than a month four dynamos were in operation, and 100 lights had been subscribed.

On January 14, 1884, the Common Council voted to accept the Hartford Electric Light Company's proposal for street lighting and to give the experiment a six-month trial. On the night of May 2, 1884, 26 streetlights were put into service, as the *Courant* reported, "to the satisfaction of all who witnessed the display." And certainly the achievement was a proud one for the city, for the *Courant* further added that

ABOVE: *Hartford has always given visitors a wide range of hotels from which to choose. The Heublein Hotel was one of the better ones; its dignified comfort is apparent in this picture of the lobby.* (CHS)

BELOW: *The Thorne typesetting and distributing machine revolutionized the print industry with its quick and efficient rotary operation. Hartford publishers such as the* Evening Post, Forum, *and* Current Literature *took advantage of this progressive device to aid them with their publications. From* Hartford, Connecticut, *1889*

After the Civil War, Weed Sewing Machine Company rented unused sections of the struggling Sharps Rifle Company. Branching out from its usual sewing machine production, Weed in 1878 took a contract to produce bicycles. From Hartford, Connecticut, 1889

These two photographs were taken 25 years apart. One was in 1888, a day or so after the blizzard, and the other was in the 1910s. Both look east on Asylum Street from the corner of Trumbull. Some new construction and facade changes in the block are evident in the second view. (CHS)

Hartford was at last "on a par with its sister cities." Hartford's first 26 arc lights installed on the city's streets had displaced 163 gas lamps. Even at this early date it was agreed that the brighter lights would help reduce crime and that the savings on police-department budgets could pay for the additional cost.

Late in 1884 the Schuyler Electric Light Company moved its office and factory from New York City to Hartford. Schuyler was one of the smaller incandescent-system manufacturers, but its location in Hartford more or less established the city as a minor center of electrical-equipment manufacture. The Waterhouse Electric and Manufacturing Company was organized in January, 1886, by Hartford industrialists who had connections with such well-established firms as Colt's, Pratt and Whitney, and Billings and Spencer. Five of the directors were described by *Electrical World* as "mechanical experts." The Waterhouse plant was set up in Colt's Armory. Two other small electrical manufacturers soon were to operate in Hartford—the Mather Electric Light Company and Eddy Electric.

On May 24, 1887, David Henney secured a charter for the Hartford Light and Power Company, but only after vigorous opposition by the gas company, Hartford Electric Light, and the Hartford business community. The Hartford Light and Power Company never was really able to get its house in order, and throughout its decade of existence it suffered one embarrassment after another. In one instance, however, the Hartford Light and Power Company was able to pull off a spectacular coup—that of supplying electric power for the Hartford and Wethersfield Horse Railroad. Early in 1888 Elizur J. Goodrich, president of the Horse Railroad Company, announced that a contract had been drawn up to purchase cars and that an arrangement had been made with Hartford Light and Power to provide electricity.

On September 21, 1888, the first electrified car made the run from the car barns at 109 Wethersfield Avenue in Hartford to Main and Church streets in Wethersfield. The run was made in 20 minutes and the return in 18. With horses, the round trip had always taken a full hour. Electrification of the horsecar line spread rapidly, and by 1892 the last of the horses had been retired.

The Hartford Electric Light Company took over the Pearl Street Station of the Light and Power Company in March, 1896, and the two systems were completely

ОTEKA

integrated without interruptions of service for the customers of either company.

These developments, small as they may seem when considered individually, were symptomatic of a general acceptance of electricity. By 1890 electricity had become very much a part of Hartford's way of life, as the city streets were by then entirely lighted by electricity, several hundred homes were lighted by incandescent lamps, most of the downtown stores had been equipped for either arc or incandescent lighting, electricity was propelling streetcars, and in a few industrial plants electricity as a source of power at least had gained a foothold.

Electricity had become, by the 1880s, one of the appurtenances of urban living, and by the 1890s the same could have been said of the electric car. In the first decade of the 20th century, it would be the automobile, and here Hartford would write a small and curious chapter in the history of American technology. The story is simple, short, and sad.

Following the American Civil War, Sharps Rifle Company fell upon hard times, and as production declined sections of the plant were rented out to the Weed Sewing Machine Company and other manufacturing concerns. In 1870 Sharps was sold to P. T. Barnum, the famous showman, and production operations were moved to Bridgeport. The Weed Company then took over the entire Sharps building. Weed, as Sharps had done before, leased portions of the plant to other concerns, but Weed itself took contracts with numerous manufacturers for the production of machinery having nothing to do with the sewing machine. One such contract was with Albert Pope of Boston for the production of bicycles, the "Columbia," the first such contraption to be produced in America. George H. Day of Hartford, reputedly a "mechanical genius," was placed in charge of Pope's bicycle department.

Pope, meanwhile, was experimenting with machinery far more complex than the bicycle and, assisted by Day, he completed several prototype horseless carriages. In 1890 Pope purchased the Weed Company and changed its name to the Pope Manufacturing Company. Day became vice president and treasurer of the company. Hiram Percy Maxim was hired as his chief engineer, and in 1895, Pope, Day, and Maxim produced their first gasoline-engine automobile, the Pope-Hartford. Historians of technology agree that this production marked the beginning of the auto-

In the 1880s, Billings and Spencer Company, organized by Charles E. Billings, manufactured many steel tool items which were used in other manufacturers' products. From Hartford, Connecticut, 1889

These two photographs of Main Street were taken just two seasons apart. Looking south from Mulberry Street, it was business as usual in the fall of 1887. In March of 1888 the Great Blizzard struck. Rails were out of sight for a week, but public transportation was resumed when the wheels were taken off the horsecars and replaced with sleigh runners. (CHS)

ABOVE: *This load of Christmas trees had been brought into Hartford in anticipation of the Christmas rush in 1890. (CHS)*

RIGHT: *Some 200 acres near the Wethersfield town line were an important part of the plan for parks in Hartford. The land includes a golf course now, but earlier the "fairways" were used every spring for maypole dancing. (CHS)*

FACING PAGE, BOTTOM: *When Hartford enjoyed its brief role as the automotive capital of America, a Pope-Hartford "paddy wagon" was purchased for the Police Department. After this purchase the police no longer needed to borrow wheelbarrows to bring in suspects. (CHS)*

mobile industry in the United States. Had the Pope Company limited its production to internal-combustion-engine cars, Hartford, rather than Detroit, might have become the automotive capital.

Pope's preference, however, was for the electric automobile, and in 1897 the company began producing the Columbia Electric. In 1899 the editor of an English technical journal declared Hartford to be "the greatest center of activity in the automobile industry today." Pope's choice was a bad one. The electric automobile was then simply not practical. Furthermore, the Pope Company became involved in a lawsuit with Henry Ford, and Ford won his case. By 1912 the Pope Company was defunct.

Oddly, considering that Hartford was so much involved in automobile production, the "newfangled machine" was slow in being accepted by residents of the city. As streetcar service was excellent and railway service was of the highest standard, many Hartfordites preferred to use public transportation rather than purchase an automobile.

The Pope-Hartford was a handsome automobile, but it was expensive, and for those who preferred to "buy Hartford," it was a choice between a Pope-Hartford and no car at all. Then, too, there was the influence of the Hartford Electric Light Company, which shared Thomas A. Edison's belief that the electric automobile would triumph over that fueled by gasoline. It was in this confidence that a small fleet of electric cars was built up to completely replace the horse-drawn vehicles that had served for 20 years as the standard equipment for Hartford Electric Light.

In 1909 the Light Company took the Hartford sales agency for the General Vehicle Company, a Long Island City, New York, manufacturer of electric trucks. But the "G. V.," despite considerable advertising on the part of the company, did not become popular. Although Hartford Electric Light was able to provide complete repair and battery service for battery-driven vehicles, there were, during the first year, only three electric trucks, other than those owned by the company, under the vehicle department's care. And somewhat ironically, at about the same time that the Hartford Electric Light Company began its full-scale battery-charging service, the company began replacing its own electric cars with gasoline-driven Fords. In 1912, in fact, the Elmer Automobile Company, the Hartford Ford agency, featured a picture of the Hartford Electric Light Company's fleet of Fords in one of its advertisements. Although the company kept a nominal "G. V." agency through World War I, few trucks were sold, and in 1922 Hartford Electric Light began to liquidate this phase of its operations.

Horses long remained a part of everyday life in Hartford. As late as 1910 several pieces of Hartford's fire-fighting equipment were horse drawn, and trash collection was completely by horse and wagon. Even at that late date there were several livery stables with horses for hire, and there were still 20 blacksmiths plying their trade in the city.

A pioneer in the manufacture of bicycles in America, Albert Augustus Pope contracted Weed Sewing Machine Company to build the "Columbia," the first American-made bicycle, in May 1878. An advocate of electric automobiles, Pope turned from bicycles to manufacturing "Columbia Electric" automobiles in 1897. From Cirker, Dictionary of American Portraits, *Dover, 1967*

Albert Pope's greatest contribution to Hartford was his gift to the city of the 75-acre Pope Park in 1895. This large expanse was close to the Pope factory, and it served as the recreation grounds for the thousands of working-class families who occupied that part of the city southwest of the State Capitol.

Significantly, Pope Park was created while the Reverend Francis Goodwin was chairman of the Hartford Park Commission. Goodwin operated with the slogan of "More Parks for Hartford," and his plan was to have Hartford circled by parks much like the Fenway System then being laid out around Boston. At the same time that Pope Park was being developed, Goodwin persuaded Charles N. Pond to donate his large estate in the northwestern part of the city as Elizabeth Park, in memory of Pond's wife. Goodwin also persuaded Henry Keney to donate Keney Park in the North End. It was appropriate that Goodwin Park in Hartford's extreme southern end, and which completed the city's major park system, should have been named for the indefatigable commissioner.

The impetus toward parks and open spaces was paralleled by the construction of handsome new business buildings—particularly newer headquarters of the Hartford banks and insurance companies. These structures were of neoclassical design and invariably were built of granite or marble. All of this was something of a reflection of the "City Beautiful" movement that stemmed from the neoclassical architecture of the World Columbian Exposition of Chicago in 1893, and whose influences were felt in virtually every municipality in the country. In 1907 Hartford followed the example of other cities in creating a City Plan Commission for the purpose of making long-range studies regarding land use and urban beautification.

But the City Beautiful idea, while obviously responsible for a transformation of "public" Hartford, did not bring beauty to all the city's residents. The United States Bureau of Labor reported in 1905 that of the cities it had studied in regard to housing conditions, Hartford was the worst of those of its size. The bureau noted particularly that most working-class homes were without bathtubs and that the tenement occupants took their weekly baths in the commercial bathhouses located in the poorer sections of the city.

CHAPTER

XI

Modern Times

~Wars OFTEN MARK
TURNING POINTS IN HISTORY—WHETHER THE HISTORY
IS OF THE WORLD, A NATION, OR A CITY. SUCH, CER-
tainly, was the case in Hartford, for it was with the First
World War that the modern city emerged.

On the eve of the outbreak of World War I, Hartford
was enjoying a considerable economic prosperity, and
the business community, led by an energetic Board of
Trade, was most optimistic. The 1911 *Annual Report* of
the Board noted that new industries were coming to
Hartford, and that the Grand List, which then stood at
$91,037,095, represented an almost 10 percent rise
from the previous year. In typical booster fashion, the
Board estimated Hartford's population at 113,944, even
though the census of 1910 had reported only 98,915.
Hartford was then listed as Number 62 among American
manufacturing cities, and even among Connecticut cities
in that survey Hartford ranked below Bridgeport's Number 33, New Haven's 46, and Waterbury's 48.

When Austria-Hungary declared war on Serbia on July 28, 1914, most Americans expected little more than a "Third Balkan War." Nor in November of 1916 were the Connecticut voters influenced by Woodrow Wilson's campaign slogan, "He kept us out of war." The state went Republican by a clean sweep, and the Democratic *Times* declared that "Hartford regards the European war as terrible, and is glad it has no part in it."

On February 20, 1917, the Connecticut Legislature authorized an inventory of men and materials available in case of war. The industrial summary revealed that 34 Connecticut firms employing over 40,000 workers were already operating under contracts with the federal government. Among these were such Hartford companies as Colt's, Veeder-Root, Maxim Silencer, and Hartford Machine Screw. And it certainly must have been well known that the Colt plant was busily supplying the Allies with orders that were being handled through Canada.

When the United States declared war on Germany on April 6, 1917, the declaration came as no surprise, for already Governor Marcus H. Holcomb had, at the request of the Secretary of War, Newton D. Baker, appointed a State Council of Defense. Through its various subcommittees, the Council soon became the State's principal agency in coordinating the war effort.

The publicity committee undertook the formidable task of making Connecticut's people aware of wartime needs, and during the war years it sponsored hundreds of war rallies that were intended to stimulate enthusiasm for the war effort.

Food supply became an immediate and serious concern. A Junior Food Army and a Connecticut Canning Corps enlisted large numbers of children and adults, and in May, 1917, the Connecticut Assembly passed an act permitting high-school students over 14 to volunteer for farm work. Home gardens flourished, and vacant lots and institutional grounds were parceled out for cultivation by anyone who applied.

Hartford, with a relatively small population of German extraction, had no serious problem with the antialien attitudes prevalent in the larger ethnic melting pots. The committee on education, however, did carry on its program of "Americanization" under a subcommittee on "American Loyalty" and distributed its pamphlets (with such titles as *What We Are Fighting For*) to grade-school children of Hartford's immigrant families.

Of the Connecticut "Big Five"—Remington Arms and Ammunition, Remington Union Metallic, Winchester, Marlin-Rockwell, and Colt's—Colt's was probably the farthest on the way toward full-time war production when war was declared. From a prewar labor force of 800, Colt's employment soon rose to over 8,000. And, as the company found that it was unable to produce revolvers, machine guns, and automatic rifles in sufficient quantities to satisfy the demands of the United States government, it surrendered its patent rights for the duration of the war on a royalty basis. Although Colt's was the Hartford area's principal war-materiel producer, numerous small plants about the city were engaged in producing goods for United States troops and those of America's Allies.

Most of the plants producing war goods went on round-the-clock, seven-day schedules. Householders were requested to conserve electricity. Hartford soon became accustomed to "lightless nights" after the city ordered that all street lighting be discontinued, and streets were in total darkness. The adoption of daylight-saving time, too, helped conserve electricity by shifting the peak load.

Despite their wartime profits, Hartford's industries suffered from the increased cost of bituminous coal. In 1916 coal could be purchased for $3.60 a ton, but by the summer of 1917 the price had risen to $7 a ton and always there was the problem of

In 1917 the domestic science curriculum at Hartford Public High School was coordinated with the war efforts. These girls were part of the program known as the "Girls Army." (CHS)

FACING PAGE: With several quicksand faults in the Hartford area, subway construction would have been difficult and costly. Instead, trolleys provided most of the public transportation in Hartford from 1890 until they were completely replaced by buses in the 1940s. (CHS)

securing any coal at all. When war was declared, there was just enough coal on hand to last the factories and the utility companies for two months, and at no time before the end of hostilities were they able to stockpile beyond that point.

There were troubles in the labor force, too. At the Light Company, for example, 80 men, or one-fifth of the total, went into the Armed Forces. Each man who was drafted or who volunteered was assured that he would be returned, upon his discharge from service, to the same position he had held at the time of his induction. Although in retrospect the arrangement seems to have been the only conceivable one, it was far from universal. Virtually all companies held the jobs for those who were drafted, but there was usually no such arrangement for those who volunteered.

One Hartford company to be particularly hard hit by the draft and by encouraged volunteering was the Hartford Steam Boiler Inspection and Insurance Company. As had been the case in the Spanish-American War, Hartford Steam Boiler, because of the particular skills of the engineering and inspection staffs, found that more than 10 percent of its employees went into the National Service. Many of the inspectors served in the Navy, usually in charge of the engineering staff of transport vessels or fighting ships.

Such plants as Colt's Patent Fire Arms and Pratt and Whitney Tool were thought to be vulnerable to sabotage by the Germans, and guarding the plants became a necessity. Arrangements were made through the Hartford Police Department whereby supernumeraries would be on duty at all times.

In the summer of 1916 Congress passed the National Defense Act, which permitted the colleges to provide Reserve Officer Training. The program was begun at Trinity on a volunteer basis on March 22, 1917, but early in 1918 the R.O.T.C. was replaced by the Student Army Training Corps, an ill-conceived program whereby the government literally turned the campuses into Army camps. None of the colleges benefited academically from this move, for it indiscriminately filled the colleges with many young men who were totally incapable of profiting from even the much diluted form of higher education that was being carried on for the Army. Since long hours of drill left little time for study, there was a reduction in the number of academic courses. The spring of 1918 marked the high tide of the war spirit at Trinity. At an "Open Air Patriotic Service," held on Sunday, June 18, 1918, the day before commencement, Ex-President Theodore Roosevelt urged the Trinity community to the greatest heights of patriotic endeavor.

News of the signing of the Armistice of November 11, 1918, came as something of an anticlimax, as for several weeks the Hartford newspapers had been suggesting that peace was near. On November 8 a rumor spread that the war had ended, and workers in factories and offices rushed into the streets, bringing traffic to a halt. The rumor proved to be false, and the Hartford citizenry was dejected. Four days later, however, news of the real Armistice reached Hartford. This time, a spontaneous parade of some 10,000 marchers went through the city, providing their own "music" with tin horns and pans. A more sedate parade was held on April 30, 1919, when Johnny was welcomed home officially by a crowd estimated at 200,000.

With the end of hostilities, the American economy and American industry tried to return to what President Warren G. Harding was to call "normalcy." However, the city's insurance companies, particularly those specializing in machinery coverage, found that the resumption of peacetime production brought many problems. Industries engaged in war production had worked their plants around the clock and around the calendar, and by the end of the war much of their machinery was fatigued and obsolete. And a serious blow to those insurance companies involved with boilers, machinery, and industrial plants was the passage in October, 1919, of the Volstead Act, which prohibited the manufacture of any beverage of more than one-half of one percent alcohol.

The life-insurance companies, too, had their problems. When the war began, the companies offered to assist the United States government in carrying the war-risk policies that had been promised all who entered military service. Although the offer was not accepted, the Hartford insurance companies made a contribution (and a costly one at that) of their own by continuing at no additional premium all policies in force, even though the policyholders had been sent overseas.

The influenza epidemic of 1918 resulted in some 500,000 deaths in the United States alone, and the many death claims paid by the companies placed a heavy strain upon Hartford's insurance industry. Each company met all of its claims, although several companies recovered a portion of the loss by reducing the amount paid to stockholders in dividends.

Hartford insurance had survived the war quite well, but the manufacturing companies were less fortunate. War contracts had ended, and there was the difficult transition to peacetime production. Even those industries that were able to make the change were still beset with the problem of obtaining sufficient coal to operate their machinery. On November 1, 1919, the miners went on strike, demanding a 60 percent pay boost, a six-hour day, and a five-day week. The strike was short, and the union settled for a 14 percent pay increase, but hardly had the coal strike ended when a railroad strike was called.

On November 2 the United States Fuel Administrator ordered 40 carloads of coal destined for Hartford to be held in railroad yards. The Hartford consignees feared that there might be a total cutoff of the supply. Such was not the case, but the long-range consequence was a rise in the price of coal to an unbelievable $17.50 a ton.

BELOW LEFT: The opening of the new armory marked the closing of the old. The cavalry was mustered for the occasion, and the First Regiment Armory on Elm Street was torn down shortly thereafter. (CHS)

BELOW: Teams clear snow from a pond for skaters in Riverside Park. It was a tedious process, and if a horse broke through the ice, the city closed the pond to skating. (CHS)

Labor felt that it had not shared in the wartime industrial prosperity, and local labor leaders, despite the huge layoffs at Hartford's factories, urged those workers who still had jobs to strike. Underwood Typewriter Company suffered a long work stoppage. Dissatisfied with Samuel Gompers' nonpartisan political stance, the Hartford Central Labor Union and 26 other labor unions formed the American Labor Party to run candidates for local and state offices in the election of 1919.

Inflation rose at about the same rate as unemployment. Between July, 1914, and November, 1919, according to figures provided by the National Industrial Conference, all household budget items had increased 82.2 percent. When a group of Hartford women organized the Hartford Housewives League, a spokeswoman for the group noted that the spirit of wartime sacrifice had turned to sullen anger.

Before radio or television reported the weather, this kiosk near the Old State House displayed barometers, thermometers, and updated weather forecasts. (CHS)

The anger in some quarters was far from silent, for the postwar period saw a small but extremely vocal group emerge in support of Russian Bolshevism, and there were all varieties of Communist sympathizers ranging from moderate Socialists to the International Workers of the World. The pastor of Hartford's small Greek Orthodox Church estimated that half of his congregation had been converted to Communism.

On March 2, 1919, about 2,000 persons gathered in the Grand Theatre to hear speakers from the I.W.W. condemn American capitalism and praise the Bolsheviks. Shortly thereafter, the Hartford Board of Aldermen voted unanimously to forbid either the Communists or the I.W.W. to conduct public meetings, display the Red flag, or distribute Communist literature. Violation carried a fine of $100 and imprisonment for six months.

Federal agents made numerous arrests, and the *Courant* reported that of all Connecticut cities, Hartford was probably the center of "Red" activity. Continued raids on alleged Communist gathering places filled the Hartford jail to the bursting point. Most of those incarcerated were aliens, either Russians or Lithuanians. Some of them were guilty only by association, as most of those individuals who went to visit imprisoned friends or relatives were themselves incarcerated. "Dangerous" aliens were kept behind bars for months without a hearing, and several complained that they had been denied needed medical attention. Under the direction of United States Attorney General A. Mitchell Palmer, many of the radicals were deported, some were sentenced to long prison terms, and a few were found innocent of their charges and freed. By the spring of 1920, Hartford's phase of the "Red Scare" had come to an end.

As these terrifying events were unfolding in Hartford, the business community was undertaking one of the most expansive programs in the city's history—the industrial and commercial development of the South Meadows. Actually, it had already begun in July, 1917, when the Hartford Electric Light Company purchased about 95 acres of land in the Meadows, with the intention of building a new powerhouse on the site.

Those familiar with Hartford's geography must have wondered whether the company was serious. South Meadows was then a large, low-lying tract, subject to flooding with each spring freshet, and totally unoccupied. South Meadows extended from the dike at the edge of the Colt's development southward to Wethersfield Cove. It was the Light Company's announcement that brought to public attention the hitherto-unused meadowland just two miles south of Hartford's business center, the city's only remaining area for extensive industrial development.

The City Council persuaded the United States Army Corps of Engineers to make a survey. Late in June, 1919, the Army Engineers announced that the Connecticut River along South Meadows would be widened and deepened, that the dredgings from the river would be used in the construction of a dike, and that some 1,000 acres of land would be reclaimed.

This was sufficient assurance for Hartford Electric Light, and on August 13, 1919, the company announced that a power plant would be constructed as soon as

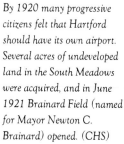

By 1920 many progressive citizens felt that Hartford should have its own airport. Several acres of undeveloped land in the South Meadows were acquired, and in June 1921 Brainard Field (named for Mayor Newton C. Brainard) opened. (CHS)

the land could be prepared. Soon the Standard Oil Company announced its intention of developing a huge oil depot on an adjoining tract.

On December 13, 1919, a writer for the Hartford *Times* rhapsodized over the future of the South Meadows. Somewhat prophetically, he visualized "two miles of busy waterfront alive with the movement of barge and boat and crane and car and noisy with the sound of whistle and bell and shouts of men, a riverside lined with docks and warehouses, areas studded with factories ... an industrial center laid out with fair streets and parkways, [and] somewhere in it a flying field with facilities for aircraft carrying passengers or mail or aerial express." The South Meadows project soon received the enthusiastic support of the Chamber of Commerce, and the estimated $300,000 to be spent in land reclamation was generally regarded as a sound municipal investment.

Without waiting for the construction of a dike, the Light Company began work. A railroad siding was built as soon as the spring flood of 1920 had subsided, and during the summer thousands of tons of fill—mostly coal ashes—were brought in from the Dutch Point Power Plant and by the Edward Balf Company, which had the municipal ash-collection contract. Actual construction was begun in the fall.

The building of the South Meadows plant came at a most opportune time. As was true in all cities that had been engaged in war production, unemployment had remained a problem. The policy agreed upon by Hartford manufacturers was one of dismissing women employees not supporting families and hiring discharged veterans in their stead. But this replacement was not an even exchange, for most of the Hartford factories had either closed or gone on short shifts. With 1,000 men on the construction force, the South Meadows project certainly was welcomed.

The power plant was not the only major construction then under way on the South Meadows. The new airfield—soon to be named Brainard Field in honor of Mayor Newton Case Brainard—was being laid out, and this busy activity attracted the curious, especially on Sunday afternoons. Light Company officials were much concerned that the not-altogether-welcome visitors might be injured, and guards were stationed at the approach to their tract. On May 2, 1921, the guards refused to allow several members of the Hartford Aviation Association to use the road that crossed the Light Company's property. Hartford's corporation counsel sharply

Hartford police wore civilian clothes on the job until 1860. By 1920, when this full-dress review was photographed, uniforms were an established part of the force. (CHS)

reminded the company that the deed under which the land had been acquired clearly specified that the road should be kept open forever to all who wished to use it. With this, the unpleasant incident was closed. The airport was dedicated on June 12, 1921, the second municipal airport in the United States. The dedication of the new Light Company plant was on December 19, 1921.

South Meadows developed slowly but steadily, as one business after another located there. Oil-storage tanks came to stand next to warehouses, and wholesaling businesses, particularly those dealing in foodstuffs, located near the Regional Market, a public facility that opened in 1952. With the development of Bradley International Airport in nearby Windsor Locks following World War II, the size of Brainard Field was greatly reduced by the laying out of new streets, a move that limited the airport's usefulness to small planes. A considerable portion of the "lower" Meadows was later taken up by the city's sewage-treatment plant.

In 1925 the Pratt & Whitney Company brought Hartford into the Air Age when its small plant began to produce small, air-cooled Wasp airplane engines for both the Navy and commercial use. Soon the company began turning out the 525-horsepower Hornet engines. Within 10 years the work force at P & W rose from 25 to 2,000, and the company moved its main production to East Hartford. This small beginning resulted in United Aircraft, which soon included Hamilton Standard Propeller and Sikorsky Aircraft, all part of the corporation now known as United Technologies, the largest employer in New England.

The Hartford Foundation for Public Giving also was established in 1925. The agency grew into the largest dispenser and coordinator of public philanthropy in Connecticut. The forming of the foundation was the culmination of the history of philanthropy in Hartford, a city long noted for its giving and its givers.

The history of private philanthropy in Hartford began in 1809, when the Hartford Female Beneficent Society was organized, as its charter declared redundantly, to

afford "relief to needy indigent females." In 1822 what is now the Institute of Living was incorporated as the Hartford Retreat for the Insane. In 1842 Daniel Wadsworth endowed the Wadsworth Atheneum, the first art museum in New England. In 1852 the Hartford Young Men's Christian Association was organized, just a year after the first YMCA had been founded in Boston. Fifteen years later the WCA (later the YWCA) was inaugurated. Hartford Hospital was started in 1854, and other hospitals followed. In 1898 the Congregation of the Sisters of Saint Francis opened Saint Francis Hospital, and in 1923 the Hartford Jewish community organized the city's third general hospital—Mount Sinai.

Hartford also saw the creation of the more obviously "social service" agencies. The Woman's Aid Society was organized in 1878, as the purpose was stated euphemistically at the time, "for the reformation of fallen women," although in later years its attention was directed toward the assistance of unwed mothers. In 1884 the Open Hearth Mission began care for homeless men, operating on the philosophy that none should be fed, clothed, or sheltered without at least a token payment. The Open Hearth's transient guests sawed cordwood in exchange for some minimum of human comfort.

With the establishment in the early 1890s of what were to become the Family Service Society and the Children's Services, charities in Hartford assumed their modern character. These organizations, together with the Visiting Nurse Association (1901), the Charter Oak Council of the Boy Scouts of America (1914), and the Greater Hartford Girl Scouts (1920), saw the city operating with the full complement of social agencies assumed in a community of Hartford's size and collective economic means.

These were the major charities, but over the years associations were organized by both Christians and Jews for the relief of members of the several sects within each faith. And there were also the Widows' Society (1847); the Hartford Orphan

Asylum, begun in the 1860s as an adjunct of the Female Beneficent Society and later to become the Child and Family Services of Connecticut; the Watkinson Asylum and Farm School for Orphan Boys; and the Union for Home Work, organized in 1872 by Mrs. Samuel Colt to farm out sewing work to indigent widows in their homes. The Union would, by several mergers and reorganizations, ultimately become Hartford Neighborhood Centers.

Through the years the contributions to the various agencies were generous, and periodically there were small-scale fund drives. Trustees and their friends remembered the institutions in their wills—sometimes with what were regarded at the time as large sums. Although each incorporated charity hoped to build up a productive endowment through bequests, it was the "dead hand" of the testator that threatened to tie up well-intended sums of money whose original purpose no longer existed.

Early in the 1920s trust officers of two Hartford banks—Maynard T. Hazen of the United States Security Trust Company and Clark T. Durant of the Hartford-Connecticut Trust Company—had faced problems arising from wills. As they shared their thoughts with Arthur Pomeroy Day, the Hartford attorney reputed to have drawn up more wills than any other member of the city's legal profession, they decided to set up a public foundation that would enable banks and trust companies to hold donated funds in perpetuity and to appropriate the income from these funds to community betterment. In 1925 Hazen and Durant persuaded the Connecticut General Assembly to pass an act authorizing the creation of the Hartford Foundation for Public Giving.

The foundation received considerable publicity in the local press, but the community-trust idea was slow in finding acceptance in Hartford, as bankers and attorneys never attempted to apply any pressure in favor of the foundation, for fear that an imperfect understanding of the foundation on the part of the client would suggest conflict of interest.

Several Hartford residents made modest bequests to the foundation, and in 1936 the first distribution was made. Between that date and 1980, however, the Hartford Foundation for Public Giving accumulated assets of $45,175,052 and made distributions of over $25,000,000 to social-service agencies, education, and the arts.

The decade of the 1920s—sometimes called the Roaring Twenties, the Prohibition Years, or the Jazz Age—meant bootlegging, the Charleston, and the ukelele. There was something of a moral change, many would have said a moral decline, as women smoked cigarettes, bobbed their hair, rolled their stockings, and shortened their skirts. Schoolteachers were reprimanded by their principals for wearing skirts that reached only to the knee, and office employees were discharged for cutting their hair. Cocktails became popular, as hosts and hostesses attempted to stretch their illicit and expensive whiskey. All of this was attributed to the letdown that followed what was then referred to as the "Great War." But it also reflected what most people regarded as a new national prosperity, as well as a new materialism, or a greater concern for the new creature comforts that reflected a higher material standard of living.

Charles Lindbergh, shortly after his transoceanic flight in 1927, received a rousing welcome in Hartford and other cities. He is seen here standing in an open touring car as it proceeds slowly along Main Street. (CHS)

These were carefree years, and as the decade was drawing to a close few individuals cared to admit that business conditions in Hartford were not all that might have been desired or that there were portents that all was not well with the national economy. By early 1929 the coal and textile industries were in difficult circumstances, and oil producers were suffering from a cutthroat price war that had resulted from a glut of petroleum products. Farmers were trying to sell unmarketable produce, and there were many farm failures and mortgage foreclosures, which, in turn, bankrupted lending institutions from Maine to California. By September even the great building boom, which had contributed so much to the postwar prosperity, had collapsed, and construction slumped to 25 percent below the level of the preceding year.

These conditions were reflected ominously in Hartford. Factories went on short schedule, and hundreds of workers lost their jobs. Hartford newspapers reported an unusually large number of business failures and personal bankruptcies, but the heaviest blow to the local economy fell when the Hartford Rubber Works moved to Detroit. By September 19, the prices of corporate shares on the New York Stock Exchange stood at an all-time high, and the profits of millions of Americans were measured—on paper, at least—in the billions. In early October stocks took a sharp downward slide, and by the middle of the month the leading industrial issues were losing from 5 to 90 points in a single day. Then came "Black Thursday," October 24, 1929, when stock plummeted by 50 to 100 points. Millions of stockholders wanted to sell, but none wanted to buy. The great crash had come, and the Depression had begun.

Connecticut was a highly industrialized state, and all of these effects were soon to be felt. The Manufacturers Association of Hartford reported in 1931 that 81 factories that then employed 36,250 persons had kept 8,873 employees on their payroll in excess of their production demands in an effort to spread the work. A year later the Connecticut Department of Commerce reported the doleful news that more than 1,000 Connecticut firms had gone into bankruptcy, and that these companies had liabilities of more than twice their assets. By the fall of 1932, eighteen Connecticut banks had failed, and by 1934, sixteen more were in the process of liquidation.

The actual employment statistics were equally depressing. A factory-employment index prepared by Metropolitan Life Insurance Company revealed that industrial employment for 1932 was 54 percent below that of 1929, and a Connecticut Commerce Department report indicated a 40 percent decrease in payrolls from 1929 to 1932.

Hartford suffered during the Depression, but there were elements in the city's economy that softened the blow. It is an axiom in the industry that insurance lags behind other businesses in both entering and leaving depression periods. Thus, with a large proportion of Hartford's gainfully employed population on the payrolls of the city's many insurance-company home offices, there was a relative security during the earlier Depression years. Also, several major building programs were undertaken during this period, and these projects kept a large number of construction workers on the payroll of local contractors. During the 1930s Trinity College erected a new dormitory, a chemistry laboratory, a million-dollar chapel, a field house, and a dining hall. In 1931 Hartford Steam Boiler Inspection and Insurance Company began construction of a new office building with the twofold purpose of availing itself of the low cost of building materials and relieving unemployment in the community. Bushnell Memorial Hall also was built between October 1928 and January 1930.

Following the stock-market crash, political and business leaders attempted to

This overview of a part of Hartford's West End was photographed in the 1920s showing the then incomplete campus of the Hartford Theological Seminary. The seminary has now moved to smaller quarters nearby, and the University of Connecticut Law School is about to occupy these buildings. (CHS)

keep up morale. In December, 1929, the mayors of Connecticut's principal cities joined in expressing an optimistic outlook for 1930, and Hartford's city fathers took pride in a nationwide survey that placed Hartford among the 25 best-lighted cities in the United States.

But times of economic distress are hardly times for civic boasting, and the City authorities decided to trim sail. There could be no appreciable increase in City taxes, as the property holders had made clear their opposition to any such measures. In fact, in September, 1931, thirty-five Hartford manufacturing firms petitioned the City for a reduction in taxes, and they held out the threat of moving their plants from Hartford if their demands were ignored.

Budget cuts were the order of the day, and one of the first municipal services to suffer was lighting. In March, 1932, the City ordered the elimination of every third streetlamp, 19 of the 80 traffic signals, and the entire floodlighting at Brainard Field. Dispensing with the Christmas lighting—a saving of a mere $240—in the downtown shopping district was too grim a thought for the merchants, and the Chamber of Commerce undertook to raise the money among the Hartford retailers. The money was raised, albeit with considerable difficulty, and the lights were put up as usual.

Perhaps the plight of the unemployed was best symbolized by the "hunger march" in the spring of 1932, when on several occasions hundreds of the unemployed—although certainly not all of them from Hartford—surrounded the State Capitol and presented petitions demanding a state appropriation of $12,000,-000 in direct relief to the unemployed.

Hartford's business community generally was agreed that the problem of unemployment was a local matter that should be solved on the local level and, if at all possible, by private charities. In October of 1931 the Hartford Community Chest had set a campaign goal of $1,090,063, of which $250,000 was to provide work for the unemployed.

Gallup and Alfred, at the corner of Asylum and Haynes streets, sold records along with Victrolas on which to play them. A three-dimensional replica of the Victor trademark, "His Master's Voice," sits by one of the Victrolas. (CHS)

But this attitude was not to prevail. Franklin Delano Roosevelt was elected President in 1932 by such a spectacular majority that the result was interpreted by many as a repudiation of the Hoover administration's ineffectual measures to end the Depression. And with the new Democratic President came a predominantly Democratic Congress, willing and eager to enact bold legislation in the interest of recovery from the Depression and reform of the social and economic systems from which many of the new legislators believed the Depression had been bred.

The new President had little difficulty in convincing his Congress that recovery could best be achieved by a policy of raising the prices of commodities, services, and labor, while at the same time strictly regulating American industry and expanding the federal program of public works. On June 16, 1933, Congress created the National Recovery Administration (NRA), an agency whose function would be to prepare and supervise a series of codes of fair competition and employment for each of the nation's major industries. The act set aside the long-standing antitrust laws, as the codes were directed toward intraindustry cooperation rather than the competition encouraged by the Sherman and Clayton acts. A general code prohibited the employment of persons under 16 years of age, set the maximum work week at 40 hours, and established a minimum wage of 40 cents an hour.

In all, 557 separate industrial codes were adopted. All were thrown together hastily, and it was apparent from the beginning that the larger corporations had dictated the terms. However, Section 7 of the National Industrial Recovery Act (NIRA), the clause that specifically granted labor the right to organize, was later to cause many a regret to those corporation executives who had encouraged it.

The evening of Tuesday, September 19, 1933, was designated by the National Recovery Administration as NRA Night, and across the entire nation there were parades. In Hartford 20,000 persons, virtually all of the city's gainfully employed, marched. There were 100 floats, 500 decorated trucks, and 30 bands. All Hartford people who were fortunate enough to have work joined in singing *Marching Along Together* and *Happy Days Are Here Again.* Unfortunately, happy days were not really here.

Although the NIRA at first had been hailed by organized labor, Hartford's union leaders soon became extremely critical of the act, branding it the foe of the workingman. Small businesses, too, ignored the codes and joined the opposition. Even big industry, under whose sponsorship the act had been introduced, had cooled, and by the spring of 1935 the NIRA had few friends. All were relieved when the United States Supreme Court, on May 27, 1935, declared the act unconstitutional.

The NIRA was but one of many pieces of New Deal legislation under which the Hartford manufacturers were to chafe. The Social Security Act of August 14, 1935, caused some confusion, for several of the companies had just instituted their own generous contributory retirement plans. The Guffey-Snyder Bituminous Coal Stabilization Act of August 30, 1934, contained price-fixing features that threatened to keep the price of fuel at a high level. The act was declared unconstitutional, however, in May, 1936.

Hartford benefited immeasurably from the programs of the Works Progress Administration (WPA), later the Works Projects Administration, which was created on May 6, 1935. In Hartford, streets were repaired, parks were improved, and public buildings were refurbished. There also were projects of a more ephemeral nature, and these were criticized as "leaf-raking" jobs or "busy work."

Although the primary intent of the WPA was to provide work for manual

Theodore Roosevelt waves to the crowd from an electric car motoring down Pearl Street. His police escort consists of six policemen mounted on Columbia bicycles. (CHS)

laborers, other projects involved artists, actors, and musicians, and here Hartford was to benefit. Hartford had an unusually large number of musicians who were out of work. With the popularity of motion pictures, the theaters had dispensed with their pit orchestras, and radio, in an effort to cut costs, had reduced the number of musicians used in the broadcasting studios. To take up the slack, the WPA created the Hartford Symphony Orchestra. Similar orchestras had been set up across the country, but this was one of the few to survive the elimination of the WPA. Local support was able to keep the symphony going, and it was to become one of the better orchestras in a city of Hartford's size, giving its own regular concert series and later serving both the Connecticut Opera Association and the Hartford Ballet Company.

One of the few bright spots of these Depression years was the celebration during the summer of 1935 of the tercentenary of Connecticut's settlement. In Hartford the theme of the celebration was "Progress." The festivities—which included pageants, concerts, art shows, and dramatic performances—ran from April through October and culminated in a huge parade on Columbus Day.

When spring came, however, the Tercentenary Celebration was only a memory, as Mother Nature dealt Hartford a most unkind blow. January and February of 1936 were cold and snowy months throughout New England, and snow piled up in almost unprecedented quantities. During the second week in March temperatures rose rapidly, and as the mountains of snow in New Hampshire and Vermont melted, the Connecticut River began to rise.

By Thursday, March 19, Hartford's previous high record of 29.8 feet, set by the May flood of 1854, had been passed. The Connecticut River Bridge was closed, and families in the low-lying East Side were evacuated quickly. Hundreds of persons were removed, some from second-story windows, by Coast Guardsmen who navigated their whaleboats through the "canals" that once had been Front Street and its adjacent lanes and alleys. Bushnell Park became a huge lake. All highways out of Hartford were impassable, and thousands of displaced persons huddled in buildings on higher ground, while City authorities doled out what food and blankets were available. By Friday the high-water mark of 35 feet above normal river level had been reached. Bellboys in hip boots splashed through two feet of water in the Bond Hotel's lobby, handling the luggage of guests who had been brought by boat from the railroad station two blocks away. By Saturday the flood stood at 37.5 feet.

The flood of 1936 was the most destructive in Hartford's history. The cost was five lives and $35,000,000 in property damage, and it was particularly unfortunate that the flood had come at a time when Hartford was just beginning to shake off the effects of the Depression.

In 1938 Nature struck again, with the most severe hurricane in the city's history. On September 21 at 4 p.m., the hurricane struck with full force, leaving the city a shambles: streets blocked by fallen trees and utility poles, crushed automobiles, stranded trolley cars, and debris from hundreds of destroyed or damaged buildings. The Connecticut River rose rapidly, and an army of City employees, WPA workers, and college students and other volunteers began to strengthen the dikes. Fifty-pound bags of sand were piled one atop another by the soon-weary workers. By 5:30 p.m. on Friday, September 23, the river attained a height of 35.1 feet above normal, held at that crest until 10 p.m., and then slowly began to fall. Again, there was the heroic evacuation of the East Side, where many small shopkeepers, still making payments on loans taken out following the disaster of 1936, were threatened with bankruptcy. Fortunately, most of these businesses were able to receive aid through the Federal Disaster Loan Corporation.

Concentric circles are caused by a bandstand's reflection in the floodwaters covering a corner of Bushnell Park. The Traveler's (Insurance Company) Tower and its reflection are also apparent. (CHS)

This was the last such disaster to hit Hartford, for even before the flood and hurricane had struck, elaborate provisions were being made to erect a system of dikes from North Meadows, past the low-lying East Side, and down the river to the Wethersfield line. This project, the last one carried out under the WPA, was not completed until 1941, but it enclosed South Meadows plants and Brainard Field, which had been outside the older and obviously ineffectual barriers. Thus, the danger of flood has been virtually eliminated.

Hartford would recover from floods and hurricanes, as she would from the Depression, but it would not be through the WPA or other federal agencies. Rather, it would be World War II that would revitalize the city's economy and make Hartford once again a major center of military production.

On Sunday, December 7, 1941, the day that President Roosevelt said would live in infamy, the Japanese Air Force attacked the United States Naval Base at Pearl Harbor, Hawaii. On December 8 Congress declared war against Japan, and on December 11 the Axis powers declared war on the United States.

But long before the declaration of war, the United States had been preparing feverishly for the conflict. Lend-lease and the unprecedented defense appropriations of 1940-1941 had transformed a Depression-ridden nation into an "arsenal of democracy," as President Roosevelt called it. Within a year more than 6,000,000 workers were added to America's payrolls, and unemployment virtually was eliminated.

In Hartford the rate of defense production was somewhat in advance of that of the nation as a whole, as such plants as Colt's, Billings and Spencer, and Pratt and Whitney Tool turned out vast quantities of metal and plastics on contracts with British, French, and United States governments. The most talked-of defense industry in the Hartford area was, of course, United Aircraft. At its Pratt & Whitney plant, United Aircraft was producing airplane engines in prodigious quantities, and the marvel was that the plant, which just a few years before had employed about a score of men, was now utilizing thousands, and that the facilities for production were growing as rapidly as construction workers could build.

With Hartford's rapid industrial expansion came an unprecedented influx of people. Workers with varying degrees of mechanical skills came from other parts of New England, from the industrial centers of the Midwest, and from the rural South. Housing became a serious problem, and even the large-scale program of government-sponsored, low-cost apartment construction soon proved to be inadequate. A reliable estimate of the time was that during 1941 alone there were 18,000 newcomers to the city. Hartford's central position in a highly industrialized state prompted the Army and Navy Munitions Board to place the city on the list of 14 "most vital strategic industrial areas in the country," and it was this presumably vulnerable position that caused Hartford to take careful measures for civilian defense.

As part of its effort to conserve food and scarce, war-needed materials, the federal government instituted a program of strict rationing. Hartfordites, however, were notorious for their refusal to observe gasoline rationing, and in 1943 the *Courant* noted that gas sales were more than twice the amount allowed by law. During the war years many women who never had worked before found employment in the factories.

During 1944 economic conditions in Hartford remained relatively stable, despite a slight decrease in industrial employment during the fall, when optimism concerning a possible end to the war prompted some departures by migrant workers. But the summer of 1944 was one of disaster for the Hartford community. On July 6 a tragic fire in the Ringling Brothers Circus tent took the lives of 168 persons, many of them children, and injured 500 more.

While such local news was monopolizing space in the Hartford papers, faraway events were bringing the war closer to its end. On August 15, 1945, the Japanese surrendered, and the most devastating war in history was over.

Then the victors came home. The Hartford insurance companies and banks had kept all jobs open for the men and women who had served, but even these found housing scarce. Many a returned veteran with a war bride, or recently married to the girl who had waited for him, was obliged to live with relatives. Even when rented quarters could be found, rents were extremely high and going ever higher.

The unskilled had little chance in the job market, but the federal "G.I. Bill of Rights" provided for college education or on-the-job training, which held veterans out of the work force and allowed them to raise their vocational ambitions. The G.I. Bill enabled Trinity College to return quickly to a normal collegiate life. It actually helped Hillyer College (founded in 1879) to emerge as a full-fledged institution of higher learning and to set it on its way toward merging, in 1957, with the Hartford Art School and the Hartt School of Music to form the University of Hartford. Also to profit from the postwar boom in higher education were St. Joseph College (conducted since 1932 by the Congregation of the Sisters of Mercy) and Hartford College for Women (begun in 1933 as a "depression branch" of Mount Holyoke). Rensselaer Polytechnic Institute set up the Hartford branch that would become the Hartford Graduate Center.

One of many presidents to visit Hartford, Woodrow Wilson greets citizens with a tip of his hat. (CHS)

Probably the worst threat to American economic well-being in the post-World War II years was inflation. President Harry S. Truman was aware of both the economic dangers and the popular feeling against wartime controls, and within a matter of months, price controls on nearly all commodities and services were ended. Congress also lowered the federal income tax slightly. Although prices remained at the wartime high levels, serious inflation, except in rents, did not particularly trouble the Hartford consumer until the outbreak of the Korean conflict in June, 1950.

World War II hardly had ended when a grassroots movement for municipal reform began among Hartford's citizenry—particularly the college-trained business and professional people—who had become dissatisfied with Hartford's city government, with its antiquated ward representation and the resulting favoritism and political patronage. To effect the reform, the Citizens Charter Commission was formed by members of both the Democratic and Republican parties. The commission's goal was to achieve a city government under a nine-member council to be elected from candidates who would run at large and without party designation. Although the idea was opposed by the old-line politicians, it received unexpected popular support, and in December, 1946, a completely new type of municipal government went into effect. The *Times*, abandoning its long-standing partisanship, proudly declared that "the citizens are at last on the top."

Also effective during the decades of the 1940s and 1950s was the Greater Hartford Chamber of Commerce, a particularly farsighted group that then represented the younger (or middle) management levels of Hartford's retailing, banking, manufacturing, and insurance concerns. And it was indeed the Chamber, under the leadership of its president, Arthur J. Lumsden, that would provide the impetus for the large-scale urban renewal projects launched in the late 1950s.

Meanwhile, the country once again had become involved in war. On June 25, 1950, the North Korean Army crossed the 38th Parallel, and on that same day President Truman ordered General Douglas MacArthur and the American military forces stationed in South Korea to lead a formidable counteroffensive. The Korean War meant the tightening again of government controls, the reimposition of the draft, the beginning of a most alarming spiraling of inflation, and a drain upon the city's labor force that was just enough to cause uneasiness in Hartford's personnel offices. Once again Hartford's war industries boomed, and once again interest turned to civil defense, as air-raid shelters were improvised in public buildings, factories, and even homes.

Also to be noted was a significant population shift. Between 1950 and 1960 approximately 56,000 people moved into Hartford, while during this same decade 95,000 others moved out. This reshuffling represented a loss of almost 10 percent of the city's population. Most of these outward moves were to such nearby communities as Bloomfield, East Hartford, Windsor, and Wethersfield, each of which experienced a population growth proportionately larger than Hartford's loss.

Hartford's racial makeup was also changing. In 1950 Hartford listed 13,000 blacks; the census of 1960 counted 25,000. Hartford, like Connecticut's other large cities, rapidly was becoming the home of the blacks and the home of the poor. In 1960 Hartford had one-third of all families living in the 29-town Greater Hartford Metropolitan Region, but it also had more than 50 percent of those families with incomes of less than $5,000, and just under 20 percent of those earning more than $10,000. Furthermore, the lowest-income families were concentrated in the largely black North End, while the more affluent families were to be found in the western portion of the city near the West Hartford line.

Dwight Eisenhower gives a victory sign on one of his trips through Hartford. (CHS)

Equally as important as the absolute decline in the population of the City of Hartford from 177,397 in 1950 to 162,178 in 1960 was the amazing growth of the Greater Hartford Metropolitan Region. In 1950 the nine surrounding towns—West Hartford, East Hartford, Bloomfield, Windsor, Windsor Locks, Wethersfield, Enfield, Avon, and Simsbury—were inhabited by a total of 133,145 persons, while 10 years later the suburban population stood at 224,286. Here Hartford's long-range problems were to be seen plainly. Cities in the American South and West almost invariably had annexed all contiguous, populated territory, and such cities showed steady population growth with each new federal census. Hartford did not have this seeming advantage, as each suburban community stood firmly by its refusal to be annexed to the city.

And yet, all of the surrounding towns were appendages to the city. Most of the residents of the towns worked in the city, did their major shopping downtown, and relied upon Hartford's cultural institutions for both entertainment and edification. Municipal boundaries remained, but Greater Hartford had by 1960 become a total community of almost 400,000. By 1970 the United States Bureau of the Census would place Greater Hartford in the Hartford-New Britain-Bristol Standard Metropolitan Statistical Area as number 33 in the country, with a population of 1,035,195.

In this process of population redistribution, Hartford had become, as the urban specialists described it, "ghettoized." The economic and social conditions of Hartford's blacks were aggravated further in the spring of 1958, when the City of Hartford announced plans for one of the largest programs of urban redevelopment ever undertaken by an American municipality. The plan was to level most of the supposedly substandard buildings that lay between Market Street and the Connecticut River—an area some four city blocks in width and a dozen or so in length—and to erect three high-rise office structures, a large hotel, headquarters for the city's major radio and television stations, extensive underground parking facilities, and a modern shopping mall.

The development, named Constitution Plaza, was completed in 1962 with financial backing by Travelers Insurance Company, and it won nationwide acclaim for its architectural design and its overall concept as a downtown business and financial center. Unfortunately, the Plaza project was far from successful, for although the office buildings soon were rented to near capacity, the shopping mall, from the beginning, consisted chiefly of empty storefronts.

Constitution Plaza replaced the old Italian East Side, and the city fathers, lured by the prospect of federal slum-clearance money, soon began the destruction of the southern portion of the black North End, the Polish Sheldon Street area, and a considerable portion of the Colt village.

Constitution Plaza did not contain a single dwelling unit, and its former population scattered to all parts of the city and to the suburbs. Many of the Italian families and businesses came to concentrate in the Franklin Avenue area. There, much of Little Italy was preserved, even to the extent of reintroducing the Italian Festa held each year since 1978. A similar exodus was noted in the case of the Sheldon Street area Polish-Americans. These geographic moves often represented upward social mobility, as the immigrants and children of immigrants were absorbed, through education, hard work, and personal ambition, into the area's middle class.

For the blacks, however, there was little choice, for as the Windsor Street area was leveled, black families simply pushed farther northward, moving eventually into the Blue Hills sector, which formerly had been predominantly Jewish. And all the

The Old State House, shown in this picture with the Hartford National Bank building behind it, has been meticulously restored. Courtesy, Old State House Association

while, a steady influx of Puerto Ricans to the North End led to further uneasiness as blacks gave the newcomers something less than a hearty welcome.

Traditionally, Hartford's blacks had been passive in their attitude. Early in 1963, however, the attitude was changed, when a small but articulate group of white college students and seminarians organized the North End Community Action Project (NECAP). These activists, affiliated with the Northern Student Movement, moved into the ghetto, tutored black children, encouraged voter registration, picketed the homes of slumlords, led a "kneel-in" at a local restaurant, and even headed a sit-in at City Hall.

They were encouraged, and sometimes actively courted, by a revived National Association for the Advancement of Colored People (NAACP), the International Ministerial Alliance (IMA), and the Congress on Racial Equality (CORE), the local chapter of which was organized by the Reverend Richard Battles, pastor of the Mount Olive Baptist Church and a friend of the Reverend Dr. Martin Luther King, Jr. When the more radical Black Muslims appeared on the scene, the older black groups were mildly distrustful. Battles, however, found all activists kindred souls and, according to the *Times* of November 26, 1963, one said, as he pointed to his breast, "All of us Negroes have a little bit of Black Muslim down here."

The Horace Bushnell Memorial Hall, which seats 2,500, has presented lectures, symphony concerts, and other events since the 1930s. Courtesy, Horace Bushnell Memorial Hall

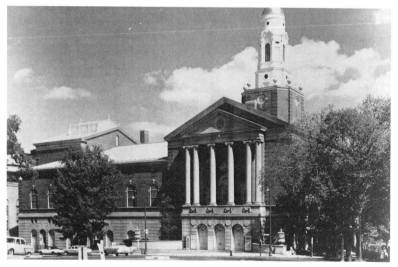

Although a proposed NECAP school boycott was called off, the Hartford Board of Education quickly got the message and resolved to improve the educational opportunity of black children. As 95 percent of Hartford's blacks lived in the North End, the city was operating virtually two separate school systems—one for the whites and another for the blacks. The Board of Education was genuinely determined to rectify the situation and turned to the Harvard University Graduate School of Education to devise a plan for school integration.

The Harvard Plan called for building several new middle schools on the fringe between white and black sections and, as Hartford's white population was declining so rapidly, busing black children to predominantly white suburban schools. The plan met with fierce resistance, as the white population of the city objected to the middle-school proposal, and the suburbs offered little assistance. Consequently, the Board of Education began a $42-million school-building program that totally ignored the Harvard recommendations and kept the schools as segregated as they had been before. In 1966, however, Project Concern, a pilot program of the federal government, began busing blacks from Hartford schools to West Hartford, Farmington, Manchester,

South Windsor, and Simsbury. Local resistance, both in the city and in the towns, precluded total success.

Hartford's blacks had become active in programs to improve their condition, but there was little to show for the effort. In 1967, for instance, Hartford had 5,816 families, mostly black, on its welfare rolls at an annual cost of more than a million dollars. Urban housing, where blacks could rent, was in short supply. Puerto Ricans, who were arriving daily, were just as "ghettoized" as the blacks. Events in Hartford soon would take a turn for the worse, as they became tied up with the turmoil that in the late 1960s beset college campuses as well as the ghettos of virtually all American cities.

Although the assassination of Dr. King in April of 1968 provided the immediate spark, discontent and unrest in Hartford had been festering for a long time, stemming in large part from the unpopular Vietnam War and the painfully slow progress being made in the Civil Rights movement. Cities across the nation already had had serious race riots with extensive loss of life and property. Hartford's turn came in the summer of 1968, when residents of the North End set fires to buildings, obstructed the flow of vehicular traffic, and assaulted police officers and fire fighters. During the oppressively hot and humid 1968 Labor Day weekend, residents of Hartford's North Main Street area rioted and burned down the Ropkins Branch of the Hartford Public Library. Although the building was close to a fire station, the rioters prevented the fire fighters from laying their hoses, and the structure was completely destroyed.

Much credit for successfully dealing with this critical situation was given to the Hartford Foundation for Public Giving, which immediately pledged a considerable portion of its allocations to the needs of those minority groups whose disadvantaged situation was being demonstrated so openly. The foundation always had allocated funds with the residents of the North End in mind, and a major contribution of $20,000 had just been made in 1964 toward establishing a Hartford branch of the National Urban League. The difference in 1969 was the approach. Crash programs were financed in part by the foundation to try to buy time until sounder, long-range programs could take over, and to attempt to correct basic conditions rather than just alleviate their symptoms.

The foundation was the first to admit that there were errors of judgment, but such is invariably the case in a crash program of any sort, and the heroic efforts were not without the seemingly inevitable disappointments. Nevertheless, the foundation was able to report in the *Yearbook* for 1970:

> The democratic way is slow and fumbling, but eventually tolerance and faith in the basic decency of most Americans, black and white, will win out, and a better society will emerge.

There can be little doubt that the foundation-sponsored programs went a long way toward pouring oil upon troubled waters.

During this period of urban unrest, which extended well into the early 1970s, Arthur J. Lumsden of the Greater Hartford Chamber of Commerce led top corporate leaders in creating the Greater Hartford Corporation and the Greater Hartford Process, one of the most extensive programs in the nation to deal with urban problems. As part of that effort, the Greater Hartford Community Development Corporation (DEVCO) was created to initiate housing rehabilitation in the North End and to acquire land to build a "new town" in Coventry. Because of understandable opposition from the residents of that quiet, rural town some 15 miles from Hartford, the "new town" idea was abandoned.

Hartford's greatest failure in the 20th century was to provide adequate housing for low-income families, but there certainly were persistent efforts from all sides to make Hartford more pleasant for those who chose, or who were obliged, to live there. One of those most concerned for the improvement of the quality of life in the city was Elizabeth L. Knox, who, after having served for 12 years on the Hartford City Council, died in 1966 and in her will endowed the Knox Foundation with the specific intent of beautifying the city. As Miss Knox expressed the idea, the "spiritual" slums, as well as the physical, must be removed if the city is to become truly beautiful. The Knox Foundation, particularly in the mid-1970s, was especially helpful in providing outdoor entertainment and recreation for those who had long since come to be called Hartford's "disadvantaged."

Hartford never became the place of beauty visualized by Miss Knox, but there were genuine efforts to make it so, and several of them have stories of their own. None is more interesting or, indeed, more circuitous than that of the spectacular piece of sculpture by Alexander Calder that is a bright spot of downtown Hartford. The story goes back to 1906, when Ella Burr McManus left $50,000 to build a memorial to her father, Alfred E. Burr, an early publisher of the Hartford *Times*. Mrs. McManus' will stated that the memorial "must be artistic in design and humane in purpose, preferably a drinking fountain for both human beings and animals." By the time Mrs. McManus' fund was available, horses were fast disappearing from the streets of Hartford, and so, after much study as to the appropriate use of the bequest, the trustees decided to use the legacy to construct a public library. Architects drew plans that, being clearly "artistic in design," were fully in keeping with one of the provisions of the will. But the probate judge, ruling that a library is not "humane in purpose," rejected the proposal.

However, the story was to have a happy ending, although neither human beings nor animals were to benefit in quite the way Mrs. McManus had intended. By 1960 the reinvested income had swelled the fund to more than $1,000,000, and the trustees again came forth with a proposal to meet, in part at least, the terms of the will. This time they were able to persuade the probate court that a huge mall with a fountain and a piece of sculpture would be both appropriate and acceptable. In September, 1966, an agreement was signed between the Trustees of the Ella Burr McManus Fund, the Wadsworth Atheneum, and the City of Hartford. The mall was constructed on Main Street on land between the Atheneum and the Municipal Building and directly opposite the office of the Hartford *Times*. In addition to carefully laid walkways and plantings of trees and shrubs, the mall featured a fountain and Calder's massive steel sculpture titled *Stegosaurus*. The project finally was completed in 1973.

Stegosaurus provoked much comment. Councilwoman Margaret Tedone was displeased: "From the Council offices," she remarked, "it looks like a great big piece of metal dropped there, like debris, from a plane crash!"

Nor did Mayor George Athanson approve: "One day I see this THING going up. I don't mind being Calderized, but I don't want to be Stegosaurusized! Why was a two-ton dinosaur known for its miniscule brain chosen?"

James Elliot, former director of the Wadsworth Atheneum, defended the selection by explaining the sculpture's artistic merits: "In spite of its lumbering, primordial quality, it is beautifully realized in semiabstract form [and] ... a spectacular addition to the downtown cityscape."

Even more controversial was the *Stone Field Sculpture* of Carl Andre, located in

What once were private homes have been remodeled to accommodate professional or commercial tenants. The University Club (shown here) preserves some of the quiet charm of the 19th century on Lewis Street. Courtesy, University Club of Hartford

the minipark just south of First Congregational Church. There, on August 22, 1977, 36 large boulders were placed in six parallel rows, ranging from one to 11 rocks and forming a huge triangle that covers most of the grassy plot. Immediately, the *Stone Field Sculpture* raised the question of whether it was a work of art or a spoof. Most observers seemed to be unfavorably impressed, despite the claim that Andre was the leading name in a new "minimalist" school of sculpture, and they were shocked to discover that Andre's fee was $87,000. It was little comfort to learn that the Hartford Foundation for Public Giving and the National Endowment for the Arts had shared the cost of the artist's fee—plus $6,500 for an "expert" to choose the sculpture.

Hartford's old theaters, several of which had once been famous for their splendid presentations by traveling companies, had given way to motion pictures, but legitimate theater returned to Hartford in 1964 with the creation of the Hartford Stage Company, a professional, nonprofit repertory theater that began operations in makeshift rented quarters in downtown Hartford. The company performed to full houses nightly, and in 1977 it dedicated its new multimillion-dollar, 350-seat theater on the corner of Main and Trumbull streets.

In June, 1971, the first Greater Hartford Civic and Arts Festival was held on Constitution Plaza. Here music, drama, dance, painting, and sculpture were brought together for a week-long gala. Throughout this aesthetic sampling there were concerts by the Hartford Symphony, school bands and choruses, rock groups, and Gospel singers. There also were performances by the Hartford Ballet Company, the Mark Twain Masquers, and the Hartt Opera Theatre. More than 50,000 persons attended the first festival. For several years following, the festival was repeated, and each year the number of participating organizations increased. Attendance at the 1974 festival was more than 150,000.

But the program of greatest long-range potential toward encouragement of the

BELOW: Mark Twain is one of Hartford's most famous citizens. He lived in several states before settling in Connecticut in the 1870s. (CHS)

BELOW RIGHT: Some years before Mark Twain lived in Hartford, he was a river pilot on the Mississippi. Apparently he instructed architect Edward Tuckerman Potter to create some resemblance of a Mississippi riverboat in the design of the Twain home. Courtesy, Kingswood-Oxford School

arts in the Greater Hartford area was set up in 1971, when the Greater Hartford Chamber of Commerce created the Greater Hartford Arts Council, a fund-raising organization intended to make a united appeal on behalf of all the arts to Hartford-area business and industrial corporations. The Greater Hartford Arts Council's first campaign (1972) raised $303,000 from 85 companies; the 1973 campaign raised $364,000 from a greatly broadened base of 155 companies; and the 1974 campaign raised $507,000 from more than 200 corporations.

Somewhat related to the arts is the Hartford Architecture Conservancy, organized in 1973 with the intent of preserving what was left of Hartford's older buildings that had either historical or aesthetic interest. Although many quite correctly regarded the idea as one of locking the stable after the horse had been stolen, the conservancy has done noble work in preserving numerous remaining examples of Italianate and Victorian architecture. Operating on the concept of recycling and working with a small revolving fund, the conservancy frequently has stayed the wrecking ball and secured purchasers who have made the once-condemned buildings both beautiful and serviceable. Several buildings on lower South Main Street, "The Linden" in particular, and an entire block of Congress Street were restored with the blessing of the conservancy. An especially pleasing restoration was that of the Cheney Building at 942 Main Street, built in 1876 and designed by the distinguished architect H.H. Richardson. The structure was refurbished during the late 1970s for retail shops, offices, and luxury apartments.

Every city, and indeed every community, has a focus. In earliest Hartford this focus was, of course, the meetinghouse. In the 19th century it was probably the city hall, especially as Hartford's particular City Hall was—in addition to being the seat of municipal government and a police station—a market house and an auditorium for public gatherings.

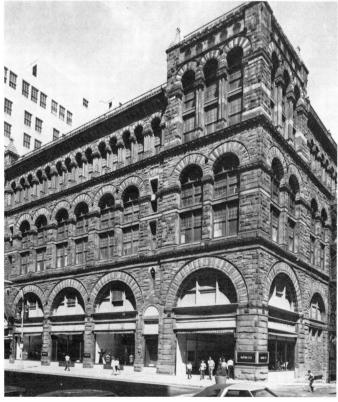

In time, however, and as public and private transportation dispersed the population to the outlying areas that were to become Greater Hartford, even this focus declined in importance. Furthermore, as Hartford's offices dismissed their workers at four-thirty, and as Hartford's stores no longer remained open in the evening, that hour saw an exodus of thousands of white-collar workers and an almost complete absence of humanity on the downtown streets. One former Hartfordite, who made a considerable name for himself in the entertainment world, described nighttime Hartford of the 1960s as a "cemetery with electric lights." His unflattering description was painfully close to being accurate.

By the late 1960s every self-respecting city in America had come to assume that a civic center was one of the necessities of urban life. Impetus for a Hartford Civic Center came from the Greater Hartford Chamber of Commerce, which soon persuaded the City Council to give official support and the Aetna Life & Casualty Company to provide the necessary financial backing.

The Civic Center provided an interesting example of an urban project undertaken with both public and private funding. In 1970 a Hartford referendum approved a bond issue of $30,500,000 to build the Coliseum, and at the same time, Aetna Life & Casualty invested $35,000,000 in the shopping-mall portion of the complex. Shortly thereafter Aetna Life & Casualty was joined by International Telephone and Telegraph Company in erecting the adjacent Sheraton Hotel.

The Civic Center opened on January 5, 1975, and to a considerable degree it lived up to expectations as the catalyst for revitalizing downtown Hartford. Literally dozens of new restaurants opened in the immediate vicinity, and on the nights the New England Whalers were playing a home hockey game or a rock-and-roll band was performing, the central city became alive once more, for a few hours at least.

At 4:19 a.m. on the morning of Jan. 18, 1978, just a few hours after thousands of fans had gone home after a University of Connecticut basketball game, the roof of Hartford's new coliseum collapsed under the weight of snow and ice, crumbling with a prolonged roar into the concrete bowl of the arena below. Miraculously, because of the hour of the collapse, no one was hurt. But the tangle of rubble left by the collapse of the futuristic "space frame" roof, its steel beams looking like matchsticks snapped by the footprint of a passing

ABOVE LEFT: *The profitable lifetime of an office building is said to be 55 years. The American Industrial building is the tall brick structure on the right. Built in 1921, it was demolished two years short of that life expectancy. (CHS)*

ABOVE CENTER: *There was no place for it in a new development planned for the area, and one Sunday morning in 1974 the American Industrial building fell in less than 30 seconds. (CHS)*

ABOVE: *Explosive charges toppled the structure into vacant space to the north.*

FACING PAGE: *In this 1973 view of Hartford's changing skyline, the Traveler's Tower continues to top all other high-rises, including One Financial Plaza which was still under construction. The modern buildings seem to dwarf the white steeple of Center Church. (CHS)*

TOP: In the early 1970s construction was begun on a civic center that would enclose a shopping mall connected to a sports coliseum. The feature of this arena was its "space frame" roof—a three-dimensional web of small structural members put together on the ground and then jacked up to rest on four corner posts. Courtesy, The Hartford Courant

ABOVE: On the morning of January 18, 1978, the roof of the Veterans Coliseum collapsed. Fortunately no one was in the building. Months of investigation did not uncover the cause. The Veterans Colosseum has since reopened with an increased seating capacity and with a traditional truss construction of its roof. Courtesy, The Hartford Courant

giant, at first glance appeared to have left downtown Hartford's renaissance in ruins. The aftermath of the collapse of the Civic Center, however, was to become one of Hartford's finest hours. Nearly immediately, city leaders coined the slogan "Bigger and Better" and immediately launched plans to rebuild an even larger arena. Whalers fans founded the "91 Club" and made the tedious trek up the interstate to Springfield's dingy arena to watch games, while the Civic Center was being rebuilt. Their faith was rewarded. When the Coliseum reopened in February 1980, now New England's largest sports arena, the Whalers had gained admission to the National Hockey League.

In the 35 years following World War II, Hartford had experienced profound change, and even the city's type and function had undergone a noticeable transformation. Many of the factories that once lined the Park River had been razed or stood as empty reminders of Hartford's earlier industrial preeminence. Most of the core city's industrial operation had been relocated to industrial parks in the suburbs and beyond, and this had encouraged a migration of skilled industrial workers to the outlying areas. Even into the late 1970s, the central city remained a primary base of retailing, insurance, banking, and state government, but even here there were exceptions. Shopping centers were developed in many suburban communities, including the huge, new Westfarms mall on the Farmington-West Hartford line. Ultimately, the development of giant suburban malls on the periphery of Hartford would prove the death knell for downtown's retail hub. Connecticut General Insurance Company, later CIGNA, had moved to Bloomfield, and state government agencies built large office buildings in Wethersfield and other suburbs.

The Greater Hartford Chamber of Commerce was determined to halt the exodus of at least the insurance companies to the suburbs, and in this effort the Chamber was at least moderately successful, although several companies, including Aetna and The Hartford, also built large suburban complexes. Other corporations, however, chose to build new headquarters in Hartford's downtown. Among these, the most notable was the structure called One Financial Plaza, known locally as the "Gold Building" for its gold-glass exterior. This was built in 1974 as the headquarters of United Technologies Corporation, and at the time was the largest rental office building between New York City and Boston.

The Gold Building was not to be the end of downtown's building boom; it was in fact the beginning of a new period of peak aspirations for Hartford. As the 1980s began, new entrepreneurs in steel and glass would emerge to drive Hartford's skyline ever higher. Thirman L. Milner, Hartford's first black mayor, would call for a "new era" with city government representing all the people but having a special concern for the city's new majority—the growing communities of African Americans, Latinos, and West Indians who were already reshaping life in Connecticut's capital city.

Hartford was always a riverfront city, until a succession of disastrous floods in the 1930s convinced community leaders to block the city off from the Connecticut River by a series of dikes and highways. A 20-year effort by River-front Recapture, Inc., to bridge the dike and highway barrier culminated on September 3, 1999, with the official opening of a landscaped plaza and terraced steps, a structure that reunites downtown and the riverfront. Courtesy, the Hartford Courant. *Photo by Stephen Dunn*

The five Kellogg brothers did lithography that added to Hartford's renown in the mid-19th century. They covered a wide range of subjects, including war, romance, the Bible and, of course, Hartford. Shown here: (right) "Don't Wish You May Get It;" and (below) a view of William Henry Harrison's campaign headquarters on the corner of Asylum and Trumbull streets, a site which the Brownstone Restaurant now occupies. (CHS)

These portraits of Samuel
Burr and his wife, Rebecca
Stillman Burr, were painted
in 1792. At that time Mr.
Burr owned the largest store
in Hartford, located on Burr
Street which is now the north
end of Main Street. (CHS)

The Putnam Phalanx, named
for General Israel Putnam of
Revolutionary War fame, was
organized in 1858 as a
"marching club." It has taken
part in most Hartford
parades since that date. These
gentlemen were officers of the
Phalanx in the 1860s. (CHS)

The library (facing page) and the billiard room (below) in Mark Twain's home are now furnished either with pieces owned by the Clemens family or with items appropriate to the years they lived in Hartford. The opulence of the interior complements the riverboat theme of the exterior. Courtesy, Mark Twain Memorial

RIGHT: Referred to as "America's Pioneer Institution for the Handicapped," the American School for the Deaf was founded in 1817. It is pictured here on a Staffordshire china platter from the same era. (CHS)

Hartford has long been known as an "insurance capital" and as a seat of heavy industry. Large manufacturers appreciated Hartford's easy access to transportation and raw materials. Those advantages attracted many small factories too. On two of the postcard ads pictured here are companies not as well known as giants like Colt or Pratt and Whitney. Imperial Egg Food "beats the world," and Williams Root Beer Extract was "the perfect temperance drink." Also pictured is an ad for Phoenix Insurance Company, one of Hartford's oldest.

Charles N. Pond donated his large estate including this house to the Hartford Parks Commission. The estate, in northwestern Hartford, became Elizabeth Park, named in memory of Pond's wife.

The third building from the right was once the office of Phoenix Insurance Company. When it was built it was the tallest office building on this section of Main Street. In this view we can see the effects of modern growth—the old Phoenix Insurance building is now dwarfed by its neighbors.

MAIN STREET LOOKING SOUTH, HARTFORD, CONN.

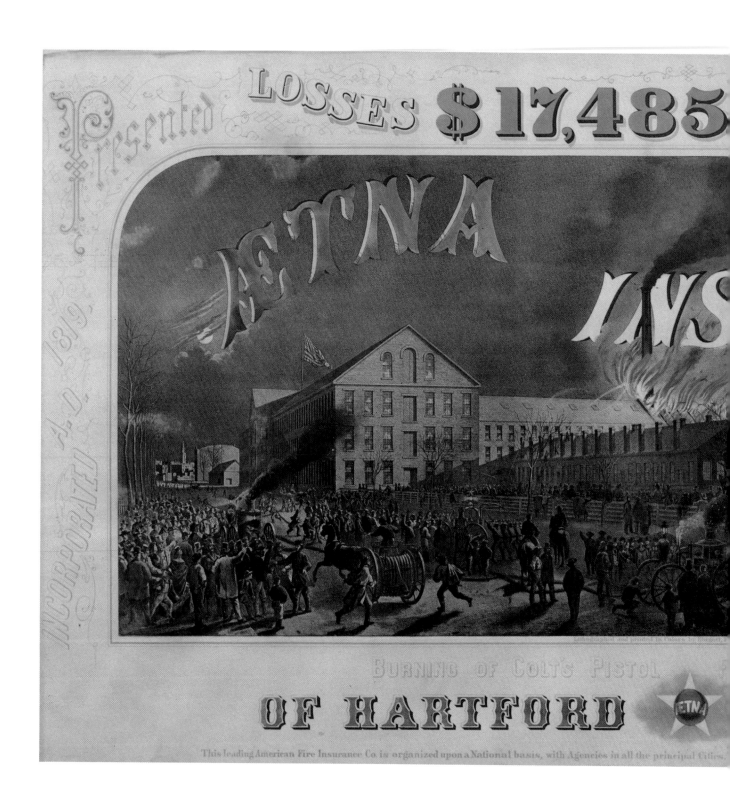

LOSSES $17,485

ÆTNA

INS

Presented

INCORPORATED A.D. 1819

BURNING OF COLT'S PISTOL

OF HARTFORD

ÆTNA

This leading American Fire Insurance Co. is organized upon a National basis, with Agencies in all the principal Cities.

Aetna and other Hartford insurance companies gained many customers because of their exemplary record. When other insurers declared bankruptcy to avoid compensating their customers after disasters, Hartford companies honored all claims. In this ad depicting the 1864 destruction of Colt's Armory, Aetna proudly proclaims the more than $17 million paid to their customers. (CHS)

Before the United States Postal Service was organized, local postmasters issued their own stamps. These came from the Hartford Post Office. (CHS)

Captain Joseph Wadsworth supposedly hid the Connecticut charter in an oak tree when the English-appointed Governor of New England came to rescind Connecticut's self-rule. The Charter Oak then became a popular subject for artists and storytellers. It was nearly 1,000 years old when E.W. Clay painted this watercolor of it in 1834. (CHS)

In 1855 Samuel Colt built his armory on Hartford's South Meadow. At the time it was the world's largest, individually-owned factory. He also established a private ferry for those employees who lived in East Hartford directly across the river from his armory. (CHS)

The late afternoon sun highlights a portion of the west facade of the State Capitol. In 1870 the State of Connecticut chose Hartford over New Haven as the permanent site of state offices. After many construction mishaps, cost overruns, and much bureaucratic mismanagement, the capitol building opened 10 years later. (CHS)

The Wadsworth Atheneum was not the only Hartford arts facility with big expansion plans in recent years. The Bushnell Center for the Performing Arts completed a $45 million expansion with the opening of the new 907-seat Belding Theater in late 2001. Credit: the Hartford Courant. *Photo by John Long*

For a mid-sized city, Hartford is blessed with a vibrant arts community. But some arts organizations, like the Hartford Ballet, whose dancers rehearsed at The Bushnell in 1997, have struggled economically during the 1990s. Courtesy, the Hartford Courant. *Photo by John Long*

The University of Connecticut women's basketball team commands a powerful loyalty across the state, and the annual showdown against its archenemy, the University of Tennessee Volunteers, is a major event on the state's sporting calendar. During the UConn women's first-ever game at the Hartford Civic Center in 1997—a sellout, of course—UConn's Nykesha Sales saves a ball by throwing it off a Tennessee player on the way to a 72-67 UConn win. Courtesy, the Hartford Courant. *Photo by Brad Clift*

Nobody's fans are more ardent than those of the UConn women. During UConn's first game in the Hartford Civic Center in January 1997, Ginger Nieman and her friend Brenda Keane, both of West Haven, Connecticut, cheer UConn toward victory. Courtesy, the Hartford Courant. *Photo by Marc Yves Regis*

CHAPTER
XII

From Summit to Struggle

~ **A**fter Edna Negron Rosario's family arrived in Hartford in 1958 from Puerto Rico, the teenager would accompany her father, a chaplain, to visit the tobacco work camps in Windsor, just north of the city. At that time, the workforce was made up of migrant Puerto Ricans, men who came to Connecticut under contract to labor, under the hot, humid tobacco tents that blanketed much of the Connecticut River Valley under massive white fabric cocoons.

The work was hard; life in the camps was bleak. The long, low wooden buildings where the Puerto Ricans slept reminded Negron of concentration camp barracks. The pay was pitiful, and the workers felt a world away from their families at home. As part of his ministry, Negron's father brought the necessities of life to the workers—food, toothbrushes, towels—and, especially, companionship. "I remember how dark it was at night; there were no lights there. It seemed to be overwhelming, the darkness. Somehow, the stars weren't as bright as they were in Puerto Rico," said Negron, who grew up to be a school principal in Hartford, a state legislator representing the city, and later, the regional director of the Puerto Rico Federal Affairs Administration for Connecticut and Rhode Island.

As tough as life there was, the tobacco camps were to become a powerful force shaping Hartford during the last half of the 20th century, because they were a gateway for two migration streams that would transform the ethnic face of Hartford between 1960 and 2000. During and after World War II, the tobacco camps not only brought workers from Puerto Rico, but men from Jamaica and other Caribbean islands. Many West Indians and Puerto Ricans stayed, finding work in Hartford's factories and later bringing wives, children, and parents from the Caribbean.

By the end of the 20th century, Hartford had become the most Puerto Rican city in America, with Puerto Ricans making up one-third of the city's population. When two of his brothers hoisted Eddie A. Perez onto their shoulders in November 2001 as the victor in the city's first mayoral election of the new century, one member of a group that started on the lowest rung of the economic ladder 50 years before had attained Hartford's political summit. After engineering a major reform of the city charter in 2002, vesting power formerly held by the city manager and city council in the mayor's office, Perez was poised to become the most powerful politician in Hartford in decades as he sought in 2003 to be the first "strong mayor" elected after the change. He hoped to use that power to boost the city's abysmally low rate of homeownership, strengthening the middle class and putting Hartford on the same upward path as smaller, resurgent New England cities like Providence and Portland.

Hartford has always seen cycles of boom and bust, dating all the way back to the 18th century, when a series of wars temporarily boosted the city's economy, only to see it fall back again once hostilities ceased. Rarely, however, was the cycle of boom and bust to be more stark and painful than in the 1980s and 1990s. But viewed across the span of the second half of the 20th century, the dominant trend for Hartford was down, in terms of population, wealth, and political clout. Although they lacked the political tools of a "strong mayor," Perez' three predecessors—Thirman L. Milner, Carrie Saxon Perry, and Michael P. Peters—were unable to stop Hartford's continuing impoverishment, in good economic times as well as bad.

Early on a December morning in 1981, the day after he was sworn in to office, New England's first popularly elected black mayor walked up the steps of Hartford City Hall to begin his initial day of work. The year 1981 was the first in Hartford's history in which whites were no longer a majority in the city, but Thirman Milner's path to the mayor's office had been anything but easy. Despite the watershed defeat two years earlier of Deputy Mayor Nick Carbone—and by extension the Democratic political machine that had controlled the city council—the NAACP had told Milner that he shouldn't run because a black politician would never be elected mayor of a New England city. And indeed, Milner did lose the Democratic primary by 94 votes to incumbent George Athanson. But the Milner campaign quickly discovered irregularities with absentee ballots cast in the primary. When one of Milner's campaign workers recognized the name of her elderly grandmother—a woman so infirm she could not even speak—on an absentee ballot, a hurried investigation followed. A few days later, a Superior Court judge overturned the primary. Milner easily defeated Athanson in the rematch, and took the general election in November.

Thirman L. Milner lost his initial primary bout with incumbent Mayor George Athanson, but a judge overturned the result because of voter "irregularities." Black North End voters, suddenly seeing that the election of Hartford's first black mayor was possible, powered Milner to an easy victory in the rematch. The day after his primary victory, Milner (on the right) looks over election returns with two of his mentors, state Senator Wilber G. Smith and Bishop David J. Billings, Milner's former boss. Courtesy, the Hartford Courant

After the Civic Center roof collapse in 1978, Whalers fans formed the "I-91 Club," commuting up the highway to games in Springfield, Massachusetts. Hartford fans were overjoyed when a rebuilt and expanded Civic Center reopened in February 1980— with the Whalers now admitted to the National Hockey League. Courtesy, the Hartford Courant

Now, a month after that victory, Milner was walking through the monumental atrium of city hall for the first time as mayor. He got as far as the glass doors labeled "Office of the Mayor"; the doors were locked. Three city employees hurriedly searched through their key rings, but nobody could find a key. New England's first black mayor needed a locksmith to get into his office for the first time.

Inside, another surprise was in store, due apparently, Milner suspected, to the ire of the Democratic hierarchy. The office had been stripped clean of paper— not a file had been left behind. The mayoral records were later located, but Milner never could bring himself to use them. He started his files from scratch, as if this December morning was the start of a new era in Hartford's history.

But during his ensuing six years in office, a time that in many respects was Hartford's most buoyant period during the second half of the 20th century, Milner was to discover his ability to change people's lives in Hartford was more symbolic than real. That realization started with the very first constituent who showed up in his office that day. The tearful woman had a personal problem that she needed the mayor to fix: She believed her daughter was in danger of becoming pregnant. The mayor, she told Milner, had to prevent it.

"I think it did some uplifting," Milner said years later of his election. "But it also, I think, brought on some people expecting more miracles than realizing what government was all about. I think a lot of people soon found out that . . . you can have political harmony, but without economic empowerment, things are not basically going to change. The color at city hall changed, but the economics did not change very much in the city of Hartford."

Indeed, even as downtown boomed during Milner's term, Hartford's poverty rate only climbed higher.

But downtown, the economy was looking up at the start of the 1980s, way up, as the tallest office towers in Connecticut rose around the newly reopened and expanded Hartford Civic Center coliseum. The Civic Center's prime tenant, the Hartford Whalers, had joined the National Hockey League in 1979, and Hartford, with the second-largest symphony orchestra in New England and one of the nation's best art museums in the Wadsworth Atheneum, with its powerhouse insurance companies and banks, appeared to be similarly making the transition to the major leagues of American cities. At least from the point of view of downtown, there seemed little doubt that the booming

By the early 1980s, it seemed that the finance, insurance and real estate sector would successfully supplant manufacturing as the foundation of Hartford's economy. In the fall of 1982, a freight train pulls out of Hartford in front of the steel skeleton of what would become CityPlace, a 38-story office tower that would be Connecticut's tallest building. Courtesy, the Hartford Courant

Above left: The Wadsworth Atheneum Museum of Art hired renowned Dutch architect Ben van Berkel (at right) of UN Studio to come up with a design for its ambitious expansion plans. The nation's oldest public art museum, the Wadsworth has long been the crown jewel of Hartford's art scene, but the museum hopes to raise its national profile with a significant expansion. The status of the expansion plan is uncertain in 2003, however, following a shake-up of the museum's Board of Trustees. Van Berkel views a model of his concept for an expanded museum with Sylvia J. Smith, the principal in charge of the project for Fox and Fowle Architects (left) and Tobias Wallisser (center), creative director at UN Studio. Courtesy, the Hartford Courant. Photo by Bob MacDonnell

Above right: For a small city, Hartford has a vibrant arts scene, including Dance Connecticut, whose members rehearsed in 2001 at The Bushnell for their performance of The Nutcracker. Courtesy, the Hartford Courant. Photo by John Long

finance, insurance and real estate sector would successfully replace manufacturing to power the city's economy. For the first time since the years right after World War II, Hartford's population was growing as the insurance companies' demand for young financial services workers, who moved into city neighborhoods like Asylum Hill and the South Green, added to the city's growing West Indian and Puerto Rican communities. And with launching Riverfront Recapture, Inc., Hartford in 1981 began the long effort to correct one of its worst mistakes, the severing of downtown from the Connecticut River. Riverfront's mission was to bridge the flood dike and interstate highway that had walled the city off from the great river since the 1940s.

"Hartford is experiencing a gold rush of sorts," The *Hartford Courant* reported that fall, "and just about everyone wants a share of the booty." Developers were expected to pump more than $1 billion into projects during the ensuing three years, creating 5,000 construction jobs and 5 million square feet of new and renovated office space in the city. Anxious to use the building boom to fight Hartford's chronic poverty, neighborhood groups like Hartford Areas Rally Together (HART) were pushing city officials to set aside up to 35 percent of construction jobs on some projects for city residents.

The expansion of local insurance giants like Aetna Life & Casualty, and the law firms, accounting firms, and banks that provided them with services, had produced a serious shortage of office space downtown. By developing new financial vehicles that invested corporate pension fund dollars in real estate across the country, Aetna and other insurers had opened a spigot on billions of dollars of capital that poured into Hartford. Aetna's real estate chief, Bill Russell, watched his division double in size, and with Aetna's other insurance lines also booming, the real estate division was kicked from the crowded home office on Farmington Avenue to downtown Hartford, as Aetna rushed to develop space for its growing army of workers. Because of its strong job base in financial services, "the city of Hartford was uniquely poised to benefit from that explosion of the economy," Russell said. "We were euphoric. Everything was falling into place."

Developers felt the euphoria, too. Across Asylum Street from the Civic Center, a partnership that included developers Allan Hutensky, Richard "Skip" Bronson and an Aetna real estate subsidiary was building the tallest building in Connecticut, 38-story CityPlace. On the riverfront, Houston developer Gerald Hines was building a signature new headquarters for the Hartford Steam Boiler Inspection and Insurance Company. Those were just two of a half-dozen major office tower projects that were either under construction or on the drawing boards in the early and mid-1980s—projects that resulted in gleaming new steel and stone headquarters for the city's banks and insurance companies. Hartford also continued its long predilection for relentlessly devouring its past, demolishing buildings like the 1912 Hartford-Aetna building, the city's first skyscraper, to create space for new office towers (some of which were never to be built). Still, much historic architecture was renovated into housing for the young corps of financial and insurance workers who were so much in demand by Hartford insurance companies and banks, as Congress Street's old buildings and other blocks south of downtown were renovated into stylish

An obelisk in Hartford's Ancient Burying Ground carries the names of Hartford's first settlers. The obelisk is in front of CityPlace, Hartford's tallest building, a symbol of the modern city. Courtesy, the Hartford Courant. Photo by Fred Barnes

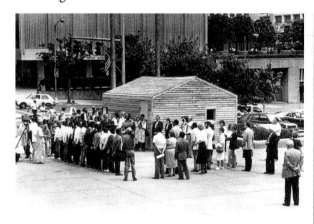

Above: *As Hartford celebrated its 350th birthday in 1986, a replica of the settlement's first schoolhouse was built in downtown Hartford. Courtesy, the Hartford Courant*

Right: *Frank Lloyd Wright called Connecticut's capitol "ridiculous" because of its mishmash of architectural styles, but it is now considered one of the most splendid buildings in the state. Here, fireworks explode above the gold dome during the state's 350th anniversary celebration in 1985. Courtesy, the Hartford Courant. Photo by Steve Silk*

Facing page: *Developer Anthony F. Cutaia, pictured here in 1988, wanted to build New England's tallest building, the 59-story Cutter Financial Center, on this site between Trumbull and Lewis Streets in downtown Hartford. But Hartford's real estate bubble burst before the project ever got started. Courtesy, the Hartford Courant*

Above left: *Small, independently owned stores, businesses like Danny's Grocery, are a foundation of Park Street, the main commercial artery of the city's Latino community. Courtesy, the* Hartford Courant. *Photo by Patrick Raycraft*

Above right: *The 2000 Census showed that as a percentage of its population, Hartford had become the most Puerto Rican city in the United States. Vendor Hilda Lebron sets up her stand on Park Street. Courtesy, the* Hartford Courant. *Photo by Patrick Raycraft*

townhouses. Everybody seemed drawn to the inevitable promise of the real estate boom. Even Nick Carbone, the abrasive and dogged political boss whose alliance with Aetna chief John Filer in the 1970s resulted in the Civic Center, a liberal politician who refused to wear a tie as a point of honor, was now a real estate developer.

By 1986 the real estate bubble was inflating so rapidly that one developer paid $11 million for less than an acre of land near the Civic Center and Bushnell Park—triple what a rival developer had paid for a nearby site just a year before. The Cutter Realty Group, which paid the record price for the real estate between Trumbull and Lewis streets, would say only that it had "special things" in mind for the property. Less than a year later, Cutter's president, Anthony F. Cutaia, announced plans to build the tallest office building in New England. The project was more typical of a real estate venture in midtown Manhattan than Hartford: Capped by a gold dome, the Cutter Financial Center would stand 59 stories tall, including 46 floors of offices and 100 luxury condominiums. At 878 feet tall, Cutter would be nearly 90 feet taller than the Hancock Tower in Boston. Some critics charged that Cutaia wanted to build a monument to himself rather than Hartford, but the Cutter project was symbolic of downtown's ascendant ambitions, and the fact that the Hartford of the 1980s was a community in which confidence, even arrogance, was not in short supply. "We have started something that will change Hartford for the next 50 years," Cutaia, never one to soft-pedal a promise, told reporters after unveiling the Cutter project at a glitzy reception at the Hartford Club attended by Governor William A. O'Neill and Mayor Milner.

As Hartford paused to mark its 350th birthday, the city appeared poised for a prosperous future in which a vital downtown would stretch unbroken from the North End to the emerging Latino neighborhoods of Park Street, and from Union Station to a riverfront reconnected to the city. "Planners Foresee Dying Suburbs, Vital City," the *Courant* announced in a story that peered 50 years into that utopian future on the occasion of the city's birthday. Even Milner couldn't contain his optimism, declaring that Hartford would become "New England's gateway."

As downtown celebrated its prosperity, however, there were troubling signs in some neighborhoods. "With the increased economic boom of the 1980s, no significant effort of any magnitude was made to alter the underlying economic disadvantages experienced in Hartford's black neighborhoods," said a report by the Urban League of Greater Hartford, "The State of Black Hartford." The report noted lowering high school and college graduation rates

among Hartford's blacks, in addition to other problems. The region's suburbanization after 1950 had steadily drained Hartford's political clout as the central city comprised an ever-smaller share of the region's voters. The number of poor people in the city climbed steadily, however, growing from 26,000 in 1970 to over 36,000 in 1990, a 20-year period in which the city's overall population dropped by nearly 20,000. The low- and moderate-income blacks and Latinos who made up an increasingly large share of Hartford's population were disproportionately dependent not on insurance and finance jobs, but on the declining manufacturing sector. As late as 1980 nearly one-third of the city's Latino workers were employed as machine operators, fabricators, assemblers, and in other manufacturing jobs. But as factories moved away, or as technological changes and the end of the Cold War blunted demand for the products Hartford had made, manufacturing work grew increasingly scarce in a city that had bottled, distilled, or assembled everything from A-1 Sauce and Smirnoff vodka to Underwood typewriters and M-16 rifles. After losing half its manufacturing jobs in the late 1960s and early 1970s, Hartford lost half of its remaining manufacturing jobs during the 1980s. By 1990, 45 percent of Hartford's Latinos, and one-quarter of the city's blacks, were below the poverty line.

Cracks also were appearing in downtown's real estate boom. By late 1989, Cutter Realty owed the city $360,000 in back taxes, and Cutaia was asking the city for permission to revise his plans. Nobody was truly prepared, however, for the economic meltdown that was to follow.

"Everything was just as hot as a pistol," said Bill Farley, a veteran downtown real estate broker who was part of many big deals of the 1980s. "Everybody saw this demand continuing, because at that time, no insurance company had ever laid off a person, other than for rape or something like that. There was kind of a tacit understanding that if you made it through the first three years, you had lifetime employment."

But the world was changing, and those changes would ride hard on Connecticut's capital.

On a late summer day in 1990, six banks forced Colonial Realty into bankruptcy, saying the Hartford-area real estate empire lacked the resources to repay $40 million of debts. The massive con that the founders of the real estate conglomerate—Jonathan N. Googel, Benjamin J. Sisti, and Frank Shuch—perpetrated didn't just damage an already-faltering economy, it struck at the psyche of Greater Hartford. During the 1980s, many in the Hartford area saw an investment in Colonial's real estate empire as the closest there was to a sure thing. Thousands of Connecticut investors bought a stake in Colonial, investments that ranged from $25,000 to $1,500,000 a person, to finance their retirement or a child's college education.

"Nearly 6,000 people . . . are facing a grim reality," the *Courant* reported the year after Colonial's collapse in 1991. "Dreams they wanted to achieve through Colonial investments—retirements, second homes, new businesses, college educations—have turned to nightmares. Beyond their financial losses, Colonial investors have been wounded emotionally. Many are estranged from the friend or family member who suggested they invest with the firm. Others, their self-confidence shaken, blame themselves for naivete. Most say they will have a hard time trusting anyone again."

Shuch, Colonial's chief financial officer, later committed suicide after he was arrested by the FBI on fraud charges. Googel and Sisti ultimately went to prison. More than 40 banks that made loans to Colonial, its officers, or the company's investment partnerships said by 1991 that they were owed more than $325

The principals of Colonial Realty—left to right, Jonathan N. Googel, Frank Shuch and Benjamin J. Sisti—said they launched their dealmaking in the telephone booth pictured here. By the late 1980s, the trio said they were worth $75 million, as they oversaw a $1 billion real estate empire. But when that empire collapsed in the early 1990s, in part due to the trio's fraud, thousands of Connecticut investors lost their savings, contributing to Greater Hartford's economic woes during the period. Googel and Sisti went to prison; Shuch committed suicide. Courtesy, the Hartford Courant. Photo by Michael McAndrews

million by Colonial. Colonial's collapse dealt another blow to an economy that already had been slowed by defense cutbacks, over-inflated real estate values, structural changes in the insurance industry, bank failures, and a national recession. More than a decade later, Hartford had yet to fully recover.

With the city's insurers battered by their overindulgence in real estate during the 1980s and a national economic slowdown, Hartford suffered massive layoffs in the early 1990s. Unemployment in Hartford doubled in the early 1990s, and the number of finance, insurance and real estate jobs in the city—the sector that had powered the economy so surely during the 1980s— declined by a third through the mid-1990s. Connecticut lost 159,000 jobs, almost 10 percent of the state's total employment, during what economists came to call "The Great Recession." The concept of the secure, almost parental, relationship insurance workers enjoyed with their employers—people commonly used terms such as "Mother Aetna" in Hartford—was obliterated as insurance companies were forced to become more competitive, and as segments of multi-line insurers were chopped up and resold, mostly to corporations that were not based in Hartford. Hartford County's population actually began to decline as economic refugees left the region to search for work. By 1993, with Cutter Realty owing $3 million in back taxes, the city decided to put up for auction the land that was to hold New England's tallest skyscraper. "There was no banging gavel, no auctioneer taking bids from the audience," the *Courant* reported on one of the largest foreclosure sales in the city's history. "In fact, there was no audience. Just a couple of lawyers sitting at a card table." Not a single bidder stepped forward to claim real estate that had fetched more than $300 a square foot seven years before. "It's a sign of the times that the property would be worth less than the taxes owed," said one of the lawyers overseeing the sale.

In 1991 and 1992 alone, 31 Connecticut banks failed under the weight of bad loans and were seized by federal regulators, including 11 in Hartford and its suburbs. The sudden appearance of a flock of federal regulators to demand the keys to a failed bank almost seemed to be a weekly civic ritual.

"The Great Recession" proved the ruin of several Hartford landmarks, including G. Fox, the University Club and a downtown diner, the Marble Pillar. The 133-year-old German-American restaurant closed in July of 1993. The restaurant auctioned off its furnishings, equipment and antiques the following month. Lin Crabtree of Glastonbury, who bought an 1880s-era clock, was one of many people who came to the auction to buy a piece of history. Courtesy, the Hartford Courant

Below left: With Hartford mired in a deep recession in the early 1990s, the $12-million renovation of the Old State House was a bright spot for downtown. Workers raised the 200-year-old building on jacks to rebuild the building's foundation and add underground museum space. Courtesy, the Hartford Courant. Photo by Cecilia Prestamo

Below right: During 1991 and 1992, when 31 Connecticut banks failed, the sudden appearance of banking regulators to take over a failed financial institution almost seemed to be a weekly event in the Hartford area. Depositors got this notice outside the failed Bank of East Hartford in 1991. Courtesy, the Hartford Courant. Photo by Stephen Dunn

In 1997, 22 years after the Hartford Whalers began playing in the Civic Centro Coliseum, team owner Peter Karmanos decided to move to North Carolina when he and the state could not agree on terms for constructing a new arena for the team. Whalers' captain Kevin Dineen, long one of the team's most popular players, takes a final lap around the Civic Center ice after the last Whalers game in Hartford. Courtesy, the Hartford Courant. Photo by Tom Brown.

Banking institutions that had been part of the city's history for more than a century, including Connecticut Bank & Trust, the largest banking failure in the history of New England when it went under in 1991, were soon no more. Weakened by the real estate bust, local banks and insurance companies went through an unprecedented wave of consolidation during the 1990s. Housing values began to rise in the late 1990s, but the median sale price of a home in the Greater Hartford region was 12.4 percent lower by 2002, when adjusted for inflation, than it had been a decade earlier, one study found. Corporate icons like Travelers insurance, whose executives had been at the heart of the city's power structure for decades, were swallowed up by larger corporations based in other cities. With Hartford's largest employers no longer local companies headed by executives who lived in the community, it became unthinkable that a CEO would invest tens of millions of dollars in a local civic venture, as John Filer had done in the mid-1970s, having Aetna develop and manage the Civic Center mall.

With a governmental system that consisted only of a state government and inwardly focused city and town governments, Greater Hartford lacked the civic machinery to address some of its biggest problems. By the early 1990s, for example, the Hartford Whalers were warning that the team would leave unless the franchise could find a way to boost revenues. Ultimately, that would mean building a new arena for the team. For an impoverished city government that had not yet completed paying off the debt on the Civic Center, that was an impossibility. Elsewhere in the country, county governments frequently helped finance new arenas during the 1990s, but in a region without county government, the problem fell to the state. Ultimately, Whalers owner Peter Karmanos abandoned Hartford at the end of the 1997 season when he couldn't reach a deal with Governor John G. Rowland for a new arena. Regional efforts at economic development were unfocused and of limited effectiveness.

The 2000 Census revealed the full extent of the wreckage the 1990s wrought upon Hartford and its suburbs. By the end of the decade, the region had 28,000 fewer jobs than at the start of the decade. Hartford County had the largest decrease in median household income—a $2,000 drop, when adjusted for inflation—of any county in the six New England states. Hartford lost 11 percent of its population; only four of the 243 cities in America with more than 100,000 people lost more population by percentage. And in a city that as recently as the 1980s had unashamedly billed itself as "The Insurance Capi-

tal of the World," job losses were so large that a majority of workers who lived in Hartford now had to commute outside the city to find work. As recently as 1990, 59 percent of Hartford workers had earned their paychecks in the city.

Few days during the Great Recession were darker than the cold Friday in January 1993 when G. Fox & Co. closed its downtown Hartford department store, a victim of sprawling suburban malls and the economy. With its stainless steel art deco marquee and its majestic escalators that carried shoppers up into the building's riches as if toward heaven, the department store was a cultural and commercial touchstone during 146 years of retail history on Main Street. Models got their start in the classy Connecticut Room; kids grew up never forgetting a pre-Christmas visit to the toy department. Beatrice Fox Auerbach, the late president of that great palace of shopping, had a nearly mythical status in Hartford: A frequently repeated tale held that the city's notoriously poor high-way design was a result of demands by "Mrs. Auerbach" that exit ramps de-posit potential shoppers near the downtown doorways of G. Fox.

But on that last day, the store's tawdry exit made memories of past glory all the more bitter. Liquidation had reduced the store's merchandise to a 50-foot square of items, including a few tables of shoes, some greeting cards, and a pile of artificial Christmas trees. Dust coated the historic department store's marble art deco pillars. An antiques hunter scurried through the store, hoping to scrounge deco furniture or fixtures.

"Mrs. Auerbach," said one of the final customers as he surveyed the sad scene, "is probably spinning in her grave."

On a Friday afternoon in May 1992, two days after a jury acquitted the white police officers who beat black motorist Rodney King, while images of rampag-ing black mobs in Los Angeles played across the nation's television screens, 300 black Weaver High School students walked out of class and marched down-town to protest the verdict. Much of the central business district panicked, as rumors spread that mobs were rampaging in North Hartford. The Civic Cen-ter mall and G. Fox closed; insurance companies told workers they could go home early. In a disturbing echo to the riots in the late 1960s that drove many whites out of Hartford, the interstate was jammed with frightened suburban-ites fleeing the city.

The gulf between the races—and between city and suburb—exposed by that flight was sobering, but Carrie Saxon Perry was to remember that Friday

Carrie Saxon Perry was the first black woman elected mayor of a northeastern city when she took office in December of 1987, and she attracted national publicity as a result. Perry always saw herself as an advocate for the people, perhaps even more than as the leader of the powerful machine of city government. Her populist emphasis was one reason she lost the support of local business leaders and others. Courtesy, the Hartford Courant

afternoon as the finest hour in her six years as mayor. Throughout that tense time, Perry, a disarming presence in one of the trademark hats she always wore in public, shuttled from school to street corner, reminding whatever group she encountered of the Reverend Martin Luther King, Jr.'s teachings on nonviolence. She ended up walking with the students as they headed downtown, and at the end of the day, the worst damage was a broken window in a store on Main Street. "We got to the streets; we talked to those students," Perry remembered years later. "It was a high point because it sort of symbolized the fact that people believed the city was worth saving . . . . It was high point not so much because I led the march. It was a high point because people followed."

Perry's election in 1987 had been another first for Hartford; she was the first black woman elected mayor of a Northeastern city. Perry had spent her earliest years in an unheated railroad flat on Russell Street, an area later erased by urban renewal, and she always saw herself, she said in an interview years later, as an advocate for the poor and working-class people she grew up with, rather than as a member of Hartford's ruling elite. The city's corporate leaders saw her as something less than a sister-in-arms. When Perry and her allies on the city council campaigned for national health insurance, and approved a resolution taking the insurance industry to task for redlining and other problems, local insurance executives were not amused. Addressing city hall in a speech to the Hartford Downtown Council during the 1993 mayoral campaign, Ronald E. Compton, Aetna Life & Casualty Company's CEO, asked: "Would you please tell us whether you want the insurance industry in Hartford or not? Just let me know, will you?" Perry believed she was wrongly portrayed by the media, the *Courant* especially, as anti-business. But at a time when Hartford faced major economic problems, Perry and corporate leaders like Compton never came close to forging the working alliance that the city needed so badly.

Many of the economic and social forces battering Hartford were beyond the scope of city government. Others were not. During Perry's term, the incidence of rape, robbery, and aggravated assault in Hartford hit 20-year highs. And by 1993, gang violence sparked a wave of shootings across the city, as the number of homicides jumped from 14 to a record 57 in a two-year period from 1992 to 1994. Gang problems were not new to Hartford, but the fear that gripped the city during those months was perhaps the final, mortal blow to the civic self-assurance Hartford possessed during the 1980s. Perry and the city council seemed powerless to stop the violence.

Michael P. Peters, a longtime Hartford firefighter, was hardly a household name. But as a former chairman of the Hartford Redevelopment Agency, he also knew many of the city's top developers and business leaders, and as a member of the Democratic town committee, he had been a significant player in South End politics for a decade. More than 20 years in firehouses across Hartford had given him a street-level fluency with the city's neighborhoods. Within the firehouse, his ability to connect with and organize people already had given him the nickname "The Mayor." Now, the politician in Peters saw an opportunity. "The city was going [down] basically, and again being a firefighter, working in the neighborhoods, I saw it happening in front of me. The gang violence was out of control," Peters remembered in an interview years later. "So what happened was, I woke up, it was a Sunday morning, and I said to my wife, 'I'm going to run for mayor.' She laughed. I said, 'What are you laughing at?' 'Well, number one,' she says, 'you're a white guy.' I said, 'That's a good point.' She said, 'Not for nothing, Michael. It's going to be very difficult for you to win, because it's an African American mayor you're going to be running against.' Then I called my family together; they all kind of laughed, too. Then my mother said something very profound, as we're all in my living room, and I'm asking them to support me for mayor. My mother said, 'I'll tell you what, let's support him, and then when he loses, it'll be out of his system.' I thanked her for her support, and off we went."

Peters didn't exactly have matinee idol looks; he had little aptitude for policy, and he spent so many evenings in city bars that the *Courant* bestowed him with the title of "Night Mayor." "New York City never sleeps," the newspaper noted in a 1997 profile. "In Hartford, that distinction belongs to the mayor." But his blunt, self-deprecating humor—columnist George Will would gener-ously call Peters "part Falstaff and part Fiorello LaGuardia"—helped Peters

With the city's economy in shambles, and city neighbor-hoods coping with an epidemic of violence, Hartford voters decided it was time for a change in 1993, electing a city fire-fighter, Michael P. Peters, as mayor. Peters was no political neophyte, having run a savvy campaign and quickly becoming a fine—and very funny—public speaker. Courtesy, the Hartford Courant

connect equally with business leaders and the homeless. Peters finished a strong second to Perry in the Democratic primary in September, and defeated the incumbent mayor as a petitioning candidate in the general election. Years later, Perry was still angry at the city's Democratic leaders, feeling they had deserted her to let Peters win.

Peters saw his role as one-part political rainmaker, tapping the new Democratic administration in Washington for federal dollars, and one-part ambassador to the suburbs. Using some of that federal money, along with federal racketeering laws and combined city and state police patrols, the city cut the homicide total to 23 by 1996. By 1997 federal prosecutors had convicted 55 gang members, solved four murders, and ended a two-year drug war between the Latin Kings and Los Solidos gangs. With a failing school system, and the city facing perhaps its worst economic times in the modern era, Hartford began trying extreme measures to reverse the city's fortunes. In 1994 the school board reached an agreement to make Hartford the first city in America to turn over management of an entire public school system to a private company—Education Alternatives, Inc. (EAI). The EAI experiment brought few lasting improvements to the schools, and was quickly terminated, but by 1997, the state legislature had voted to take over the Hartford schools, with the support of Peters and other city leaders. The previous week, the Hartford Whalers had played their final game in Hartford. "I lost the Whalers, and I lost the school board in one week. Great. This is awful. But we are going to be okay," Peters told a reporter in his typical optimistic-no-matter-what style. Despite the mayor's cheerleading, the silver lining was tough to find. The state was to run the Hartford schools for the next five years. Peters' most lasting legacy might be his partnership with John Wardlaw, the head of the Hartford Housing Authority, to initiate what became a $100 million-plus effort to raze the city's crime-ridden public housing projects and replace them with lower-density apartments, suburban-style, owner-occupied single family houses and commercial development. The ultimate success of that venture remains far from clear; however, one effect appears to have been to increase the burden of poverty in surrounding neighborhoods as the poorest of the poor moved out of projects.

Ultimately, in Hartford's "weak mayor" form of government, in a city with less taxable property than its suburb of West Hartford, a political heavyweight

Above left: *When Presidents Dwight D. Eisenhower and John F. Kennedy came to Hartford in the 1950s and 1960s, they spoke in downtown Hartford. When President Bill Clinton came to Hartford in 1999, he visited Latino merchants on Park Street, and the newly completed Artists Collective building on Albany Avenue, an African American arts and culture organization—reflecting Hartford's new ethnic identity. At the Artists Collective, Clinton reacts to a joke from Governor John G. Rowland about the $1.7 million home Clinton was buying in New York state. Courtesy, the Hartford Courant. Photo by Patrick Raycraft*

Above right: *The Greater Hartford Open has been a summer tradition in Central Connecticut for more than 50 years. Phil Mickelson, who became the tournament's first back-to-back champion after winning in 2001 and 2002, blasts out of a bunker on his way to tying a course record with a nine-under-par score in 2001. The tournament will be called the Buick Championship starting in 2004. Courtesy, the Hartford Courant. Photo by John Long*

NBA star Ray Allen, who played at the University of Connecticut, is an important part of the community. Here, Allen attends a celebrity boat ride on the Connecticut River in Hartford, a fundraiser for his Ray of Hope Foundation. Courtesy, the Hartford Courant. Photo by David Roberts

with significantly more power than Peters was needed. That turned out to be Governor John G. Rowland, a Republican who grew up in another poor Connecticut city, Waterbury. Rowland failed to keep the Whalers, but the following year, in early 1998, the governor proposed a record $350 million state-financed development plan for downtown Hartford, including construction of a convention center and 1,000 units of housing. In secret, the chief executive of the The Phoenix Home Life Mutual Insurance Company, Robert W. Fiondella, had already been working with planners Bill Mead and Josiah "Cy" Kirby for several years on a dramatic plan to reconstruct the riverfront. As reporters began sniffing around, Fiondella was forced to go public, unveiling the Adriaen's Landing project later that spring. Named after Dutch explorer Adriaen Block, the project included somewhat fanciful plans for a museum to be built atop Interstate 91, a convention center, an indoor stadium, and other attractions. But when the *Courant* trumpeted "THE $1 BILLION BABY" in banner headlines the next day, an interested party 100 miles to the north took notice. Robert K. Kraft, the owner of the New England Patriots, was frustrated with his inability to get Boston and Massachusetts politicians to help

Hartford lost the Whalers, but it looked like the city was poised to grab another major league sports franchise after Governor John G. Rowland inked a deal with Robert Kraft, owner of the New England Patriots, to bring the National Football League team to a new stadium to be built in downtown Hartford. Here, Rowland (left) presents Kraft (right) with a Connecticut license plate after the state legislature approved a finance package for a $374 million stadium in December 1998. Five months later, the deal was dead. Courtesy, AP. Photo by Bob Child

pay for a new stadium for his National Football League franchise. Whether Hartford was, from the very beginning, nothing more than a useful foil for Kraft's stadium ambitions in Massachusetts remains unclear. In any case, once Kraft signed a deal with Rowland in November 1998 to have Connecticut taxpayers finance a $374 million stadium on Hartford's riverfront, Massachusetts leaders and the NFL got serious about keeping the Patriots near Boston. Massachusetts succeeded and Rowland, who failed to fully comprehend the environmental and engineering limitations of the proposed Adriaen's Landing site, didn't. But even after the Patriots deal collapsed in April 1999, Rowland continued to push the Adriaen's Landing plan. By 2003 Hartford's riverfront was becoming a massive construction zone, as the largest convention center between New York and Boston began rising above Interstate 91, and crews cleared space for a housing, entertainment, and shopping district. There was a new $92 million football stadium, too, but it wasn't in Hartford. It was across the river in East Hartford, and the main tenant was University of Connecticut football rather than the Patriots.

Adriaen's Landing was not the only significant building project in Hartford. In 1999 Riverfront Recapture completed its two-decade effort to reconnect downtown with the Connecticut River, opening a pedestrian plaza over the interstate. The G. Fox building, derelict for nearly a decade, had been converted into the new home of Capital Community College. Former Trinity College president Evan Dobelle had led a successful effort to build the "Learning Corridor," a $110 million campus of public schools that linked the Trinity campus with the Institute of Living. The Bushnell completed a $45 million expansion, adding a new 900-seat performance hall and becoming the Bushnell Center for the Performing Arts. At the Mark Twain House, construction began in 2002 on a new $15 million visitors center designed by noted architect Robert A. M. Stern. Adjacent to Adriaen's Landing, the Wadsworth Atheneum Museum of Art was also pursuing ambitious expansion plans, although the recession that began in 2000 left the outcome uncertain.

Still, as the decade ended, there was a sobering reminder that the city had not come close to recapturing the economic success of the 1980s. The 2000 Census showed that Hartford's poverty rate had reached 31 percent. If Connecticut was a country, it would be the world's wealthiest nation, a study by local economists showed. Yet, Connecticut's capital had the second-highest poverty rate among all large U.S. cities, trailing only Brownsville, Texas.

The past 20 years have seen Hartford evolve into a more varied and diverse ethnic stew than the white-black-Puerto Rican triad that marked the city into distinct areas of ethnic turf in the 1970s and 1980s. In North Hartford, Jamaicans have emerged as a leading commercial force; south of downtown, Peruvian entrepreneurs are renovating rundown apartment buildings and opening restaurants. One way to see that new diversity is through the sports Hartford plays: a weekend visitor to Keney Park might be able to take in a cricket match played by teams made up of immigrants from Jamaica, India, and Guyana. In Colt Park, teams wearing the national colors of Peru, Mexico, and other Latin American countries will be playing soccer. At the start of a new century, it has become increasingly difficult to assign ownership of any particular neighborhood to a single ethnic group. An intricate ethnic mosaic is also emerging along many of the city's commercial corridors. In Parkville, Vietnamese and other Asian merchants provide much of the commercial horsepower, while Brazilians, taking advantage of an existing base of Portuguese speakers, are building their influence. In "Little Italy" along Franklin Avenue in the South End, Italian-

American businesses increasingly share space with Latinos and Bosnians who are opening restaurants, travel agencies, and other businesses.

A more polyglot—a more global—city represents a powerful opportunity for Hartford in a world that is growing ever more global. The question is, as those groups gain influence and wealth like earlier waves of immigrants, will Hartford be able to hold onto them? Or, as in earlier decades, will they simply migrate to the suburbs, leaving only the poor behind? At the start of a new century, Hartford is entering a pivotal period. Will Adriaen's Landing, the most ambitious downtown development project in a generation, lure private investment back to the center city? As the school system comes back under the control of a local board, will city students sustain the progress they made under state administration? Will the new strong-mayor system, in which the mayor is the dominant political force rather than the city council and city manager, provide more effective political leadership? Can Eddie Perez succeed in his bid to increase Hartford's depressed homeownership rate, thereby bolstering the city's middle class?

The biggest problem for Hartford on the cusp of the new century is that the city's boundaries have become a kind of filter, continually intensifying the concentration of poverty within the city's 18 square miles during good times as well as bad. The history of the past 20 years strongly suggests that unless a way can be found to break that mold, Hartford—and the Greater Hartford region—will continue to struggle, even if downtown makes a comeback.

CHAPTER

XIII

Chronicles of Leadership

~ WHEN THOMAS HOOKER AND
HIS FOLLOWERS CAME TO WHAT IS NOW HARTFORD IN
1636, THEY BROUGHT WITH THEM DEEPLY HELD
Puritan convictions. However, they had not left their
homes in Massachusetts because of religious dissension.
They moved west in search of better opportunities for
themselves and their children.

Until the early 19th century Hartford could hardly be
called much more than a provincial, agricultural town.
As the alternate capital for the colony and state of Connecticut, its major economic activity consisted of trade
via the Connecticut River. Most of the warehouses,
shops, and services depended on that trade. The
embargo and ensuing War of 1812 temporarily slowed
down even that activity.

Once the conflict was over Hartford began to change
economically. This was due in large part to what has
always been the city's major resource—people. Its leading citizens were ready to give support to new industries
in those pre-Civil War years. Others, residents and those

from other towns, brought ideas which they believed could become successful enterprises.

Some of these fledgling industries failed because of the turmoil of a free economy. But, as the following pages indicate, many succeeded beyond the greatest expectations of their founders. Hartford's banks provided much of the needed capital, the railroad's arrival in 1839 opened up new markets, and workmen, often from the surrounding countryside, proved to be easily trainable in a variety of crafts and skills. Hartford had a solid base upon which to build its future.

The city's early industries produced furniture, silverware, and leather goods, and included recognized printing and publishing firms. Other manufacturers developed steam engines, boilers, heavy machinery, and firearms. All of them benefited from water power as a convenient source of energy. Insurance companies expanded in size and number throughout the century, making Hartford well-known, at least by name, all over the world. Not only have they provided employment for countless thousands, but their contributions to the community have helped to enrich the quality of life for Hartford.

A characteristic of 19th-century America was the arrival of people from Ireland, Germany, Italy, Poland, Russia, and many other countries. With their coming Hartford became more metropolitan and new businesses and services reflected the importance of these people to the economic and cultural life of the city.

By the beginning of the 20th century Hartford had become a major American industrial and financial center. Gas, electricity, water, as well as the new automobile and the soon-to-be "aeroplane," were indicative of how far the city had come. Its relationship to surrounding towns was growing closer as corporations formed and branched out to the suburbs.

Hartford's industrial expertise was of vital importance to the nation's defense efforts during the wars of this century. Aircraft engines, specialized component parts, and wiring, among many other products, were manufactured in the area. While important in and of themselves, these defense industries developed new areas of technology. Industries change over time and so too, Hartford's enterprises will continue to evolve. Today, the city is a center of financial services, healthcare and aerospace companies. While once known as the "Insurance City," today there are fewer than a half-dozen such companies based in Hartford.

Hartford can boast of a rich cultural and educational environment, modern communications outlets, and excellent health facilities which offer residents of the capital region the best facets of modern life. Thomas Hooker and his followers would find little to relate to today in the community they founded, but they could take satisfaction in knowing that their early struggles had helped to produce an attractive, modern American city which respects and takes pride in the accomplishments of the past.

THE BUSHNELL CENTER FOR THE PERFORMING ARTS

Over the last seven decades, more than 28 million people have experienced The Bushnell Center for the Performing Arts. In addition to bringing symphony orchestras, dance troupes and the best of Broadway to Hartford, The Bushnell has staged cooking classes, spelling bees, ice shows, magic acts, circuses, rodeos, war-relief efforts, naturalization ceremonies, political conventions, lectures, graduations, awards ceremonies, charity benefits and other events, including a 1996 Presidential Debate.

The Bushnell is approaching its 75th anniversary in 2005, and has become more than a beloved venue. In its mission as "a center for the benefit of the public," The Bushnell is a home for local arts organizations and a presenter of renowned performers from around the world. Through the years, The Bushnell has adapted to embrace ever-changing and diversifying art forms and tastes—remaining mindful of the transformative influence of the arts in daily life, and of the opportunity to benefit the region by bringing arts, education and community together.

Mikhail Baryshnikov, one of the most celebrated artists in the dance world, launched his recent tour in Hartford, gracing The Bushnell's Belding Theater stage for two sold-out performances in May 2003. The engagement was a co-presentation of The Bushnell, Dance Connecticut and Baryshnikov Dance Foundation. Photo by Thomas Giroir

The Bushnell's new 90,000-square-foot addition, built adjacent to the current Mortensen Hall, opened in November 2001 and includes the 900-seat Belding Theater and such amenities as a café, gift shop, classroom and reception space. Photo by Robert Benson Photography

It all began when Dotha Bushnell Hillyer (1843–1932) wished to pay tribute to her father by creating a "living memorial"—a place where the community would come together to celebrate life, and where art in its many forms would elevate people's spirits.

The Reverend Horace Bushnell (1802–1876) was an esteemed minister, philosopher, and civic leader. Although he spent his early life in rugged existence on his family's farm, at age 21 he enrolled at Yale and spent his next 10 years earning four degrees. An early advocate of public parks and waterworks, he believed in the redeeming and soothing powers of green spaces, or "common ornamental grounds" as he referred to them.

In 1879, daughter Dotha Bushnell married philanthropist Appleton Robbins Hillyer, founder of the Aetna National Bank of Hartford and director of the Aetna Life Insurance Company. Dotha's dream was to create a lasting gift to the community in which her family lived and thrived—and to commemorate her father's commitment to public service—by constructing The Horace Bushnell Memorial Hall, adjacent to Bushnell Park.

This dream was accomplished with meticulous planning and a bit of luck. In 1919, Dotha took an inheritance of $800,000 and invested it in the stock market. She drew up the Articles of Incorporation for the memorial, stating that it should be a "center for the benefit of the public." She asked for design advice from friend William H. Mortensen, who later became mayor of Hartford and managing director of The Bushnell for more than 40 years. The chosen architectural firm, Corbett, Harrison & MacMurray, used The Bushnell's design as a prototype for their next project, Radio City Music Hall in New York.

By 1928 Dotha's initial stock market investment of $800,000 had grown to over $3 million. She withdrew her monies in December 1928, shortly before the great crash, and created a nonprofit corporation and a charitable trust to provide construction funds and a modest endowment.

The Bushnell's exterior echoed architectural elements of Hartford's Old State House in the Georgian Revival style, including a tall Ionic portico and gold-domed cupola. The Hall's art deco interior was considered innovative and daring at the time. Overall,

Katharine Hepburn with Bushnell managing director William H. "Bill" Mortensen before her first Hartford performance in the play Without Love, *presented on April 27 and 28, 1942.* Hartford Times *photo by Ted Kosinski, from The Bushnell's Shepherd M. Holcombe Archives*

With the existing 2,800-seat Mortensen Hall booked to capacity, the new 900-seat Belding Theater that opened in 2001 has enabled The Bushnell to present new arts and entertainment options and better accommodate local arts organizations in multiple performance spaces. The expansion has also provided an economic boost by bringing more people to downtown Hartford. Photo by Robert Benson Photography

the architecture intentionally reflected the persona of Horace Bushnell: the conservative, traditional exterior symbolizing his role as a minister and philosopher; the warm, vivid interior reminiscent of the contemporary, forward-looking man.

After two years of construction The Bushnell's opening night on January 13, 1930 was a resounding success. People arrived via trolleys, in new cars or on foot, dressed in black tie and gown. Dotha, however, was too ill to attend, so she experienced the three days of opening ceremonies through a radio broadcast piped into her home by WTIC. Although Dotha lived less than a block away, in her frail health, she only set foot in the Hall once.

Over the years major performing artists from vaudeville to classical have appeared on The Bushnell stage, including Jolson, Chaplin, Toscanini, Bernstein, Horowitz, Rubenstein, Perlman, Pavarotti, Sills, Olivier, Hayes, Garland, Brando, Baryshnikov and

Channing. The Bushnell has additionally provided a podium for such visionaries as Winston Churchill, Eleanor Roosevelt, Helen Keller and Martin Luther King, Jr.

The late Katharine Hepburn, four-time Academy Award winner who was born and raised in Hartford, first appeared professionally at The Bushnell in April 1942 in *Without Love*, a comedy written especially for her by Philip Barry, who also wrote one of her best-known film roles in *The Philadelphia Story*.

In recent years, theatre at The Bushnell has expanded to include the biggest of touring Broadway musicals, including *Cats, The Phantom of the Opera, Les Misérables, Miss Saigon, Disney's Beauty and the Beast, Showboat, Ragtime, Rent* and *Mamma Mia!*

Reminiscent of its founder's planning, the Board of Trustees saw an increasing need for expansion of The Bushnell. In 1998 a five-year capital campaign was begun with a goal of raising $45 million to construct a new theater and to increase the institution's endowment. The campaign ended in 2003, having raised $48 million.

The addition built adjacent to the current Hall, and completed in 2001, includes the 900-seat Belding Theater, the Autorino Great Hall for receptions and smaller performances, and several amenities including a café, gift shop, classroom space and more restrooms and elevators. With the existing 2,800-seat Mortensen Hall booked to capacity, the expansion has enabled The Bushnell to present new arts and entertainment options and better accommodate local arts organizations in multiple performance spaces. The expansion has also provided an economic boost by bringing more people to downtown Hartford.

Architects Wilson Butler Lodge, Inc., of Boston and Schoenhardt Architects of Simsbury carefully integrated the new facility with the historic Hall and with the Nationally Registered Historic District surrounding it. The design of the new exterior harmonizes with the stately façade, reinterpreting the use of brick, stone, and copper. But unlike the existing build-

ing, whose symmetry and classical motifs create a formal appearance, the addition is openly transparent and deliberately extroverted.

Beyond the theater walls, The Bushnell has been providing arts-in-education programs within Greater Hartford schools for the last decade. The Bushnell's nationally recognized program, PARTNERS (Partners in Arts and Education Revitalizing Schools), is a cross-community effort presently serving nearly 7,000 students in 32 schools and 17 districts. Since 1993, PARTNERS has offered classroom-based, arts-infused instructional units that are integrated into school curricula, and directly linked to state and national standards. Each unit combines children's literature and a variety of art disciplines to create age-appropriate, hands-on arts activities that improve literacy, enhance self-confidence, encourage creativity and foster the understanding and appreciation of diverse cultures.

The Greater Hartford community has fully embraced the "New Bushnell." Audience attendance and contributions to support theater operations and arts-in-education programs have surpassed expectations. These results continue to illustrate the relevance of The Bushnell's nonprofit mission as "a center for the benefit of the public."

Opened in 1930, The William H. Mortensen Hall is steeped in history and heritage. But, with age, certain physical, mechanical, and aesthetic needs in the theater have been highlighted for restoration. Work will be completed in time for the 75th anniversary of the opening of The Horace Bushnell Memorial Hall in January 2005, returning the auditorium to its original splendor. Courtesy, The Hartford Courant

CONNECTICUT CHILDREN'S MEDICAL CENTER (CCMC)

While it's the youngster who is in need of medical attention, Connecticut Children's Medical Center (CCMC) in effect treats the entire family.

One of only 58 free-standing facilities in the United States dedicated to the healthcare of children among the nation's roster of 5,000 hospitals, CCMC has carved itself a special niche. A couple of anecdotes help tell the story.

Because of an asthmatic condition, a three-year-old boy makes regular visits to the architecturally unique hospital located at 282 Washington Street in Hartford.

"We call him one of our frequent fly-ers," said Tom Hanley, director of public relations. "When he took a fall and needed some stitches, his mom drove him to the nearest hospital. When they were finished, he asked, 'Where's my ice cream? Where's my pajamas with the cartoon figures? Where is my movie?'"

When the local hospital had no answers, the child turned to his mother and said, "Get the keys. We're going home."

In another example a father wrote to Connecticut Children's: "It was just as important that you paid attention to my wife's anxiety about what was happening to our child as you did to the child's medical condition."

At the opening ceremonies dedicating Connecticut Children's Medical Center on April 2, 1996, a monument was unveiled reading, "Celebrating a new era of healing, hope and health for our children."

Larry Gold has been the president and CEO of Connecticut Children's Medical Center since March 1997.

"That's important to us," said President and CEO Larry Gold about the hospital that serves 150,000 children's visits a year for primary care, specialty clinics, emergency visits and inpatient units. "Kids take their cues from their parents on how they should react about going to the hospital."

Connecticut Children's attempts to give their young patients "a sense of ownership about the process. Just because a kid is sick doesn't mean he or she has to stop being a child," Gold said.

For example, when a child is facing the prospects of surgery, the hospital attempts to bring the family in beforehand to check out the operating room and see all the people wearing funny clothing and masks. "Experiencing that for the first time would scare any four year old" says Gold.

The youngster is allowed to put the surgical mask on and play with the blood-pressure cuffs. The technicians will even X-ray a toy to get that there's-nothing-to-fear message across.

On the day of the surgery, the child will be taken to the operating room in a battery-powered Ferrari, Barbie convertible or G.I. Joe jeep. "You don't know how many times we will hear adults say, 'Gee, I wish I was treated that way when I go to the hospital,'" Gold said.

Yet what Governor John Rowland called "one of the jewels in the crown of the state's health-care system" in his 1998 State of the State Address was not all that warmly embraced when the concept of a fully dedicated children's hospital, a relatively new phenomenon at the time, was first proposed for Connecticut in the early 1970s.

The suggestion spawned opposition and public hearings at the state level. A major hurdle was overcome when the Hartford Chamber of Commerce sponsored a study by a prestigious healthcare consultant that ended up endorsing the concept of a free-standing children's hospital dedicated to providing tertiary care for youngsters and the spectrum of pediatric services.

What was to become ranked in *Child Magazine's* top 20 among the best children's hospitals in the country evolved from the consolidation of the pediatric programs and personnel from three institutions: Hartford Hospital, Newington Children's Hospital and the University of Connecticut School of Medicine, John Dempsey Hospital.

The 123-bed facility opened on April 2, 1996. "It came about," Hanley said, "after an incredible amount of community examination of the health-care needs of children up to the age of 18. We are the only hospital of its kind in the state."

Newington Children's Hospital spearheaded the initiative with the two hospital partners to design a new children's hospital from the ground up to address the pressing

Connecticut Children's Medical Center in Hartford is the state's only freestanding, independent hospital exclusively dedicated to the care of children.

health needs of children that were not being met in a system that fragmented pediatrics among three institutions.

Newington's location was also a problem—seven miles from the heart of Hartford with no public transportation service. Hartford's youngsters and, more importantly, their parents could hardly get there.

"Our team brought together some terrific expertise when the three hospitals consolidated," Hanley said. "Because of our national reputation, we are also recruiting excellent pediatric surgeons and physicians from all over the country. We have great capacity to do the job, from open-heart surgery to cancer cases to complex spinal fusions, right here." No longer do Hartford-area youngsters with significant health issues have to go to Boston or New York.

"Right here" is across the street from the traditional-looking Hartford Hospital with its straight lines. CCMC was designed with children in mind—lots of curves and configurations.

"Imagine a building that looks like a children's science museum," Hanley said.

Full of natural lighting, the CCMC facility broke ground architecturally for a

Creating an environment where kids feel comfortable and safe is as important as quality medical care. At Connecticut Children's Medical Center, kids get to drive themselves to the operating room and parents may accompany them while anesthesia is administered.

children's hospital, earning *Modern Health-care Magazine's* No. 1 award for architecture. Hundreds of visitors from all over the world come to borrow ideas. There are lots of inviting things for children to look at and touch. Even the artwork on the premises was either inspired by children or created by them.

"All of that is part of the medical equation," Hanley said. "Being ill is scary enough. Having a child sick is anxiety enough for a parent. A hospital should be an inviting place."

A philosophy of family-centered care permeates the CCMC. Children and families were surveyed about adding home-like touches. Each inpatient child has a private room and restroom. Parents are encouraged to spend the night. As Hanley said, "we tried to put hospitality in the hospital."

Family sleep rooms are also situated near the intensive care unit (ICU) and the neonatal ICU. There is no charge for parents to use these facilities.

"We want the parents to be true partners in their child's health," he said, "and be involved at all levels of decision-making, from the diagnostic room to the bedside.

There is more to CCMC than "feel-good medicine," though. All of the pediatric medical specialties are available at Connecticut Children's. It is a leading center in redesigning care for children with asthma, giving them better control of their disease. The foremost pediatric authority on children's digestive diseases practices at CCMC. Experts on minimizing the pain of medical procedures and surgery performed on children are changing practice at Connecticut Children's and at children's hospitals across the country. It does great work as a teaching hospital for the University of Connecticut School of Medicine. Each year, 60 pediatricians take part in the center's residency program.

"We replenish the supply of pediatricians and doctors in Connecticut and southern New England each year," Hanley said. "I really believe we are raising the bar of healthcare quality for children."

CONNECTICUT LIGHTING CENTERS

Originally, both Arthur and David Director had designs on teaching careers.

The father-son force behind Connecticut Lighting Centers holds great respect for what happens in the classroom and for the people who mold young minds as mirrored by some of their philanthropic initiatives.

Arthur, the company board chairman, actually sampled the classroom experience after his 1952 cum-laude graduation from Central Connecticut State University with a degree in business education.

His son David, now president of the two-location operation that has taken their lighting business to the next level, originally had plans to become a physical education instructor, but instead chose a marketing major at Quinnipiac University, where he earned his diploma in 1981.

Arthur was raised in Norwich, where his father owned a liquor store. Upon graduating from college, he realized that he could not afford to teach, as the starting salary being offered for high school teachers was approximately $1,800 a year in 1952. Instead, he began applying the business acumen and basics, which he had planned to teach in the classroom, in the for-profit world.

Arthur, David, Edythe Director—the Director Family.

For 20 years into the early 1970s, Arthur developed into an executive with the Red Wing Oil Company, a large distributor of gasoline, heating oils and heating equipment—and, later, the Chevron Oil Company that purchased their distributor.

Early on, Arthur kept his connection to schooling, serving as an instructor in the evening adult education program. His wife Edythe, whom he met on the Central Connecticut campus, also did her share of teaching in the VISTA program.

In 1968 Thomas Industries, one of the premier manufacturers and suppliers of lighting fixtures and equipment in the nation, decided on a bold move into the world of retail by building showrooms, which they leased out.

"That was something of a new marketing concept," David said. "Lighting manufacturers and suppliers did not sponsor retail outlets. Thomas was trying something unique."

For whatever reason, the Hartford showroom of what was already known as Connecticut Lighting Center was not working out. One of the principals who happened to be David's godfather, cast about for options. His gaze fell upon Arthur, whom he knew was not all that satisfied with the Chevron chapter of his life. Arthur had little or no experience in the lighting business, but was considered very astute in evaluating companies prior to acquisition.

"I took my two-week vacation in August of 1972 to observe and evaluate the business," Arthur recalled. "It certainly was not retail-oriented; it was mismanaged and was on the verge of bankruptcy. However, my gut feeling was that there was great potential. On a handshake, I became a partner and assumed my share of the business's $250,000 debt."

Total sales for 1972 totaled only $236,000 with seven employees. Today, aided and abetted by a second location in Southington, Connecticut Lighting Centers do in excess of $14 million in business a year with 70-plus employees.

Today, Arthur Director has been recognized for his many achievements and contributions in his community, state and business organizations. The ultimate trade recognition was his election to the American Lighting Association's Lighting Hall of Fame.

The ink was hardly dry on David's Quinnipiac cum-laude diploma when he joined the family business full time in 1981. His mother has been part of the business as well, serving as a buyer of lamps and lighting accessories. When the elder Director retired in 1994, moving up to board chairman, David assumed the company presidency.

"I now have the perks job," Arthur said. "I represent the company at all the good things: charity golf tournaments, chamber of commerce affairs and all kinds of community functions"—and at many of the "give-back" events that the Directors support in the communities they serve, such as the annual leadership-development conference for middle-schoolers that the Connecticut Lighting Centers sponsor at Quinnipiac through the Connecticut Association of

Schools. The middle school that creates and operates the best leadership program during the academic year receives a cash prize and a statewide award named for Arthur Director.

Father and son have donated tremendous amounts of time and talent to many organizations such as the Rushford Center, the Interfaith Golf Tournament, B'nai B'rith Lodge, Northern Middlesex YMCA, Middletown Rotary Club, Big Bother/Big Sister, youth sponsored organizations, the Jaycees, the United Way, the Better Business Bureau of Connecticut and many other community-service agencies.

"Once you get involved and do a good job at it," Arthur said, "they tend to come back to you when help is needed."

"My father brought me up," said David, who, with his wife Carol, are raising three children—Todd 16, Jenna 13, and Brett 10—with this philosophy: If you are going to take from the community, be prepared to give something back. That was a great lesson."

The sports-loving family accomplishes two objectives—supporting the University of Connecticut's national power basketball programs and sharing their good fortune with youngsters—each holiday season. The company buys 1,000 tickets to a game for children, who might not be able

to afford the price of admission.

With the largest collection of lighting, ceiling fans and home accents in New England, Connecticut Lighting Centers cater to shoppers who like to gain a sense of how what they are buying will look in their homes or work spaces. Instead of being hidden inside warehoused boxes, the selections are within artistic and eye-pleasing view.

Knowledgeable sales personnel guide the customers through glittering arrays. With their impressive inventories and showrooms, if you can't find what you are looking for at their lighting centers, chances are you won't find it at all.

"The retail lighting business today is highly diverse and customer oriented" said David, who believes that the best proof of the centers' "unique niche in the market-place" is to visit his locations after stopping at a "Big Box" outlet.

"Our motto is, 'We sell solutions, not lighting.' People come to us because they have lighting needs, issues or problems, and we can offer solutions, because we have knowledgeable sales personnel, a large inventory of products to offer and displayed showing applications. We help solve their problems and it doesn't cost the customer any more."

David looks forward to heading for his office. "I love what I do," he

Since 1968 a Brainard Road landmark.

said. "It seems to get better and better. This business is dynamic and changing every day. There is nothing static. The challenge is always there. You certainly don't get bored."

The father-son tandem subscribes to the three maxims that too many businesses somehow lose track of in the sprint to bottom-line success.

You are only as good as the people who work for you. Connecticut Lighting's average for employee longevity is nine years, with many in management past the two decade mark.

The biggest mistake a retailer can make is losing touch with what the business is all about and giving the number-crunchers more clout than the people in the trenches.

A customer can very easily become a friend, which is great, because a friend becomes your best advertising medium. And the Directors have the repeat business to prove it.

EMPLOYEE FAMILY PROTECTION, INCORPORATED

It was a chance encounter over a cup of coffee at a small-town Connecticut pharmacy that inspired Charles "Charlie" Stepnowski to explore the idea that eventually became Employee Family Protection Incorporated (EFP), a firm that has survived for 25 years as one of the leading benefit communications and voluntary benefit marketing firms in the nation.

The year was 1978, and as Charlie stepped out of the Franklin Pharmacy—complete with an old-fashioned soda fountain and luncheonette—he struck up a conversation with close friend Charles Smith. It seems that Smith and fellow life insurance underwriter Jon Webber were starting a new firm that would market voluntary life insurance products to employers and employees of the Hartford area. Smith needed a "hands on" person to help him get started in this venture. The deal was cemented only a few months later, following yet another chance encounter at the pharmacy.

Although Franklin Pharmacy is now defunct, the concept for EFP, formed at its counters, continued to evolve. It wasn't long before Charlie, the son of a trucker and rigger, found himself the president and chief ex-

Sales and administration working closely to provide innovative solutions.

ecutive officer of EFP, which was incorporated on February 16, 1979. His partners served on the board, while Charlie went about the business of building a foundation for the firm, working temporarily out of a conference room at Smith's insurance agency. Two weeks later, the company found a more permanent headquarters at 1177 Silas Deane Highway, Wethersfield, Connecticut.

Charlie brought to the table more than 13 years of experience in the personnel and

Michael Stepnowski, and his father, Charlie Stepnowski, will lead EFP well into the 21st century.

labor relations field. Having worked primarily for hospitals and medical centers, he was intimately familiar with a sobering reality: that most employees rarely scrutinize their benefits until they find themselves in the middle of a medical crisis. In a way he had never anticipated, the former adjunct professor of personnel and labor relations was about to put his graduate work in social demography to practical use.

"We help people to make changes in their benefits programs as their lives change," Charlie says, explaining the company's mission in layman's terms. "We are not the traditional purveyor of insurance programs. Rather, we believe in emphasizing education and communication as a means to better educate workers on what they have (in benefits) and how to improve upon that." EFP's clients include manufacturers, distributors, retailers, banks, hospitals and, most recently, municipalities.

In its first year, EFP obtained four clients representing in excess of 1,000 eligible employees. Today, the firm boasts 500 clients representing 300,000+ employees. Known for its customer service, EFP sees to it that every employer is assigned a service rep that personally visits the organization regularly, ensuring that every employee understands his benefits. EFP offers strong administrative support, including toll-free customer service and electronic case management.

On May 1, 1979, EFP made its debut at the Hotel Sonesta, introducing its services to insurance professionals. The ensuing summer months found the company forging ahead in marketing, recruitment of staff and training. In July a young marketing and sales professional named Kevin Foster joined the firm, concentrating on building brokerage relationships and obtaining clients in Connecticut. A benefit enrollment staff of four was in place by August. The company's initial product offering was a voluntary life insurance product underwritten by the Travelers Insurance Company.

By early 1980, diversification became the order of the day. EFP expanded over the next four years, forming relationships with both clients and new carriers. One of those relationships—with New York State Security Mutual Life Insurance of New York (SML) —was to prove valuable to the company's future.

Early 1983 marked a period of challenge and transition, a critical juncture for the firm. Charlie, with his wife Roseann, was now raising three young children, was stretched to the limits of his energy and resources, and the company required additional capital. After conferring with his partners, they decided that the best way to ensure the company's long-term growth was to sell 100 percent of EFP to SML in September 1983. Charlie was retained on a three-year management contract.

"We had, and still have, a great, ongoing relationship with SML. It gave us the capital resources to build internal structure, including computer hardware and access to sophisticated technology," says Charlie.

From 1983 to 1987, EFP expanded not only its geographic presence but also its product offerings. It also estab-

EFP board members discuss a future expansion plan.

lished a relationship with the Connecticut Business and Industry Association (CBIA), as well as the New York State Business Council.

By late December 1987, when the calendar reminded him that his contract was up for renewal, Charlie decided to repurchase 100 percent of the company from SML. He and Roseann, as EFP's sole purchasers, had now seen EFP come full circle.

Pivotal in the forward momentum of the firm was a key addition to the staff in 1996: Michael Stepnowski, the president's son. Michael led the firm in a new direction, emphasizing employee communication and the expansion of marketing efforts. A year-long series of meetings with clients to assess their needs bore fruit in enhanced broker-client relationships. Now the vice president of marketing and sales, Michael has far surpassed the original two-year commitment he had pledged to his father's firm. "Benefit communications is what it is today because of Michael," says his father.

Benefit communications has also been enhanced by the development of a company website. Although EFP's website (efpnow.com) has existed for five years, it is redesigned and expanded on a regular basis. It allows employees to readily access their specific benefits online for information and services.

"We do our job well," says Charlie with

pride. "Our marketplace is expanding from small to mid-size to large employers." He adds that an anticipated increase in governmental regulation, as well as shrinking profit margins, will challenge EFP. But he is confident that the company has the right mix of people and skills to meet, and exceed, expectations.

Charlie, who chooses to give something back to the Hartford community through membership in the Chamber of Commerce, UNICO (a service club), and sponsorships of charitable events for nonprofit clients, was recently inducted into the National Association of Professional Enrollments Hall of Fame—a fitting bookmark to note the company's 25th anniversary.

From the seed of an idea that sprang out of a chance meeting at a small-town pharmacy, EFP has blossomed into a big-town sort of company that has led to better communication and education among employers and employees throughout Hartford, the Northeast and the nation. And, just as Charlie once admired the personalized service of an old-fashioned business like Franklin's Pharmacy back in the 1970s, he can proudly say today that his 25-year old firm is well on its way to emulating the same high standard of customer service and satisfaction.

GERBER SCIENTIFIC, INC.

H. Joseph Gerber devised an invention, the Gerber Variable Scale®, after conceiving an elastic pajama waistband as a way to solve a complex mathematics problem. Referred to as the most revolutionary engineering tool since the slide rule, the Variable Scale would be the first of his and the company's many inventions that would change the face of industrial automation.

Born in Austria in 1924, Gerber grew up building self-playing musical instruments, inventing magnetic circuit breakers and dreaming of starting a company that would make crystal radios. By the time he reached his teens, however, Europe was experiencing the atrocities of the Hitler regime, and Gerber was imprisoned in a Nazi labor camp. His son David later said that "it was a childhood shortened, as the Holocaust shook the pillars of his world. But this force could not diminish his recognition of the beauty as well as the horrible abuses of technology, his desire to contribute to society despite its weaknesses, and his optimism to dream of the future."

At the age of 15, Gerber jumped from a train leading to a death camp, and he and his mother escaped to the United States. Gerber relished all that this country offered. Motivated by his dreams, he learned English, held down a full-time evening job and was cap-

Gerber Technology develops and supplies integrated software and hardware automation systems to the apparel and flexible materials industries.

H. Joseph Gerber, 1924-1996, founder of Gerber Scientific, Inc.

tain of his soccer team—all while finishing high school in half the usual time. Gerber then completed his studies at Rensselaer Poly-technical Institute in record time to become a graduate engineer. In 1950, at the age of 26, the DuPont Company sponsored *Young Man in a Hurry*, a nationally-broadcast Broadway play about Gerber's life. In 1953 H. Joseph Gerber was honored as one of the "10 Most Outstanding Young Men in America."

In 1948, The Gerber Scientific Instrument Company was incorporated to refine and

manufacture Gerber's original Variable Scale. Since then, Gerber Scientific has been a leader in bringing innovative products to market across many industries. The company's drafting machines played an integral role in the design of the first jumbo jets. During the same time the space program used the company's machines to design contour maps of the moon. In the 1960s Gerber's photoplotter became the tool of choice for TV picture tube manufacturers. In the following decades, Gerber helped save the jobs of countless workers in the garment industry by creating the GERBERcutter®, a machine able to quickly cut large quantities of multiple-layered fabric. Other technological breakthroughs of Gerber, David J. Logan, and other inventors at the Gerber companies included the world's first numerically-controlled high precision line drawing plotters, automated sign making machines and automated systems for the manufacture of prescription eyeglass lenses.

H. Joseph Gerber died in 1996—two years after receiving this country's highest award in technology from President Clinton—The National Medal of Technology. With more than 675 U.S. and international patents awarded to his name, and several inventions on display at the Smithsonian Institution in Washington D.C., H. Joseph Gerber was one of the most prolific inventors of his time. As he was remembered at the company's 50th anniversary in 1998, "His generous spirit, his quiet fervor, his joy in playing with an idea, his inventive genius, his courtly charm, his boyish restlessness and his boundless enthusiasm are dearly missed by all who knew him. But he breathed life into his ideas and our company, and he left us wonderful opportunities and the heritage of a truly amazing and important story: a story of the birth of a visionary enterprise, the affirmation of our basic values and a life of heroic proportions. So today, we go into the future with dreams that put butterflies in our stomach, with abilities that open up vast new horizons of products that existed only in the minds of dreamers, and with principles that continue to make a healthy company, a good community, and a livable world."

Gerber Scientific, Inc. today is a leader in providing innovative, end-to-end customer solutions to the sign making and specialty graphics, apparel and flexible materials, and

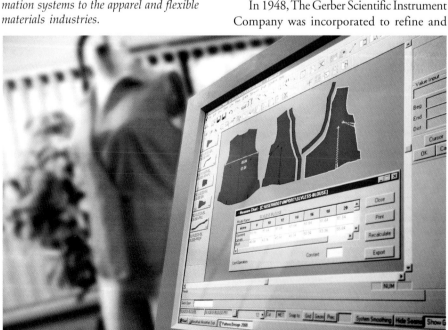

Gerber Scientific's headquarters in South Windsor, Connecticut.

Gerber Coburn provides computer-integrated lens processing systems for the ophthalmic industry.

advanced computer-aided design and manufacturing systems for the sewn and flexible materials industries; Gerber Coburn, a world leader in ophthalmic lens processing systems; and Gerber Innovations, a pioneer in rotary-machining die tool production systems for packaging industry applications.

Building on its legacy of radical innovation under the leadership of President and CEO Marc T. Giles, Gerber Scientific continues to pursue new ways to drive innovation and deliver world-class service. In 2003 alone, the company launched more than 30 new products and added over 45 new patents to its portfolio of over 1,000 active patents. The company's software products, computerized manufacturing systems, supplies, and services are fully integrated for maximum customer support and flexibility. With 65 percent of its revenues derived internationally and 55 percent of its employees located outside of the United States, the company today does business in over 115 countries around the world, and sees continued growth opportunities for extending the reach of all its businesses globally. The scope and scale of its combined global resources enable Gerber Scientific's individual business units to leverage each other's strengths and share efficiencies for operational excellence.

ophthalmic lens processing industries through its five business units; Gerber Scientific Products, a world leader in developing and manufacturing computerized sign making and specialty graphics systems; Spandex, a leading global distributor of high-performance software, equipment and materials to the sign making and specialty graphics industry; Gerber Technology, a world leader in

Gerber Scientific Products develops and manufactures computerized sign making and specialty graphics systems.

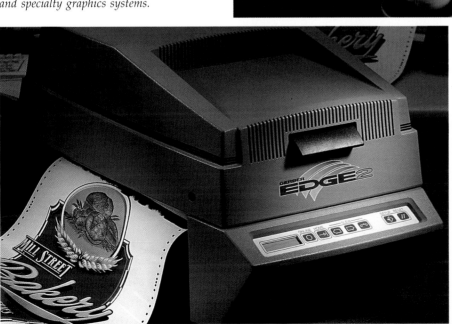

Listed on the New York Stock Exchange (NYSE: GRB), Gerber's headquarters is in South Windsor, Connecticut, with major facilities throughout the United States, Europe, Asia, Central and South America. Sales in 2003 reached $512 million; the company employs approximately 2,150 employees. The company and Gerber family sponsor three scholarship funds: the H. Joseph Gerber 1947 Scholars Fund Endowment at Rensselaer Polytechnic Institute, the David J. Logan Scholarship Endowment at Trinity College, and the H. Joseph Gerber Vision Scholarship for high school students attending South Windsor, Manchester or Tolland High. Gerber Scientific also supports the United Way and other local charities.

179

GOLD BOND

In 1899 the bicycle frame was patented, Claude Monet created the famous water lily painting series, and people around the world awaited the start of the 20th century. That was the year Gold Bond Mattress began mattress production in Hartford, Connecticut. Now an internationally respected mattress manufacturer, Gold Bond is set to bring its success and steady growth into the 21st Century.

What keeps this 104 year-old company in competitive shape? Robert "Bob" Naboicheck, the third-generation mattress manufacturer and president of Gold Bond, believes the answer lies within each one of his employees — and himself. "You must be passionate about your company," he says. "A president and CEO must be the number one salesperson and be fair to all employees." This circle of trust and commitment has served the company well and it helped thrust it forward throughout its history. For the products themselves, comfort and longevity are essential.

In 1898 Bob's grandparents Isadore and Rebecca Naboicheck made a huge leap of faith. They emigrated from the Soviet Union to America. They believed anything was possible in their new land. The two boarded a train in Elizabeth, New Jersey, and headed north. They got off at each stop, liked Hartford the best. The couple decided to stay. With New World conviction and Old World forti-

Left: Second generation, Aaron "Butch" Naboicheck, and on the right first generation, Isador Naboicheck.

tude, Isadore determined to continue a tradition perfected back in the homeland—hand-making mattresses. In those days, small shops made similar items throughout Connecticut. There were no national mattress brands. Isadore opened his operations in a four-story brick building on North Street near the Connecticut River. By the 1920s Gold Bond was blending its own cotton—and creating the region's most highly regarded mattresses.

Business grew during those earliest days, and when the consumer society exploded on

the scene after World War II, Gold Bond's momentum accelerated. With the second generation now at the helm—Bob's dad Aaron (better known as "Butch") and his Uncle Louis—the company forged into the contract business, supplying leading universities, posh hotels, resorts and health care facilities, and above all the company's mainstay, retail stores. "The retail furniture business was different back in the 1950s and 1960s," Bob says. "There were lots of mom-and-pop shops. Folks were local and on a first-name basis back then, as compared to chain stores today. But while we now supply chain stores as well as smaller three and four-store operators, we are still very much a first-name basis company," Bob says.

Another of Bob's uncles, Max Kaminsky, joined the family business. Gold Bond was shipping well beyond the Hartford area, trucking their products throughout the Northeast. Gold Bond had grown into the country's largest independent mattress maker.

By 1995 Gold Bond expanded into its present location, about a mile away from Isadore's original plant, in Hartford's inner city. The 115,000 square foot operation contains state-of-the-art equipment and employee loyalty to rival any business, anywhere. Gold Bond considers employee intellectual capital a key asset, and company policy does not force retirement. The company employs several senior citizens. One 93-year-old worker recently retired after 60 years with the company. Bob knows each employee and is proud of his staff's ethnic diversity and multigenerational aspect. Having relatives work for the same company is not uncommon at Gold Bond, unlike some other major companies.

"We try to remain a good example of a family business. We care for our city and we are loyal to customers and suppliers. It's unique," he said.

Today, Gold Bond continues to excel at making hand-made premium mattresses and box springs. But mattresses are no longer Gold Bond's only products.

World Futon Leader

Gold Bond is also renowned for making the finest futon mattresses worldwide. What was originally a thin mat, which the Japanese rolled up and stowed each morning, the futon was to become one of the home furnishings industry's newest super-stars. Gold Bond

Early 20th century Gold Bond fleet truck.

executives saw a distinct opportunity to put a fiercely competitive sofa sleeper into everyday American homes. So, Gold Bond took the Japanese mat—and made it plusher. "It had to feel like a sofa when you sit on it," Bob explains, "We made it thicker. Comfort was our aim. The idea took hold with our retailers, and futons roared into the '80s and '90s for us all," he said. It shows no signs of slowing down worldwide. Bob's insistence on high quality (his mantra: "It's going into someone's living room, it must be comfortable, have eye-appeal and it must last at least 10 years"), laid the foundation for long-term success.

Gold Bond futon mattresses have been in great demand for customers around the globe ever since. Like its mattresses, a Gold Bond futon mattress features cotton batting made from pure cotton. The company's double-stitching ensures that seams won't unwind or split. To give each mattress extra strength, the heavy cotton twill outer shell is constructed like a box, with panels on the top, bottom and sides. Gold Bond uses automated filling machinery to insure consistency and a smooth surface. Six high-speed garneting machines produce over 5 million pounds of cotton each year, from which 4,000 futon mattresses and 1,500 pieces of conventional bedding are shipped each week.

Gold Bond presently ships to 49 states and the United Kingdom, Germany, Japan, Israel, Netherlands and Malaysia.

The company is committed to ongoing growth and recently added a top-tier man-

Quilting machine operator Edgael Cruz.

One of Gold Bond's modern tractor trailor fleet.

agement team of Dennis Ferry, vice president of manufacturing; Ray Andarowski, production manager; Alan J. Cohen, chief financial officer and comptroller; and Andy Freedman, vice president of sales and marketing. The new team brings Gold Bond vital experience from their many years in the industry. The company now has 120 employees.

Bob and his wife Alice, also a Hartford native, have three children: Candice, 23, who works in the fashion industry in Manhattan; Henry, 21, a college man who when home involves himself with employee management; and Alexander, 17, a senior in high school who is becoming educated in the sales end of the family's business. Perhaps the fourth generation will also manage the family's company one day, Bob says.

It's clear his staff thinks highly of him, and deservedly so. Bruce Alexander, public relations counsel says: "Everything Bob does, he does 100 percent."

Each year he travels to many of the countries in the former Soviet Union and Israel to help Jews in need—just as his grandparents did. He also contributes to his community in many ways. Some of the organizations he helps include the Jewish Federation of Hartford, the United Jewish Communities and the Hebrew Home and Hospital—the nursing home that his grandmother helped found. In 90 days, Bob raised $9 million for this facility. Bob has also

helped other organizations by sitting on the boards of prep schools, art institutes, the Futon Association and Connecticut Public Television. For 14 years he hosted the station's food and wine auctions. He loves history and sees collecting wine as a way of learning about the winemakers' heritages, and about other countries and cultures.

This man with many skills and interests, however, says that he's "only a simple salesman, on the road doing motivational training on how to sell Gold Bond's products."

He's proud of the company he leads. When contemplating the future of Gold Bond, Bob says that he's "very excited about the potential," with an expected double-digit increase in the next few years—which is great news for Hartford, too.

Hartford was once the nation's wealthiest city with a large manufacturing core. Now, Bob says, "Connecticut is a costly place to run a business, and few products are made in the United States now." Gold Bond regularly receives invitations to move to a less expensive state. Believing in Hartford and having loyalty to his hometown, he's always refused such offers: "We're not going anywhere; we're staying."

His grandparents would be proud of their grandson's conviction and fortitude. What started in the 19th Century along the city's waterfront, is now Gold Bond. The company reaches into yet another century, with comfort and durability paramount.

THE HARTFORD CONSERVATORY

For more than a century, central Connecticut has enjoyed a harmonious relationship with the Hartford Conservatory. This unique school for the performing arts, the first of its kind in the area, has given the gift of music to the town with an unwavering dedication.

Although born of humble beginnings, the small school was destined to grow and prosper. In 1890 Dr. Charles Hartranft, president of the Hartford Seminary Foundation formed the School for Church Musicians, dedicated to the instruction of ecclesiastical music. The school was established to serve the musical needs of the foundation.

Hartranft had experience in organizing this type effort. Prior to arriving in Hartford, he had established a conservatory and choral union in New Jersey. He used his hands-on knowledge to lead the new school through its inception.

In Hartford, Hartraft first introduced music instruction at the seminary, then created the Hosmer Hall Choral Union, which quickly led to the School for Church Musicians. The school thrived, and the seminary and town reaped the benefits.

Five years later, Mrs. Archibald Welch, a local vocalist and arts patron, made it possible for the school to become independent, in terms of business, from the seminary. Welch operated a vocal studio in her home conducted by Miss Villa Whitney White.

Our Two-Year Intensive molds students into professional dancers.

Lynne Patnode, Ed.D. Executive Director.

Together, Hartranft, Welch and White transitioned the school to a new location and name, the Hartford School of Music.

The school was successful as an independently operated entity, offering a professional retreat for many local musicians and singers to learn and practice their craft. It was able to incorporate as a nonprofit institution in 1908.

In 1926 the school relocated to a former stately turn-of-the-century residence at 834 Asylum Avenue, in the heart of the Asylum Hill district, and has called that address home ever since.

In the 1930s the modern dance movement was in full swing, and the school made a progressive decision to offer dance. Truda Kaschmann, a strong influence in the

movement, brought ballet and jazz to the program. The modern dance classes complemented the music offerings and again, the school grew.

The 1950s and 1960s brought about massive changes in American culture. The school withstood the times and social shifts in interests; however, in 1959 it did change its name to the Hartford Conservatory. The school briefly changed its name again in the 1980s, but reverted to this name in 1995.

In 1961, again through the generosity and vision of yet another Connecticut arts patron, the school was able to grow. The buildings, the Welch House and the Goodwin House, are named in honor of the benefactors that made this possible.

Today, the Hartford Conservatory has continued the tradition of providing affordable, high-quality instruction in music, dance and theater to its students. A philosophy of fostering an analytical approach to study is valued. And, each student learns to identify and build on his or her artistic strengths, rather than weaknesses. To better serve the performing arts students of the Hartford metropolitan area, the school offers two satellite campuses in east and west Hartford.

The Hartford Conservatory, which is accredited by the New England Association of Schools and Colleges and licensed by the State of Connecticut Department of Higher Education, offers an accredited two-year diploma program to educate students for careers in the performing arts. This division offers diplomas for studies in jazz and popular music, music pedagogy, dance performance, dance pedagogy, musical theater and record production.

Students may study under four different departments at the conservatory. Departments and majors include music, dance, musical theater and record production. The approximately 60 diploma tract students become a close-knit group, not only performing together, but teaching and learning from one another as well.

The school is committed to providing the best possible technical instruction available. This goal is achieved by attracting and retaining first-class professional music, dance and musical theater faculty. More than 60 instructors are on staff, and

many are active in the local area, participating in local orchestras, choral groups and performance troops.

The second division of the school is focused on the community, offering instructional services to students of all ages and abilities. More than 900 students participate in private music lessons; full ensemble program; and theory, ear training and singing classes on an annual basis, featured through the community division.

The school's mission is to provide the finest instruction in the performing arts to students of all ages and abilities in an artistically vibrant and historically rich setting. The atmosphere of the two Victorian homes lends itself to the creative and artistic environment.

The conservatory shares a deep history with Hartford and recognizes the need to support the community that has given it a home for more than a century. The school is a continual source of talent for Harford, providing entertainment for private functions and fundraisers, including local organizations such as AHOP, the Child Council, St. Francis Hospital and the International Children's Festival.

The music program serves over 600 students per year.

The Hartford Conservatory hosts professional groups such as the New England Jazz Ensemble.

Another opportunity the school takes to give back to the community is the Give Music to a Child program. This effort encourages people to donate an old instrument to a child in need. Through organizing this program, many children who would not have been able to discover the joy of music, receive the chance to learn and nurture a new talent.

It was with deep purpose that The Hartford Conservatory chose the slogan "In concert with the community" as the staff, its faculty, students and board of directors work tirelessly to show appreciation to the school's hometown. The community and the school, which share a bond of love for the arts and a tradition of mutual respect, have created beautiful music together for more than 113 years.

The Hartford Conservatory is located in two beautiful 1890 Victorian buildings.

HOSPITAL FOR SPECIAL CARE

HOSPITAL FOR SPECIAL CARE

At Hospital for Special Care, an exceptional staff of highly-skilled medical professionals works together with one ultimate goal in mind: to *rebuild lives*. Hospital for Special Care (HSC), a private, not-for-profit institution in Greater Hartford's city of New Britain, first opened its doors as a teaching facility in 1941. Today, HSC is the largest rehabilitation and chronic disease facility in Connecticut.

Both the Commission on Accreditation of Healthcare Organizations (JCAHO) and the Rehabilitation Accreditation Commission (CARF) accredit the hospital programs, which include accreditation in comprehensive inpatient rehabilitation, spinal cord injury, inpatient brain injury programs, outpatient rehabilitation, and the outpatient work-injury rehabilitation program. Hospital for Special Care is affiliated with the University of Connecticut and Yale University as a teaching hospital. By sharing a director of research with the University of Connecticut School of Medicine, HSC has expanded the scope, quality and quantity of research within its continuum, while benefiting too from the integration of complementary medicine with their traditional modalities.

Relationships and Partnerships. True partnerships foster reciprocity, a mutuality, a dance

"*This culture of care, and caring has become our mantra. It's that added dimension that makes us so distinctive. We are never business as usual. This is our formula for success.*"

of equal exchange and responsibility. HSC takes pride in not only being a premium employer, but also forging partnerships with the best caregivers and staff in the healthcare business.

The hospital's management model brings together doctors, nurses, therapists, administrators, and other healthcare professionals working in teams to focus on specific patient needs. Patient-care teams work in centralized settings to maximize interaction and communication between caregivers, patients, and their families. To support the hospital's mission "to provide exemplary rehabilitation and continuing medical care with the active involvement of patients and their families," HSC is organized into three services: inpatient and outpatient rehabilitation, respiratory, and medically-complex pediatrics.

Leading HSC's multidisciplinary team approach to providing the highest quality of care is a physiatrist, (a physician with a specialty in rehabilitation and physical medicine), and an internist. In addition, a case manager coordinates care during a patient's stay, serving as a patient advocate and someone to whom the patient, family, and professional team can look for support and information.

HSC's rehabilitation services offer both inpatient and outpatient programs designed to help patients with complex orthopedic and neurological problems become as independent as possible. Staffed by an interdisciplinary team of professionals, including a cadre of highly-skilled physical, occupational, speech, and recreation therapists, the hospital's rehabilitation unit

"*The exemplary care for which were are known, coupled with our steadfast efforts to understand, offer compassion, relate well and successfully with our patients and their families, is that special connection and hallmark for which we are so proud.*"

provides programs for people needing acute rehabilitation due to serious illness or physical trauma; longer-term inpatient neurobehavioral and chronic-care programs; and numerous outpatient services, from daylong, multi-therapy sessions to hour-long sessions for chronic back pain. The unit also

"*If, and when you may ever need us, we will be your partners in healing, your partners in care and caring, your partners in rebuilding your lives...*"

features a daily living apartment where patients and their families can simulate the home environment prior to their discharge.

The hospital's multi-level respiratory services treat individuals with serious breathing problems resulting from neuromuscular conditions, trauma and pulmonary disease. To maximize the treatment of various conditions, HSC offers three levels of care: the Close Observation Unit (COU), offering complex medical care for patients needing advanced technological intervention; the Respiratory Care Unit—including the nation's largest unit for ventilator-dependent patients—for patients needing ventilator assistance on a 24-hour basis; and the Respiratory Step Down Unit, for people requiring artificial ventilation on a less intensive basis. Respiratory services also include a nationally-recognized regional weaning center, where patients transition from long-term mechanical ventilation toward regaining their independence.

HSC is one of 23 participating organizations in a study by the National Association of Long-Term Hospitals to analyze weaning outcomes for ventilator-dependent patients. Since 1994, HSC's COU has achieved a 70 percent success rate in weaning outcomes. Nationally, the success rate is about 55 percent. A multi-center weaning outcome study is a major breakthrough in the long-term hospital business.

Hospital for Special Care's pediatric services care for children with severe and complex health problems, including those who are technology dependent. The unit's dedicated team of experts focuses solely on the requirements of the hospital's youngest patients. Treatment on the pediatric unit is highly individualized, with lengths of stay ranging from a few days to more than a year. The goal for every child, regardless of his or her length of stay, or the complexity of the child's illness, is to return home as soon as possible.

Aquatic Fitness Rehabilitation: In recognition of the importance and benefit of aquatic exercise and aquatic therapy, Hospital for Special Care opened a state-of-the-art Aquatic Rehabilitation Center on the hospital grounds in 1999. This outstanding facility has become Connecticut's Premier Aquatic Rehabilitation and Fitness Center, boasting a 27,000-square-foot facility with two wheelchair-accessible pools—a warm-water pool for

Connecticut's premier 27,000-square-foot aquatic rehabilitation and fitness center brings together fitness, athletic training, and rehabilitation in one convenient setting.

This wonderful opportunity, the magical connection and therapeutic value from horses will open up a whole new world for children and adults living with disabilities.

aquatic therapies and a cooler pool for fitness, athletic training and recreation. The fitness center offers the latest computerized cardiovascular and strength-training equipment, including equipment (Lite-gait, aquatic treadmill, FES bike) specifically designed for therapy, and accessible for individuals living with disabilities. This Center brings together fitness, athletic training and rehabilitation in one convenient setting. Memberships and package rates are also available to the public.

Sports, Training and Leadership: Hospital for Special Care's commitment to sports and fitness extends far beyond the hospital grounds. For example, HSC is the managing sponsor of the Cruisers, a team of young, physically-disabled Connecticut athletes who compete locally, regionally, and nationally in wheelchair track-and-field competitions, where many Cruisers have set several national records. Through Special Care's Ivan Lendl Junior Wheelchair Sports Camp—the first and only one of its kind on the East Coast—world-class disabled athletes provide campers with instruction in tennis, swimming, basketball, and track and field at no cost, thanks to the fund-raising success of Special Care's Annual Ivan Lendl Golf Tournament. HSC also sponsors its own wheelchair basketball team, a WAVE swim team, Skiers' Unlimited, and numerous adaptive-sports programs, clinics, conferences, and symposiums; all part of an effort to champion the cause of athletes living with disabilities through education, information and advocacy.

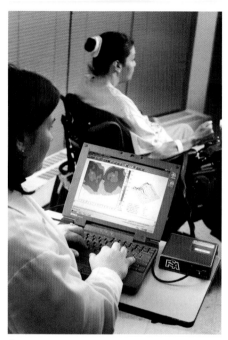

"Our unwavering focus to pioneer research, will keep us perpetually competitive and progressive in our vision, thereby reinforcing our goal to be a rapidly-evolving, groundbreaking research institution, poised to attract not only regional and national recognition, but to be a viable contender for major healthcare research funds."

A Continuum of Care: As part of its continuum of care, Hospital for Special Care provides other facilities and programs for its patients and the community at large, including Brittany Farms Health Center, a 284-bed healthcare facility specializing in subacute rehabilitation, hip and knee rehabilitation, dementia care and long-term care. Other affiliations and initiatives include: Manes & Motions Therapeutic Riding Center, a National Spinal Cord Injury Resource Center, and Special Care Dental Services (a dental program for Medicaid-eligible children and adolescents). HSC also offers numerous support groups for patients and families affected by arthritis, Guillain-Barré syndrome, stroke, head injury, Parkinson's disease, and pulmonary conditions.

The Joy of Art: The Volunteer Services' Joy of Art was created to support HSC's mission of helping patients to achieve enduring improvements in the quality of their lives. The hospital is widely recognized for its exceptional and caring work in short and long-term care rehabilitation.

The objectives of The Joy of Art are to enhance the quality of patients' lives by providing a diverse selection of art for their enjoyment, and to strengthen the bond between the hospital and the community by fostering relationships with talented artists. The Joy of Art program includes the Art Cart, which offers patients the opportunity to select and rotate artwork in their areas of the hospital; in-house art exhibitions for patients and families, visitors, staff, and members of the community; and fund-raising through the sale of artwork.

Spinal Cord Resource Center: In partnership with the National Spinal Cord Injury Association (NSCIA), Connecticut Chapter, Hospital for Special Care's campus is the new home for Connecticut's first Spinal Cord Resource Center, designed specifically for individuals faced with the challenges of living with a spinal cord illness or injury. This new, fully-accessible center offers meeting rooms, printed resources, computers, Internet access, support groups and the latest news/information related to spinal cord injury/illness for patients,

Everyday, every member of the Center of Special Care staff positively and efficiently aspires to be the best providers of care; to vigilantly nurture relationships among caregivers, patients, patients' families and fellow staff.

families, and healthcare providers. One of Hospital for Special Care's CARF accreditations is for specialized care and rehabilitation of patients challenged with spinal cord illness or injury. Spinal cord injury research is another exciting priority. Being on the cutting-edge of progress and care in this area, will enable HSC to analyze data and examine outcomes of its programs and document the benefits of specific treatments. As participants in multi-center and other clinical studies, will further distinguish them as visionaries and trailblazers, affirming their goal to be a dynamic, forward-focused institution with long-term viability and continued growth in spinal cord research.

Manes & Motions Therapeutic Riding Center: The only therapeutic horseback riding center in central Connecticut, and a member of the Hospital for Special Care Community, Manes & Motions Therapeutic Riding Center is a certified North American Riding for the Handicapped Association (NARHA) center. It is located at Wedgewood Stables in Kensington, offering children and adults living with cognitive and physical disabilities with the opportunity to enjoy horseback riding for therapeutic, recreational, sport and educational purposes. This wonderful opportunity and the magical connection and therapeutic value from horses will open up a whole new world for children and adults involved in the disabled sports and fitness programs at Hospital for Special Care.

Volunteers and dedicated staff are key to the meteoric growth and success of Manes & Motions. Therapeutic riding and its benefits have been documented for many years, going as far back as 1875. It has long been known that the human–animal bond is a powerful force in human emotions, and is one of the most important elements of this program. In addition to the emotional benefits, therapeutic riding is proven to improve muscle tone, head control, increased mobility, coordination, physical strength, confidence and self-esteem. During each session, riders enjoy a variety of games and activities designed for horseback, which motivate the rider and provide opportunities for meeting physical, cognitive, behavioral and psychological goals. The addition of therapeutic riding has the potential to expand HSC's sports, training and leadership programs in a variety of ways.

AMERICAN SCHOOL FOR THE DEAF

In 1807 Dr. Mason Fitch Cogswell was a respected Hartford physician. He lived next door to a French Huguenot family, the Gallaudets, whose son, Thomas Hopkins Gallaudet, was to become a leader in the education of deaf and hard-of-hearing persons. Cogswell's daughter, Alice, had lost her hearing from a childhood disease when she was two years old. Gallaudet, a Yale graduate, was able to make significant progress in teaching the child, causing Cogswell and other prominent citizens of Hartford to send the young man to Europe to learn the methods for instructing deaf children.

Arriving in Paris in 1815, Gallaudet visited the Paris School for the Deaf, the world's first such institution. He was instructed by Abbe Sicard, its director. Sicard's deaf assistant, Laurent Clerc, returned with Gallaudet to Hartford and became instrumental in developing the Hartford school, the first special education facility in America.

The Connecticut General Assembly granted incorporation for the American Asylum for the Education and Instruction of Deaf and Dumb Persons in 1816 and donated $5,000 toward the institution. This action represented the first legislative aid to the education of the handicapped in the Western Hemisphere. The school

The present campus of the American School for the Deaf.

opened in 1817 on Main Street in Hartford with seven pupils, including Alice Cogswell.

Word of the effort being made at Hartford spread, and in 1819 Congress appropriated 23,000 acres of public domain in the territory of Alabama for the school's use. As a result of the sale of this land, a site was purchased where the present Hartford Insurance Group is located on Asylum Hill, so named because the school was situated there between 1821 and 1921.

Much of the success of this institution was due to the work of three co-founders—Cogswell, who helped secure legislative support and funding, and organized the governing board; Gallaudet, who was a teacher and the first headmaster for 13 years;

and Clerc, the first deaf teacher in America, who implemented the instructional program and facilitated the development and growth of American Sign Language. Clerc dedicated the remainder of his life to deaf education and, through numerous contacts, brought the work of the school to the public's attention. One of the dormitories on the present campus is named in his honor, but the school is his greatest monument.

The present campus, occupied in 1921, is at 139 North Main Street, West Hartford. Over 200 faculty and staff provide instruction and services to approximately 240 full-time pre-primary through high school students, 115 adults in a variety of vocational and life-skills programs and 70 families of deaf infants and children from birth to age 3. Comprehensive services are provided to deaf and hard-of-hearing persons of all ages. The campus includes complete facilities for all activities including student life, work experience, athletics and recreation.

Modern technology has been enlisted to promote better programs, methods of instruction and communication. High-speed Internet access, specialized computer programs and video teleconferencing are among these applications. The American School for the Deaf, a pioneer in the education of deaf and hard-of-hearing individuals, is still at the forefront of its field. It is an institution of which Hartford can truly be proud.

Older students and their teacher showing the youngsters some new signs.

JETER, COOK & JEPSON ARCHITECTS INC.

Hartford's oldest and largest architectural firm, with a seven-decade legacy of award-winning projects and notable achievements to its credit, is facing the future with a "thinking-out-of-the-box" mentality.

Its third generation of leadership firmly in place, Jeter, Cook & Jepson Architects Inc. (JCJ) is implementing a vision that has already paid dividends—as illustrated by such innovations as the University of Connecticut's campus in downtown Waterbury, the Wesleyan University Center for Film Studies and Cinema Archives in Middletown, and Hartford's nationally acclaimed Learning Corridor.

In effect, this kind of creative blueprint for action is in keeping with the tradition of Sherwood Jeter Jr., founder of the architectural practice in 1936, and accomplished designer Arthur Cook, who joined Jeter in 1945 after World War II service with the Navy. The year 1961 saw the founder's son, S. Edward Jeter, come aboard following his graduation from Rensselear Polytechnic Institute (RPI). The third name on the logo belongs to David Jepson, another RPI alumnus who signed on with the growing enterprise in 1968 following a tour of duty as a U.S. Navy Civil Engineer Corps officer on Okinawa.

"Companies that have been around as long as we have," said Jepson, who is now chairman of the JCJ board, "are sometimes thought to be rather stodgy. That's not us. We know our history and are proud of it. You could call us an old firm with a renewed thirst for design excellence."

In addition to Jepson, also included in JCJ

First Church of Christ, Wethersfield, Connecticut.

Seneca Niagara Resort and Casino Masterplan, Niagara Falls, NY.

leadership facing the 21st century are another RPI graduate, Chief Executive Officer James LaPosta Jr., and President/Treasurer Peter Stevens. The leaders and the firm's staff of 105 teamed up to earn the University of Hartford's Business Leadership Award for 2003. This honor was given to the firm based upon the firm's financial return on shareholders' equity, support of employee development and its commitment and involvement in community service

Based in downtown Hartford for all 67 years of existence, and housed in its fourth location at 450 Church Street since 1982, JCJ stresses that its commitment to the city and Connecticut's business community "has never been stronger." "Equally as important," the company stated in its application for the Business Leadership Award, is that "our ability to give priority to the community which we have always so proudly called 'our home' has never been stronger."

To provide a framework for growth in a new millennium that will bring even greater competition from the architectural marketplace, JCJ restructured its approach by creating "practice groups." Each focuses on a specialty kind of project or building type: K-12 education; higher education, hospitality/leisure; interior design;

senior housing and health-care facilities; planning, and other building types.

The latter is the catchall category of future business opportunities. The "planning" practice is involved with "new urbanism" and town master planning, and master plans for educational facilities and public safety complexes. JCJ also offers services in historic preservation, facilities management, roof restoration, and financial-development analysis.

Complementing this strategy is a new-look operational hierarchy with units that focus on such essential tasks as office administration, marketing, risk management, information technology, construction administration, human resources, graphic design, and project management.

Yet the "new" Jeter, Cook & Jepson is not straying too far from the way things were when the founder, a graduate of Yale with numerous design awards, started delivering exquisite custom-made homes and commercial buildings for Hartford-area clients. "Architecture is a business," Jepson said, "but it is also an art form. Yet, what we design not only has to look good, it must be good with the highest quality of construction. It must hold up well. It must be efficient to operate. And it must be easy to maintain."

Jepson said the firm has made all of these adjustments fairly smoothly through the application of ever-improving technology.

"There is hardly any more hand-drawing," he said. "The new tools, the computers and advanced technologies are helping us do things faster and better." And it is JCJ's highly competent, high-tech staff that is leading the way.

In the 1950s, the firm expanded its mission by designing banks, educational buildings, and corporate headquarters. Some of Connecticut's oldest churches received new leases on life because of Jeter and Cook. Power companies began to commission the firm. The 1960s signaled the start of a trend, when the partners were selected to design the Bennett College Science Center in New York. It was their first commission outside the borders of their home state.

When growth crunched their office space, JCJ "hired" itself to convert the former 30,000-square-foot Swift Company warehouse on Church Street north of Union Station into office space befitting an architectural firm gaining an enhanced reputation around New England.

In the higher-education sector, JCJ's distinctive stamp is on the new student center under construction at Southern Connecticut State University and the Babson College Center for Executive Education in Wellesley, Massachusetts.

Wilbert Snow Elementary School, Middletown, Connecticut.

Modem Media, Norwalk, Connecticut.

Among more than 100 K-12 projects since the early 1990s, the firm has accumulated 25 national design awards in the last five years, including the technology-rich Woodland Regional High School, the Smith Middle School in Glastonbury, Darien's landmark Middlesex Middle School, and the Wilbert Snow Elementary School nestled in a thickly wooded site in Middletown.

The exotic Foxwoods Resort Casino in Ledyard—the largest facility of its kind in the Western Hemisphere with 1,500 rooms, an 1890s main street from a typical New England

town, and a variety of recreational venues—had a $986 million price tag, becoming the region's number one destination attraction. The Glenora Wine Cellars Inn and Conference center in Dundee, New York, near Lake Seneca, was another JCJ project, along with the Seneca Niagara Casino adjacent to the world-famous falls.

In diversifying its portfolio, the Hartford firm stretched across the country to give its special touch to the Blue Lake Casino in mountainous Humboldt County, California, and the Gila River Resort and Casino near Phoenix, Arizona.

In the corporate world, the North American headquarters of LEGO in Enfield combined both U.S. and Danish building traditions, with JCJ designers taking into account that the 103,000-square-foot creation would be home to the world leader in producing toy building blocks.

Back home, JCJ is part of the team retrofitting a six-story 1950s structure into the new base of operations for Connecticut Public Television and Radio, complete with the latest in telecommunications and broadcast technology. Other clients in the private sector include Modem Media in Norwalk and AIG Financial Products in Wilton.

Now that's what you call an old firm, with an exciting vison for the future.

LOCTITE CORPORATION

It is hard to say whether Connecticut's Loctite Corporation began in a Hartford chemistry laboratory basement or with a close relationship between father and son chemists. Along with other family members and friends, their entrepreneurial spirit, talents, and business savvy parlayed a chemistry experiment 50 years ago into a billion dollar company and revolutionized how parts are put together.

Loctite technology is part of your everyday life. Virtually every passenger car on the road today is built with a Loctite® adhesive, as are stereo speakers, washing machines, vacuum cleaners, cell phones and personal computers. Military and commercial aircraft and the space shuttle fly with the help of Loctite branded products—threadlockers, thread sealants, gasketing products, coatings and specialty adhesives.

These products are known by manufacturing and design engineers, mechanics and maintenance professionals for their ability to predictably secure parts, add reliability and often reduce assembly costs in a wide range of industries. These powerful materials hold bolts together to keep parts from loosening prematurely and seal assemblies to eliminate wear.

The Krieble homestead on Niles Street in Hartford was the first home of American Sealants Company.

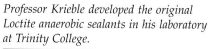

Professor Krieble developed the original Loctite anaerobic sealants in his laboratory at Trinity College.

Loctite came to be known as the primary brand and source for high quality, innovative specialty chemicals and adhesives for industry, the automotive aftermarket, and consumer needs.

Loctite Corporation, originally based in Hartford, was renamed Henkel Loctite Corporation in 2002 after being purchased in 1997 by Henkel Corporation, an affiliate of Henkel Group KgaA, Düsseldorf, Germany. Henkel's primary business was laundry detergents with a strong sales base in Germany. The companies are complementary and compatible—both are know for their entrepreneurial roots, history of technology innovation and strong brands.

Henkel's corporate slogan "Henkel – A Brand Like a Friend" echoes the close relationship loyal customers have developed with Henkel brands. Henkel is a global leader with brands and technologies that make people's lives easier, better and more beautiful. Globally there are 50,000 Henkel employees operating in three strategic business areas: home care, personal care and industrial technologies. The most recognizable brands in the U.S. include Loctite® brand adhesives, Pritt® Glue Sticks, Tangit™ Pipe Adhesives, Duck® brand duct tape and Dep® and LA Looks® hair care products. A major Henkel product brand is Persil®, a laundry detergent famous in Europe. Henkel products are available in over 125 countries.

Loctite, the brand that holds it all together, began with Vernon and Bob Krieble, a father-son chemistry team that collaborated on solving a chemistry problem. Vernon Krieble

Today, Henkel Loctite Corporation's industrial headquarters for North America is located in Rocky Hill, Connecticut.

(1885-1964) was born into a farm family in Worcester, Pennsylvania. But it wasn't any farm family. Vernon's father Jesse Schultz Krieble was a leading area farmer, head of the local school board for many years, and a director of the local bank. Jesse Krieble had helped start the school Vernon first attended.

This was an area steeped in German tradition. Vernon recalled later in his life that his family spoke only a German dialect at home and when he started at the Perkiomen School he could only say "yes" and "no" in English.

The Kriebles were descended from freedom-loving Germans from the Rhineland, who fled religious persecution in the 18th century and found refuge in the wilderness of Pennsylvania under the patronage of broadminded Quaker William Penn. Numbering fewer than 200, the small sect which settled some 20 miles north of Philadelphia were called Schwenkfelders. Above all, they prized freedom, education and hard work.

By his senior year at the local school, Vernon was class president. He enjoyed his duties and activities to such an extent that his grades fell and his father thought he had become lazy. Vernon later recalled what his father said: "He told me I'd have to get my grades up or there would be no college."

His grades shot up to near perfect. Vernon left the close-knit community for Brown Uni-

versity, where he graduated Phi Beta Kappa in 1907. When he told his father he wanted to be a chemist, Jesse asked, "Is it real work?"

Vernon assured him it was, and joined the faculty of McGill University in Montreal, Canada, as a chemistry demonstrator while completing his master's studies. In 1912 he received the Canadian Governor General's Medal for the best research paper. He was promoted to lecturer, earned his Ph.D. the following year, and was made assistant professor two years later.

Also in 1912 he married Laura Cassell (1889–1991), whom he had known since childhood from the German Schwenkfelder Sunday school back in Pennsylvania. Before long they had two children, Gladys and Robert, and Vernon's widowed mother came to live with them. The two mothers hated the Montreal winters and dreamed of warmer climates "in the South."

At that point, Hartford's Trinity College was conducting a search for a scientist who could help raise them to national prominence. Vernon Krieble had offers from Harvard and Princeton, but the proffered salaries were so minuscule he felt he couldn't raise his family. Then an offer came from a college he had never heard of before. Trinity College's position had the added advantage of a faculty house.

So in 1920 Vernon moved to Hartford to head the chemistry department at Trinity, and his wife and mother were happy to be in a

warmer climate. He received $3,000 in salary and kept a milk cow in his backyard. His mission was to make sure everyone he came in contact with became aware of chemistry in their daily lives. By 1936 Trinity had built a new chemistry building.

By 1953, son Robert (1916–1997) had a Ph.D. in chemistry from Johns Hopkins University and worked for General Electric. He also had a problem with a chemical formula, so he discussed it with his father over dinner one evening. Vernon set to work in his lab.

His persistence paid off. He discovered that this chemical liquid would harden to a tough plastic resin. The lack of oxygen and the presence of metal accelerated the hardening. The product could be used to lock nuts and bolts together—parts that were notorious for premature loosening, causing equipment failure. The problem was that it also hardened in the package. Bob mentioned that a nearby company had introduced a polyethylene bottle, permeable to oxygen. Vernon filled the bottles only half way, thus leaving a head of air, and the liquid remained liquid.

Bob's wife Nancy dubbed the new product Loctite. Professor Krieble established the

An early publicity photo showed a variety of conventional threadlocking devices, which could be replaced by a drop of Loctite® Sealant.

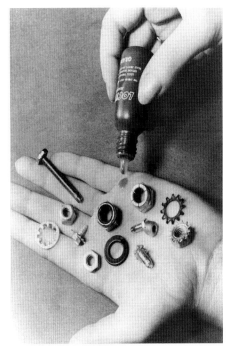

American Sealants Company, and made and distributed the product to companies in his neighborhood. In 1955 he retired from Trinity College at age 70 after 35 years, and devoted himself full-time to his new company. In 1956 the company operated from the first floor of the chemistry building at Trinity, with Trinity's blessings.

When he described his new venture to alumni, he had investors—to the tune of $100,000. Krieble called a press conference in New York and the resulting stories about Professor Krieble's "Magic Goo" led to orders and inquiries. Industrial types remained skeptical for years, though. Sales in 1956 were only $7,000. But some samples had been shipped overseas, and six years later, the overseas volume was one-fourth of sales. Foreign sales became even stronger when Jean Delmas, who had married Bob's sister Gladys, set up

American Sealants Company changed its name to Loctite Corpoation in 1963 to identify more closely with its products' brand name.

Indianapolis raceway mechanics like George Bignotti have long used Loctite® products for safety and reliability.

International Sealants SA, based in Mexico City.

Old friends said Bob, who came to work for Loctite, took a "boyish glee" every time he learned about a new use for the product. Loctite established marketing programs and targeted potential clients. They hit the road in a traveling demo lab, handing out free samples.

When an early engineer with the company visited a bicycle manufacturer he and his team were asked to put together a bike with Loctite. The manufacturer took it to the roof of the building and tossed it into the parking lot. The joints held, and they had a sale. By 1960 the company reached sales of $1 million.

Little by little they convinced engineers at companies like General Motors, Caterpillar, Black and Decker and Ford to use the adhesive as a design aid.

In 1964 Professor Krieble passed away, and Bob took over the company. He developed a corporate program such that 25 percent of future sales would come from products not yet available. Loctite acquired smaller companies making products that were compatible with their own.

Loctite marketing people coined the term "Super Glue" for a product they acquired, but Super Glue became a household name so quickly that they ended up losing its trademark to public domain.

By the time Bob retired at age 70 in 1986, Loctite had more than 1,000 products being distributed worldwide.

Innovation, listening to customer needs for product development, responsive engineering and chemical solutions continued under the leadership of Kenneth W. Butterworth, a replanted Australian, until his retirement in 1995. As 2003 comes to a close, Henkel Loctite continues a steady stream of innovative new product introductions.

Just to round things out for their 50th anniversary, Henkel Loctite cracked the technology to reformulate Professor Krieble's old threadlock liquid into a semi-solid stick form. Now it can be carried in a pocket without spilling, and it won't drip on something that should not be locked. As Ken Butterworth said about Bob Krieble, "enthusiasm and persistence will defeat pessimism and uncertainty every time."

HARTFORD FOUNDATION FOR PUBLIC GIVING

"Here to help. Here to stay." Since 1925 that phrase has embodied the commitment by the Hartford Foundation for Public Giving to improve the lives of area citizens. Through its partnership with nonprofit organizations, community leaders and donors, the Foundation is helping to build a brighter future for the Greater Hartford community.

Now the tenth largest community foundation in the country, the Hartford Foundation proudly serves the 29-town capitol region. Its service to the Greater Hartford community began with a grant of $982.52 to the Watkinson Library in Hartford. Since then, the generosity of thousands of individuals, families and organizations has enabled the

The Hartford Foundation has been proud to fund programs that use volunteers to build affordable housing for area residents.

Foundation to award grants totaling over $300 million to area nonprofits. Currently, the Foundation's permanent endowment is valued at $550 million.

This endowment enables the Foundation to make grants of approximately $25 million per year, touching virtually every aspect of life in the region—education, health, housing, arts and culture, and social services. In addition to its regular grantmaking, the Foundation has also made special commitments to address particularly pressing community needs. The most ambitious of these initiatives is called Brighter Futures, which began 12

The Hartford Foundation supports a wide range of arts and cultural programs in the city and its suburbs.

years ago to improve the school readiness of Hartford's young children. The ten-year, $10-million effort enjoyed so much success, that it has been expanded to a 20-year, $25 million project.

The arts have received strong support from the Foundation throughout its history. In fact, Connecticut Public Television and the Tony Award-winning Hartford Stage Company were established with lead funding from the Foundation. Also receiving significant funding from the Foundation is The Artists Collective—which has exposed over 1,000 children to music, drama, and dance—

and the University of Hartford for its planned opening of a state-of-the-art performing arts center for its Hartt School.

Another major focus of the Foundation has been to help nonprofit agencies improve their operating capacity and effectiveness. Initiated in the late 1980s, the Nonprofit Support Program provides grants for strategic planning, agency automation programs, board development and financial management, as well as training sessions for agency leadership.

The Foundation also plays an important role as a convener of community leaders, donors and nonprofit representatives to discuss important issues and ways to address them.

Throughout its 78-year history, the Foundation has served as a resource to charitably minded individuals, and their professional advisors, who want to make a difference in the Greater Hartford region. Currently, more than 800 funds at the Foundation are testaments to the generosity of area donors.

"The Hartford Foundation is a rallying point for people committed to the future of their community," says Michael Bangser, the Foundation's executive director. "People in Greater Hartford have taken great pride in the Foundation over the years. They have seen the impact of the Foundation and its grants."

Residents throughout the Greater Hartford region enjoy the many benefits of the Connecticut River, thanks to the efforts of Riverfront Recapture, a nonprofit organization, which has received funding from the Hartford Foundation.

PERTEL COMMUNICATIONS OF N. E., INC.

Pertel Communications of N. E., Inc. has been providing quality telecommunications services with exceptional customer care to the Connecticut area since 1986. From day one, the company has been guided by the determination, hard work and values of its founder, Charles Whaley.

Whaley opened the doors to Pertel Communications Corporation already knowing what many first-time business owners do not: how to survive. Against the odds, and not for the first time, Whaley and his partner saw the opportunity to establish a new business in Queens Village, New York. Whaley recognized the chance to provide business clients with telecommunications services at significantly lower rates than the existing large corporate interconnect companies, creating their own niche in the market.

In just a few short months Pertel arrived at a very important turning point. The small start-up made a name for itself by bidding on and winning a large contract. The Hamilton Standard (now Hamilton Sundstrand) division of United Technolo-

Pertel's corporate headquarters, 750 Main Street, Hartford.

Al Seymour, operations manager.

gies rewarded Pertel with a five-year, $1 million contract to provide telecom repair and maintenance services for its Windsor Locks facilities and outlying locations in Connecticut.

The contract was a professional coup for Pertel, as the company's competition for the bid included AT&T, SNET and nine other large established firms. The contract not only put Whaley and Pertel on the map, but formed a long-term relationship for the business with United Technologies. Whaley credits United Technologies with serving as a strong mentor and supporter during the young company's initial growth stage.

When Pertel won the United Technologies bid, it had only three employees on the payroll: Whaley, his partner and a technician. During the 13 years that Pertel served United Technologies as its primary telecom services provider, the company grew to employ more than 80.

The story of Pertel's success cannot be separated from that of Whaley's personal triumph. As a

child, Whaley would have been considered by some to be set up to fail. Born in Queens, New York, he spent his childhood in the Brownsville section of Brooklyn. At the age of seven, life dramatically changed course for Whaley: tragically, a drunk driver killed his father in a car collision. The young boy was raised by his mother in the Tilden Housing projects.

Defying statistics, Whaley graduated from Brooklyn's Tilden High School in 1976 and began his college studies. With ambition and the eagerness to learn, Whaley earned an associate's degree in applied sciences from Queensborough Community College in 1979.

Whaley's determination, coupled with his education, unlocked the door to his future. Soon after completing his degree, Whaley was hired at by General Telephone and Electronics (GTE) as an applications engineer. His career in telecommunications was just getting started. Whaley continued in his field with positions at General Dynamics, United Technologies and Memorex/ Telex. During his tenure at United Technologies, Whaley formed the relationships that would ultimately prove to be critical to the future of Pertel.

Whaley's experiences and resources gave him confidence to pursue his dream of operating his own business. He applied the determination that led him through his young life to seeing that dream become a reality. After four years of operation, the company evolved into Pertel Communications of N. E., Inc. and was established as a Connecticut corporation. The company's mission was to pursue public sector projects in the New England area.

One year later, in 1991, Pertel Communications of N. Y., Inc., was formed as a successor organization to Pertel Communications Corporation. This transition occurred following the departure of Whaley's partner in the original business. Pertel Communications of N. Y. operated from 1991 to 1996.

During the past decade and a half, Whaley has called on his early experiences to overcome adversity. Instead of folding when problems arose, Whaley kept Pertel afloat on his personal drive. Because of Whaley's determination—along with integrity, invaluable staff members and loyal customers—Pertel has survived the effects of financial and personnel issues.

The successful businessperson never forgets where he or she came from, and Whaley is no exception. He has felt, and honored, a continued responsibility to the community and those who are in need. Whaley has made it a personal and professional goal to employ handicapped individuals, recovering substance abusers, women and senior citizens in key management and technical positions. Whaley's guiding words are, "The exclusion of any human resource from the mainstream is a detriment to not only those individuals, but to the economy and success of our nation."

Pertel is led by Whaley's values. The company, through its employees, has been active in fighting breast cancer, AIDS, substance abuse, homelessness and multiple sclerosis in Hartford and New York. Staff members are also encouraged to participate in mentoring programs to guide those in disadvantaged situations.

Over the years, Pertel and Whaley have been honored by many organizations for successes and contributions. Awards include being selected as 22nd on the *Inc.* Magazine/ICIC Inner City 100 list and third on

Pertel's Windsor Locks location, 1988–1996.

the Connecticut Inner City 10 list by the Connecticut Department of Economic Community Development, as well as the Shinning Star Award by the Connecticut Minority Supplier Development Council, the SBA Administrator's Award for Excellence, *Who's Who in America, Who's Who in the East* and *Who's Who in Finance and Industry.*

Of these achievements, Whaley says he tempers his pride with the following words: "Be proud of your accomplishments, but not impressed. There is always more work to do."

Today Pertel continues to offer reliable quality technical systems support and network development services, with a specialization in structured cabling applications. The technical staff works closely with clients to design, test and maintain fixed or wireless telecommunications systems and network infrastructures. Other services include electronic office telephone systems, voice mail, automated-attendant and paging systems, and maintenance of voice/data PBXs.

The company serves Connecticut, Massachusetts, Rhode Island, New York, New Jersey, Pennsylvania, Delaware, Maryland and Virginia. Their client list included ABC Television Network, Pratt & Whitney, Sikorsky Aircraft, Otis Elevator and UConn Health Center.

The menu of services continues to evolve to meet the state-of-the-art technological needs of its clients. In the years to come, Pertel will incorporate wireless voice/data and security products, virtual intranets and physical and virtual voice over IP (VoIP) systems.

Pertel has grown to the multimillion dollar revenue mark, and the future holds the potential for further growth. However, for Charles Whaley the victory of Pertel's success has also been about the journey, not just the result.

Pertel's technicians on the job site.

P/A INDUSTRIES INC.

The company was founded in 1953 as Pneumatic Applications Company in Simsbury, Connecticut for the purpose of designing and building pneumatic tension controls and equipment for industrial applications creating several products that are trademarked and still sold today, some 50 years later, Soft-Aire Clutches and Brakes, Varatorq and Sona-Torque products are primarily used by Original Equipment Manufacturers.

In 1975 Jerome E. Finn became the major shareholder and president. The name was changed to P/A to reflect the company's new emphasis on Press Automation for the Metal Stamping Industry and moved to what is now named, P/A Technology Park in Bloomfield, Connecticut.

Using the pneumatic engineering capability, P/A designed and patented one of the first Precision Air Feeds. These compact, versatile, and inexpensive devices replaced older, less accurate mechanical roll feeders. From one model, the range has expanded to 22 models to provide exactly the right size and power for almost any strip-feeding application. The air feed was so popular it became the dominant feeding device used on power presses throughout the world and replaced hand-fed operations.

At this time, P/A marketing introduced the motto "You Supply the Press....We Supply the Rest." Several unique products were developed to further increase productivity and modernize coil handling.

Corporate headquarters.

In the early 1990s, it became clear that production speeds and efficiencies demanded a radically different approach to press feeding. P/A began to introduce numerically controlled, electrically driven Servo Roll Feeds. This development is one of the most important factors to increasing productivity within the Stamping and Fabrication Industry today.

When the electronics industry began its meteoric rise, P/A was again positioned to be a major player in producing automated equipment that was versatile, maintenance free and affordable.

P/A developed a complete line of Automatic Winders for every kind of terminal/contact manufacturer. These machines counted and wound the fragile pre-stamped parts with interleafing paper for protection. Modern PLC controls— monitored with in-house software—function flawlessly

for 24/7 production requirements

P/A's strategic plan was to develop international markets by establishing manufacturing and sales and service companies in Europe and the Pacific.

In 1994, P/A Retain Ltd. was formed in Taiwan to manufacture machine assemblies for Servo Roll Feeds. The electronics were

Transporters.

built in Bloomfield and shipped to Taiwan for sales in the Pacific Basin—China, Korea, Singapore and Australia became important markets for these products.

Believing that Eastern Europe would be another emerging market, P/A Bohemia s.r.o. in the Czech Republic was established in 1995 and our first opening to what used to be a closed market to American companies.

A Swedish company developed a unique product that would remove scrap and parts from presses. The patented product—a pneumatic feed (Transporter)—was introduced into the American Market in 1985 as an

Air feeders.

Advantage Servo Roll Feed.

alternative to belt conveyors and became an overnight success. In 1995, P/A bought Mectool Sweden AB and began marketing their products alongside their pneumatic feeders. In less than five years, production volume increased five fold!

The year of the millennium, P/A created a German sales and service company, P/A GmbH with the intention of creating a European headquarters to coordinate Sales & Service.

P/A is the only American company in the Press Automation Industry that has a global presence

Whether it's coil handling or press feeding equipment, at P/A Industries and its subsidiaries around the world, a customer can order a pre-engineered, off-the-shelf system or a completely integrated one that is custom designed to meet any particular need.

Jerome Finn, president says, " customers lead to new products, product improvements and new applications. Of course we work in research and development to develop what we believe will be the next new product our customers will need, but a high percentage of our new offerings come from working to solve a customer's application problem."

The company is also distinguished from its competitors through its warrantee to its customers. Instead of just covering parts and service, P/A provides its "POMG" —Peace of Mind Guaranteed. The company works to solve problems quickly and will do all it can to find solutions that will last forever. Customers are the highest priority to P/A as noted in the company's quality policy: "If a customer perceives a problem, then a problem exists until that perception is corrected." The company uses service and extensive procedures to manage its quality. They are committed to relentless dedication to continuous improvement.

Family owned and run, this company counts on its workforce to deliver on its high standards. "Our people are exceptionally loyal and dedicated, challenged toward independent thinking to constantly question the status quo," says Finn. "Within a teamwork environment, they work together to accomplish our goals in ways that amaze us. We measure ourselves by a simple, effective standard: whatever we say or do should be 'Fair, Honest and Reasonable' to our customers, our company and ourselves. Our satisfied customers—over 8,000 strong—tell us that our people and their enthusiasm are unmatched in the industry!"

Manufacturing facility.

Ten Up Automatic Rewind.

In 1998, the Town of Bloomfield presented the Beacon Award, their top business honor of the decade to P/A and in 1999, the Hartford Chamber of Commerce presented the Leadership Award in the Large Business Category to P/A for outstanding achievement and growth.

Jerome Finn says: "our goal is to broaden our product line, customer base and distribution system to enable us to be recognized as the World Class Leader for Press Automation."

RENSSELAER AT HARTFORD

Lifelong Learning is our Passion: 50 Years and Growing. For nearly 50 years, Rensselaer at Hartford has been Connecticut's leader in education for working professionals. Term after term, Rensselaer at Hartford has proven that it is fully committed to providing excellence in education for working professionals by delivering a world-class learning experience with 21st-century content to prepare students to lead in an increasingly technological world.

"We like to say that an undergraduate education is 'just-in-case' learning, meaning that we learn that material just in case we need it at some future state," explains Dr. Alan C. Eckbreth, the vice president and dean at Rensselaer at Hartford. "We offer our students what I would like to call 'just in time' learning. In other words, our working professionals may learn something on a Tuesday evening, and they may apply it the very next day in their workplace. Our curriculum is designed for the realities of the modern-day workplace, and in many cases is almost immediately applicable."

Rensselaer at Hartford is part of the world-renowned intellectual community of Rensselaer Polytechnic Institute, the oldest technological university in the United States.

Dr. Alan C. Eckbreth, vice president and dean of Rensselaer at Hartford.

In 1824 Stephen Van Rensselaer founded the Institute in Troy, New York, "for the purpose of instructing persons in the application of science to the common purposes of life." Excellence in education inspired the founders of Rensselaer, and innovative pedagogy remains a core value of the Institute today as it strives to achieve even greater prominence as a top-tier, world-class technological research university with global reach and global im-

pact. As a rapidly growing research university, Rensselaer is a community of learners, dedicated to discovery and expanding the boundaries of scientific inquiry. At Rensselaer, excellence is the mantra and the metric, the message and the measurement of success.

Rensselaer at Hartford (formerly The Hartford Graduate Center) was founded as a division of the graduate school of Rensselaer Polytechnic Institute in 1955, a time when rapidly expanding technologies in the aircraft and defense industries were creating a critical shortage of engineers and other professionals in the Greater Hartford area. At that time, H. Mansfield Horner, chairman of United Aircraft Corporation (now United Technologies Corporation) approached Livingston Houston with the idea of creating an educational institution geared toward working professionals in the Hartford area. Horner was motivated by recruitment and retention concerns for engineers in the Connecticut River valley; Houston responded enthusiastically to the idea.

In 1955 six tenured faculty from Rensselaer, led by Dr. Warren Stoker, moved to Connecticut and led a team of educators who began offering post-baccalaureate engineering education to 212 students, only three of whom were from companies other than United Aircraft. Buoyed by its initial success, Dr. Stoker and his associates began offering a nondegree engineering design program in 1956, and management degree and nondegree management development programs in 1959. Eight years later a master of science in computer science was introduced. In 1977 the Groton site for management degrees was opened and expanded into computer science and engineering degrees. In 1997 the centers at Hartford and Groton were "Re-Rensselaered" and merged with Rensselaer Polytechnic Institute to become a branch campus known as Rensselaer at Hartford.

Rensselaer at Hartford offers its students some of the finest educational facilities in the Hartford area. The 15-acre campus is situated just a half-mile from the Hartford city center, and a mile from the intersection of Interstates 91 and 84, two of Connecticut's major highways. Rensselaer offers its students 27 well-appointed classrooms, five distance education classrooms, five computer classrooms, the 40,000-volume Cole Library, a

An early Rensselaer classroom scene from the 1950s.

Rensselaer at Hartford is easily accessible from Interstates 84 and 91.

convenient bookstore, ample free parking and cafeteria facilities. Seminar Hall is a 100-seat facility with real-time two-way video. Rensselaer at Hartford courses are available not only at the Hartford campus, but also at a satellite center in Groton, Connecticut. The Groton regional site has five classrooms, including a computer classroom and a distance classroom, and is conveniently located near the area's major employers and entertainment facilities.

In addition to its fine facilities, Rensselaer embraces cutting-edge technology to deliver educational opportunities. RSVP, Rensselaer's signature distance delivery program, is a leading provider of graduate-level, distributed education programs for working professionals at leading corporations and government agencies all over the world. Through a variety of delivery technologies, Rensselaer offers credit and noncredit courses, graduate certificates and master's degrees. RSVP is known for excellence in content, delivery and services. It has received considerable national recognition and numerous awards. Through Rensselaer's interactive learning environment, students are able to obtain high-level knowledge while honing their analytical capabilities and leadership skills to enhance their innovative thinking.

Rensselaer at Hartford makes a concerted effort to accommodate its hardworking students. Most classes are offered in the evenings between 5:30 and 9:30, and accelerated programs are offered on Friday evenings and Saturdays. Clearly, Rensselaer caters to the needs of working professionals.

Beyond the facilities, it is the faculty members who drive the educational experience at Rensselaer. There are 29 full-time faculty, 19 in management and 10 in science and engineering. These full-time faculty, and approximately 30 adjunct faculty, are supported by a staff of more than 80—almost a quarter of whom have at least 10 years of service. Eighty-

two percent of the faculty have doctorates. Each and every faculty member has solid academic credentials and exceptional teaching skills combined with an expertise grounded in solid research. Beyond the classroom, the faculty members at Rensselaer have a wealth of professional experience in engineering, management, computer science, information technology and real-world business applications.

"Our faculty is distinguished by the fact that most of them have actually had professional careers and real-world experience," Dr. Eckbreth observes. "Only a few of our faculty have been on traditional academic paths. This is extremely important, especially when you consider that many of our students come in with 10 or 15 years in the workplace already. Particularly in the management arena, they are out there living it day in, day out. Our faculty members include many distinguished scholars who have published books and papers. But the real-world background is what distinguishes ours from traditional academic faculties."

The original academic leaders left their posts at RPI in Troy, New York, for an opportunity to bring their expertise in engineering and science to eager engineers awaiting them in Central Connecticut. Seated: Kenneth Bisshop, Warren Stoker, Gordon Campbell; Standing: Bronis Onuf, Murray Spiegel, Joseph Krahula, Valdemars Punga.

Students embrace Rensselaer's sense of mission, this passion for lifelong learning. Each course is designed to meet the needs of working professionals seeking to advance their careers and enhance their organizations' successes. Rensselaer at Hartford is one of Connecticut's leading providers of graduate education and professional development programs. Rensselaer's Lally School of Management and Technology offers an M.B.A. degree, as well as a master of science degree in management with concentrations in finance, marketing, information systems, operations management, international management and innovation and entrepreneurship. In addition, the Lally School at Rensselaer offers an Executive Master's Program, the

Rensselaer at Hartford is housed in its own eight-story building on 15 landscaped acres in downtown Hartford.

Seminar Hall accomodates up to 100 people and is fully equipped with digital projection and videoconferencing technology.

Weekend M.B.A. and the Weekend M.S. in Management (Financial Management Concentration). With innovative course offerings and flexible structures, the Lally School is making great progress toward becoming preeminent among educational institutions in integrating management and technology for innovation and value creation in the global marketplace.

Rensselaer's Department of Engineering and Science encompasses the areas of computer science, engineering and information technology. Computer science/information technology is the fastest-growing field in the global job market today. The Department of Engineering and Science is committed to a nationally recognized applications-based

computer science program that prepares professionals for the job market in computer fields. According to *U.S. News & World Report*, Rensselaer's Graduate School of Engineering is ranked 31st in the 2003 "Best Graduate Schools" guide and the Electrical and Mechanical Engineering Programs are ranked 17th and 18th, respectively.

The Department of Engineering and Science offers students master of science degrees in computer science, information technology, mechanical engineering, electrical engineering, engineering science and a master of engineering degree in computer and systems engineering. In addition, the Department of Engineering and Science offers students graduate certificate programs in computer science and information technologies such as bioinformatics and information systems, and in engineering fields such as high-temperature materials and systems modeling and analysis.

Beyond its degree and certificate programs, Rensselaer offers a full range of professional development programs and services. Professional Development Programs (PDP) are designed to provide working professionals with the critical skills they need to be effective in today's dynamic workplace. Programs generally range from one to five days in length. Training programs and workshops are available in computer and information technology, leadership and executive development, and technical and professional development.

PDP also offers services designed to help companies and individuals understand and define their developmental needs. Services include needs assessment, custom program development and executive coaching. All in all, Rensselaer provides a dynamic learning experience for those who need to balance their professional, academic and personal lives. The result is that Rensselaer graduates—executives, senior professionals, managers and individuals with high potential—become architects of their futures.

Rensselaer is dedicated to developing sophisticated business leaders who are prepared to guide their organizations in integrating technology for new products, new businesses and new systems. Rensselaer students know the value of the education they are receiving. Much of that value is

generated by interaction with other hardworking, ambitious professionals. The overwhelming majority of Rensselaer at Hartford students are indeed professionals, with an average age of 33. Nearly a quarter of all entering students already hold a graduate degree. The companies for which Rensselaer at Hartford students work include many of Connecticut's leading employers, such as United Technologies, Pfizer, CIGNA, General Dynamics and General Electric.

Rensselaer students share knowledge and experience as part of their education, knowing that they are destined to take an important place in the business community. "We have access to very high-caliber people, people who are current leaders in the workplace or people who will be the future leaders of these companies," Dr. Eckbreth explains. "We believe that our impact is really based on the fact that we are educating the high-end working professional—the leaders of the present work force and the emerging leaders."

As a Connecticut institution for nearly half a century, Rensselaer has proven to be a strong recruiting/retention asset for the region. A recent study by Appleseed, Inc., a consulting firm, found that the Rensselaer at Hartford campus is a "significant enterprise" which contributes to the regional and state economies, especially through the development of Connecticut's professional workforce.

Students enjoy the support of a sophisticated classroom environment with state-of-the-art workstations accompanied by the latest software applications and network access.

Students gather with family and friends for the traditional post-graduation picnic at the Hartford campus.

Rensselaer at Hartford has granted more than 13,000 master's degrees in Connecticut since 1955. As working professionals, Rensselaer at Hartford graduates are more likely than young-adult graduates of many other institutions to remain in the area. More than 5,700 Rensselaer at Hartford alumni—more than 45 percent—still live in Connecticut. Recently, Rensselaer at Hartford accounted for 21 percent of all master's degrees in business and management awarded by Connecticut colleges and universities, 22 percent of all master's degrees in engineering, and 26 percent of all computer science master's degrees.* "For nearly 50 years we've been a resource in terms of both recruiting and retention for employers in this region," Dr. Eckbreth says. "We have definitely fulfilled our mission of having a long-term impact as a major educational provider in the area."

Rensselaer and its graduates have contributed to the Hartford area in ways that go far beyond the world of business. Each summer for the last 22 years, Rensselaer at Hartford has sponsored a computer camp for neighborhood children. The four-week camp gives students a chance to acquire basic computer skills, to learn to use the Internet, and to create their own Web pages. In addition, the people at Rensselaer are involved in area reading programs, in Habitat for Humanity projects and in Hartford Proud and Beautiful, a city beautification organization.

It's all part of what Dr. Shirley Ann Jackson, the president of Rensselaer Polytechnic Institute, describes as creating a "communiversity," the process of bringing together the local community and university for everyone's benefit.

Rensselaer at Hartford is committed to pushing the boundaries of excellence still further. The faculty and administration are working to broaden and increase the base of corporate clients served at Hartford, create a one-year executive M.B.A. program and increase engineering enrollments in degree/certificate programs and the dual degree program with management. Rensselaer is also collaborating with Hartford-area organizations and public officials to explore the feasibility of developing a research and technology park and an incubator facility for new ventures.

Rensselaer has succeeded in preparing its graduates to meet the challenges of the 21st century. In their passion for lifelong learning and their proven ability to master the skills demanded by an increasingly technological world, Rensselaer's faculty, students and alumni personify the Institute's slogan, "Why not change the world?"

*Source: Connecticut Department of Higher Education.

SAINT FRANCIS HOSPITAL AND MEDICAL CENTER

Since its founding in 1897 by the Sisters of Saint Joseph of Chambéry, Saint Francis Hospital and Medical Center has been a leading regional health care provider. Based in Hartford, Saint Francis is one of Connecticut's largest hospitals, and the largest Catholic hospital in New England. It is licensed for 617 inpatient beds and 65 bassinets. With clinical concentrations in cardiology, oncology, women's health services, emergency/trauma care, and rehabilitation, Saint Francis provides sophisticated, contemporary medicine to the Greater Hartford community. Saint Francis has been repeatedly named among the top 100 hospitals, and the top 15 major teaching hospitals, in the United States by Solucient, a leading health care research firm. Solucient has also recognized Saint Francis as one of the top 100 hospitals for cardiovascular services.

When it opened in Hartford's Asylum Hill neighborhood, Saint Francis could accommodate 30 patients in its wards. Its first administrator was a French nun who had less than two years of nursing training in Lyons, France, and barely spoke any English. Her staff included four American nuns who had no medical experience and had never even seen a hospital. The hospital building was

Hospital administrators and religious leaders attend the groundbreaking of the McAuliffe Lying-In Pavilion, named for Bishop McAuliffe of Hartford, in 1949.

located in a vacant, run-down, three-story former seminary donated by Bishop Michael Tierney. These limitations did not inhibit its founders from aspiring to build the first Catholic hospital in Connecticut, and believing that it could become among the best in the nation.

The hospital has responded to the region's health care needs from its inception, notably in providing critical care during the 1903

Located on the corner of Collins and Woodland Streets, the original Saint Francis Hospital, which opened in 1897, had 30 beds and two private rooms.

outbreak of scarlet fever, and in 1919, when it was designated as an Army Reserve Hospital. When World War II began, Saint Francis was the first local hospital to initiate a Volunteer Red Cross Nurses Aide course.

Following World War II, the Saint Francis Hospital staff regrouped and began a new era that focused heavily upon patient care and physician training. During the 1950s outbreak of polio, it was the first to establish a post-polio program. By the mid '50s the hospital had established 11 separate specialized departments including pathology, radiology, outpatient services, anesthesiology, cardiology and obstetrics. In 1957 the cardiovascular pulmonary section was established, and a year later Saint Francis introduced the first artificial kidney in the area.

Throughout the next three decades, Saint Francis continued to grow and enhance the services and programs offered at the hospital. During this time, a Cardiopulmonary Research Laboratory, an Intensive Care Unit, a Coronary Care Unit, a Neonatal Intensive Unit, a Diabetes Care Center, an Ambulatory Care Center and a section for oncology were established. To reflect its expanding breadth of service, the hospital's name was changed to Saint Francis Hospital and Medical Center in 1976.

Until 1988, the administrators of Saint Francis were all Sisters of Saint Joseph. Mother Ann Valencia, founder of the hospital, led the hospital from 1897 until her death in 1936. Mother Mary Xavier Kilroy became the second administrator in 1937 and served in this role for eight years. Mother Bernard Mary Sheehan presided over the hospital from 1945 until 1962, when she was succeeded by Sister Mary Madeline Forcier, who served from 1962 until 1973. The last religious administrator of the hospital was Sister Francis Marie Garvey, who ran the institution from 1973 until 1988.

David D'Eramo, Ph.D., became the hospital's first lay president and CEO in 1988. Since the late 1980s, Saint Francis has experienced tremendous growth, which was achieved through key strategies implemented by Dr. D'Eramo. One included a new hospital center with a 10-story Patient Care Tower,

A hospital within a hospital, the Patient Care Tower at Saint Francis today is one of the most contemporary medical facilities in the region.

and the cultivation of medical Centers of Clinical Excellence which propelled the hospital into the national spotlight in areas such as heart, cancer, women's services and emergency/trauma care. Another strategy focused on reaching out to the Greater Hartford community through mergers and affiliations with neighboring hospitals and other health care providers.

Dedicated in 1996, the Patient Care Tower encompasses 358,480 square feet, provides 42 critical care beds, 108 replacement beds with new medical/surgical features, and 28 neonatal intensive care bassinets. Along with key affiliations, the Tower represents a signature event in the transition of Saint Francis from a single acute care hospital to an integrated health care delivery system that provides a wide range of inpatient and outpatient services in convenient locations throughout the region.

Saint Francis concentrates on several areas of expertise known as Centers of Clinical Excellence. One such area is the Saint Francis cardiology program, which was the first medical specialty section developed at the hospital in 1957. Throughout its history, the program achieved many significant milestones. Between the 1950s and 1980s, some of these achievements included the first cardiac catheterization at the hospital (1959), the first open-heart surgery (1960), pioneering studies on Mitral Valve Prolapse (1971), and the development of a Cardiac Rehabilitation Program (1976).

A significant development in the evolution of the cardiology program was the establishment of the Hoffman Heart Insti-

Nurses attend to newborns in 1910. During that year more than 200 babies were delivered at Saint Francis Hospital.

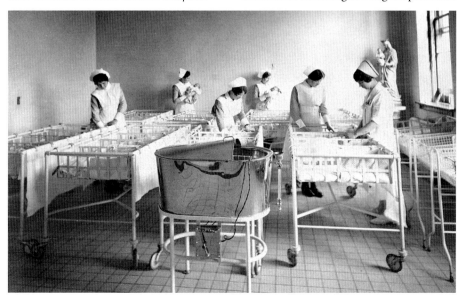

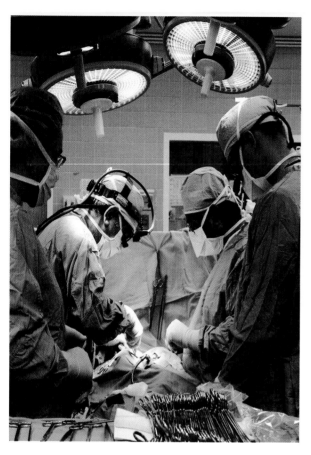

Cardio-thoracic surgeons perform more open-heart surgeries per year at Saint Francis than any other hospital in Connecticut.

tute in 1991. Named in recognition of the $2 million grant given by the Maximilian E. and Marion O. Hoffman Foundation, its purpose was to focus on areas of prevention, diagnosis, treatment of cardiovascular diseases, and the rehabilitation of patients with the disease. Two of the most frequent procedures (5,100 per year) performed by cardiologists at the institute are cardiac catheterizations and angioplasties. Cardio-thoracic surgeons perform more than 1,300 open-heart surgeries annually, which is more than any other hospital in Connecticut. In 1997 surgeons performed Connecticut's first minimally invasive port-access open-heart surgery; in 2000 the state's first transmyocardial revascularization with a carbon dioxide laser was done. In 2002 Saint Francis was the only hospital in the state to be named one of the nation's 100 Top Hospitals for cardiovascular services.

Another of Saint Francis' Centers of Clinical Excellence is the cancer program. The

section of oncology was established in 1978. In 1982 the first outpatient Oncology Center was established, and one year later the Saint Francis Chemotherapy Clinic was instituted. The Saint Francis/Mount Sinai Regional Cancer Center was opened in 1993. The two-story, 32,000-square-foot facility was made possible through a significant contribution from the Mount Sinai Hospital Foundation and houses the latest technologies such as a state-of-the-art linear accelerator and chemotherapeutic facilities.

Services provided by the Cancer Center include research, prevention, detection, evaluation, treatment, rehabilitation, and teaching. One of its technological advances was Greater Hartford's first high-dose-rate brachytherapy remote afterloader machine. This is one of the most powerful ways to treat deep-seated tumors in the endometrium, esophagus, or lungs. In 1997, the first photodynamic therapy machine in Connecticut was installed, which helped treat esophageal cancers on an outpatient basis. Radiation Oncology uses a high energy linear accelerator that makes it one of the most advanced radiation treatment facilities in the Northeast.

The center is designated as a Teaching Hospital Cancer Program by the Commission on Cancer of the American College of Surgeons, a distinction achieved by fewer than one-fifth of all hospitals in the United States.

Today, disease-specific services for patients with

breast cancer, gastrointestinal cancer, lymphoma, myeloma, leukemia, female reproductive cancer, urologic cancer and lung cancer are organized to provide a multi-disciplinary approach to disease.

Women's services is a third Center of Clinical Excellence at the hospital. From 1970 to 1992, significant advances in the obstetrics and gynecology program were made. In 1970 fathers were permitted in the delivery room for the first time. A year later a section of fetal medicine was created.

With the opening of the John M. Gibbons Pavilion in 1996, women's health services at Saint Francis were advanced. All 14 Labor-Delivery-Recovery rooms, located within the Pavilion, are equipped with rocking chairs, private baths and medical equipment that is hidden from view until needed. Other features of the Pavilion include cesarean section rooms, a family visiting area, and a neonatal

At the leading edge in lifesaving care, an Emergency Department nurse assists emergency medical technicians in transporting a critically ill patient from the hospital's helipad.

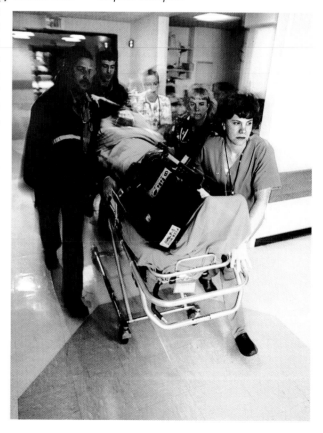

intensive care unit, which provides the most advanced level of care for critically ill newborns. The department also has maternal fetal medicine specialists who use sophisticated ultrasound technology for high-risk pregnancies.

A Comprehensive Breast Health Center was opened in 1999. Part of the efficient outpatient mission, this new center eased the diagnostic process for women. Previously, when a breast lump was detected, the patient was led through various diagnostic procedures and had to wait several weeks to learn if she had cancer. Today, on-site surgeons, cytopathologists, diagnostic radiologists, and nurse specialists, are able to provide a complete diagnosis and treatment plan in a single visit. In 2001, the Center became the first in the state to offer Computer Aided Detection, a technology that helps to identify hard-to-see forms of breast cancer.

The final Center for Clinical Excellence at Saint Francis is Trauma and Emergency Medicine. In 1989 the hospital doubled the size of this department in an attempt to meet the growing demand from the community by constructing a new Emergency/Trauma Center. The $5 million facility would serve 45,000 patients a year, including 12,000 children. Also in 1989, the hospital opened Hartford's first rooftop helipad for LIFE-STAR helicopters.

During the 1990s, Saint Francis began to expand the reach of its continuum of care by affiliating and merging with neighboring health care institutions. In 1990 Saint Francis formed an affiliation with Mount Sinai Hospital, believed to be the first such collaboration between a Catholic hospital and a Jewish hospital in U.S. history, culminating in 1995 in a formal corporate merger. In 1995 Bristol Hospital and Saint Francis Hospital and Medical Center affiliated; in 1996 an affiliation agreement was signed between St. Mary's Hospital in Waterbury and Saint Francis. Other affiliations included the Greater Hartford Easter Seals Rehabilitation Center, Inc., the Alcohol and Drug Recovery Center, and the Suffield Visiting Nurse Association.

More than just corporate or economic reorganizations, the result of these affiliations was a tangible improvement to the medical care of Hartford residents. As an anchor insti-

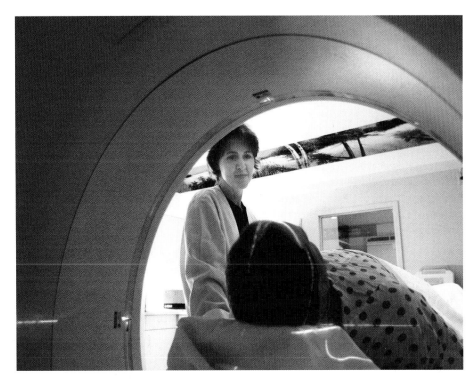

tution in a multicultural metropolitan area, Saint Francis had evolved to embrace the diversity of the city.

As Saint Francis entered the new millennium, it recognized that health care consumers were taking a much more active role in seeking out medical information and making decisions that affected their health. In addition, a number of regulatory issues were implemented to ensure greater accountability for quality performance. Saint Francis responded by creating a Department of Quality and Benchmarking in 2002. Also in that year, Saint Francis was named a Leapfrog Hospital. Leapfrog is a coalition of Fortune 500 companies and other private and public health care purchasers who provide benefits to approximately 33 million people.

One of the criteria for Leapfrog Hospital designation is the use of Computerized Physician Order Entry (CPOE), which is said to reduce serious prescribing errors in hospitals by more than 50 percent. Saint Francis is one of only 5 percent of U.S. hospitals to have implemented CPOE 10 years ago, and it is currently installing a second generation application.

In a continuing effort to improve quality performance, Saint Francis joined in a collaborative initiative with Anthem Blue Cross and Blue Shield's Clinical Quality Program

Using an ACQSIM CT scanner, one of the industry's most advanced three-dimensional computer simulation systems, a technologist creates an anatomical view of a patient in order to pinpoint the precise area for treatment.

to enhance patient safety and demonstrate that quality costs less. The pilot program, which began in 2003, evaluates and rewards mutually established measures of quality of care, clinical outcomes, patient safety and processes designed to deliver quality, affordable health care.

For over a century, Saint Francis has been guided by its mission and fundamental values. These include compassion, charity, sensitivity and attentiveness—the values that underlie the basic desire to help those in need. While Saint Francis continues to place great emphasis on the technology and scientific procedures that help diagnose, treat, and cure patients who suffer from disease, infection or injury, it has never wavered from the Catholic ideals that were espoused by the Sisters of Saint Joseph over 100 years ago that are at the heart of what Saint Francis Hospital Medical Center has been, what it is today, and what it will become.

S. H. SMITH & COMPANY, INC.

It was a great deal for both sides, with the acquisition of a manufacturer by another company—but there was a hitch. The manufacturer had been uninsured for product liability for 20 years, and the acquiring company wanted to be indemnified from any claims arising out of past actions. Enter S. H. Smith & Company, Inc. With its broad portfolio of insurance products, and its dedicated staff of experienced professionals, S. H. Smith & Company was able to arrange a products liability policy that protected the acquiring company from any claims arising from occurrences over the past 20 years that were unknown to the manufacturer. The deal was saved, the sale went through and S. H. Smith & Company once again both met and exceeded the expectations of agents and their clients.

After more than half a century, S. H. Smith & Company is the largest excess and surplus lines broker in the Northeast. Licensed to work in all 50 states, and a Lloyds of London correspondent, S. H. Smith represents more than 70 domestic and foreign markets. For certain lines in certain regions, S. H. Smith is the biggest name in the business.

The owner and president, Scott H. Smith.

"There are five things that are the keys to providing top quality service as an insurance provider," Scott Smith, the company president, explains. " They are putting together the best combination possible of price, carrier, claims, terms and conditions, and service."

As one of the largest and most successful excess and surplus line brokers in the country, S.H. Smith has become known for its unmatched expertise in areas ranging from large umbrellas to product liability, to property

exposures. S. H. Smith is also highly experienced in coverages for high tech companies, biotech, as well as in manuscripting new coverages, in particular for D&O and professional liability. The company's goal is to provide independent insurance agents with markets for hard-to-place risks, typically defined as being either unusual or unique exposure, non-standard business, needing higher limits, or needing broader coverages. To provide the highest level of service, S. H. Smith has dedicated teams and support staff for every policy offered.

One of the keys to the company's success is their relationship to their insurance carriers. S. H. Smith works with a diverse group of insurers and has developed strong relationships with underwriting professionals at key leading companies over the years. Carriers that S. H. Smith & Company represents includes AIG, Chubb, Zurich, St. Paul, Arch, Hartford Insurance, Traveler's and many more.

These relationships, built over time, allow S. H. Smith to present agents' risks to carriers in such a way that they are predisposed to write them, usually with terms and conditions successful for all. Risk categories for which S. H. Smith & Company can provide solutions include property, liability, personal lines, workers compensation, directors and officers, professional and umbrella and/or excess coverage.

More than the product lines, it is the people who make S. H. Smith & Company such an outstanding organization. The company understands that it is in a service business, and the organization aspires to be the best. By providing prompt answers, clearly worded coverage and a detailed knowledge of any client's business, S. H. Smith does business the right way, the only way to be successful in the field. Its team includes classically trained underwriters, CPCUs, CICs, ARMs, and individuals with graduate degrees in business and law. Many employees have underwriting backgrounds and have extensive knowledge and experience in writing products and programs.

President Scott Smith acquired the assets of a predecessor firm in 1982. From his primary office in Connecticut, Scott has grown the company from $2.5 million in business per year to over $130 million. Prior to creating S. H. Smith & Company, Smith worked

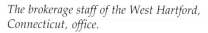

The brokerage staff of the West Hartford, Connecticut, office.

The principals of S. H. Smith & Company, Inc.

the Connecticut Development Authority and has been actively involved with the Hartford Art School, the University of Hartford, the Wadsworth Atheneum, Saint Francis Hospital and Medical Center, and the Hartford Hospital Group.

All of the professionals at S. H. Smith & Company work together to combine their vast product knowledge with an equally broad knowledge of the disposition of the market, both historically and today. They are easily accessible and pride themselves on their knowledge and experience. No matter what the challenge, S. H. Smith & Company has the talent and the expertise to bring top quality solutions to the challenges of today's difficult market.

Resourcefulness, extensive contacts and a long history of proactive service puts S. H. Smith & Company in a unique position to provide its clients and the people of the Hartford area with a unique advantage. Whether it is serving the needs of the Hartford community or meeting the fast changing challenges of the insurance marketplace, S. H. Smith & Company understands that there is no such thing as an excess and surplus of experience.

for what was then one of the largest excess and surplus line brokers in the country. Prior to that, Smith was an underwriter at a major property and casualty insurer.

In addition to Scott H. Smith, there are six other principals of the company. Neil Cross is executive vice president and branch manager of the Massachusetts office, and manager of contract/binding authority for all offices. Dennis Donovan, executive vice president, is in charge of the Professsional Liability Department. David Kinder is chief financial officer and senior vice president.

Jeffrey Parmenter, vice president, manages the Small Account/Contract Authority Department. David S. Perkins, senior vice president, is responsible for the Professional Liabilty Department in the Massachusetts office. And, John Williams is senior vice president of marketing.

S. H. Smith & Company has five office locations. Each one is fully equipped to manage any and all client needs. The home office, the heart of the company, is located in West Hartford. Over the years, S. H. Smith has worked to build the Hartford community. In addition to provid-

ing jobs and revenue for the Hartford area, staff have been involved with the Independent Insurance Agents of America (IIAA), Professional Insurance Agents (PIA), the American Association of Managing General Agents (AAMGA), and many other regional and national insurance industry organizations. President Scott Smith has served on the board of

The Massachusetts office brokerage staff.

C. M. SMITH AGENCY, INC.

For the C. M. Smith Agency, Inc., service goes beyond offering insurance to their Connecticut-based clients. The 30-year-old firm prides itself on helping clients make decisions in their best interest. C. M. Smith's areas of focus include employee benefits, executive benefits and retirement services.

Charles M. Smith found his life's work in the insurance industry shortly after he graduated from Amherst College in 1959. The ambitious Boston native started a career as an accident and health-underwriting trainee at Travelers Insurance Company in Hartford. After serving six years with the company, Smith joined the staff of Benjamin, Connor & Walker, a local insurance firm specializing in property and casualty insurance. His role was to introduce a life and health insurance division, and he quickly rose to the challenge.

In the early 1970s Benjamin, Connor & Walker was purchased by Fred S. James and Company, a national firm. Having learned his trade by serving the local community, Smith realized that a large broker was not his style, and it was time to make some changes.

Charles M. Smith, founder of the C. M. Smith Agency.

On New Year's Day 1974, Smith formed a firm in his home, with a shingle bearing his name. He knew the insurance business and—more importantly—he knew the needs of the Hartford community and its citizens.

As the agency prospered, new offices were needed to accommodate the growing firm. The C. M. Smith Agency moved to Hebron Avenue in Glastonbury, where it remained for several years. In 1983 the firm rehabbed the historic former Glastonbury Second District school building at 2252 Main Street in Glastonbury.

Smith's accomplished career included serving as president and director of the Hartford Life Underwriters Association and as a past director of the Hartford Chapter of Chartered Life Underwriters. He also served as a national speaker in his field and held qualifying membership in the Million Dollar Round Table's Top of the Table, and the International Forum, which placed him in the top 0.2 percent of life underwriters worldwide.

On January 1, 1995, the firm's 21st anniversary, John O'Connell and Baxter (Bret) Maffett purchased the company from Smith.

After many tireless years of hard work, Smith knew he had turned his company over to secure hands, allowing him to retire. At that time there were 11 employees.

Maffett had joined the agency in 1983. He received a bachelor of arts degree from Middlebury College in 1972 and a master's of business administration from the Amos Tuck School of Business Administration at Dartmouth College in 1975. Maffett holds the Chartered Life Underwriter (CLU) and Chartered Financial Consultant (ChFC) designations. He is a life and qualifying member of the Million Dollar Round Table, a member of the American Society of Chartered Life Underwriters, the National Association of Life Under-

Office site on Main Street, Glastonbury, in the former historic Second District School Building.

Bret Maffett, president of Insurance and Retirement Services, and John O'Connell, president of Employee Benefits.

writers, and The Estate and Business Planning Council of Hartford. Maffett is actively involved with a number of community organizations and industry groups. He serves as vice chairman of the Advisory Board for Jefferson House (an affiliate of Hartford Hospital) and on the Saint Francis Hospital Foundation Board.

O'Connell came to the agency in 1986. He earned a bachelor's degree from Trinity College in 1981. O'Connell has earned industry designations as a Certified Employee Benefit Specialist (CEBS) and a Chartered Life Underwriter (CLU). He serves on several boards in and outside the industry, and recently completed a term as chair of VNA Health Care, Inc. O'Connell currently serves as president of the Board of Trustees of Renbrook School in West Hartford, Connecticut.

Upon Charlie Smith's retirement, O'Connell took the position of overseeing the employee benefits department and Maffett took the role of managing the insurance and retirement services division. Incidentally, Barbara Monhardt, Smith's

first employee, served the company for 28 years before retiring in 2002.

The firm has grown significantly since its move in 1997 to bigger quarters at 100 Western Boulevard in Glastonbury. Fourteen employees made the move in 1997; Bret and John have since added 14 more, bringing the total to 28.

Today, the C. M. Smith Agency continues to be a leader in Connecticut's insurance industry. On the employee benefits side, C. M. Smith clients represent over 50,000 employees and over $400 million in annual premiums. On the retirement planning side, C. M. Smith services over $250 million in assets for clients and their employees.

The agency is more than the collective vision of its three leaders. The associates who have joined C. M. Smith have helped the firm prosper and grow, and embody the principles of business excellence forged by Charlie, Bret and John. The company's current focus is to provide brokerage and consulting services regarding employee benefits, retirement plans, executive benefits, and life and disability insurance with first-class personalized service.

The cornerstone of the firm was created from three words: expertise, integrity and credibility. These simple but powerful words are more than a philosophy: they are the basis for a long-term commitment extended to every C. M. Smith client. This commitment, in turn, has established the agency and its leaders with a sterling reputation in the business community.

With the ongoing challenge of rising health care costs, C. M. Smith can assist in revising medical plans to integrate efficient delivery systems and to optimize financing and cost-sharing. C. M. Smith's expertise extends to group life, disability protection, dental coverage, cafeteria plans, executive benefit plans, tax-sheltered annuities and 401(k) plans.

Whether a corporate client or an individual, each can be assured that they will experience the same professional and detailed attention. All clients have their needs assessed first, to determine their requirements. A plan to best serve the client is then put into action; however, the service does not stop there. The people of C. M. Smith nurture the one-to-one relationship with each client, and are prepared to meet every changing need as it occurs.

C. M. Smith Agency is always mindful of its mission to provide the most individualized customer service, even when that customer is a large company. Satisfied corporate clients include Hartford Hospital; Diageo North America, Inc.; Saint Francis Hospital; Barnes Group Inc.; Ethan Allen Inc.; and Connecticut Children's Medical Center.

The agency is well-suited to assist large employers, as it has established licenses in multiple states. In fact, C. M. Smith holds insurance licenses in 34 states beyond Connecticut, including California, Florida, Massachusetts, New York and Pennsylvania.

Smith, Maffett and O'Connell have dedicated their careers to creating a company that offers not only the best insurance options, but also long-term commitments to the services they provide. Although much in the world has changed since 1974, the C. M. Smith Agency has remained grounded on its foundation of expertise, integrity and credibility.

STANDARD METALS

There are companies in America today who still follow the "American Ideal," a philosophy that has often fallen victim to the world of higher prices and cheaper foreign product. Lost in that has been the notion of creating high-quality, durable products made in American plants and factories. Standard Metals, Inc. (SMI) has bucked the trend of buying foreign over domestic and has proven that there is still success to be experienced by doing just that.

Founded in 1980 by Stephen Buzash, Standard Metals operates as a fully-equipped non-ferrous metal service center supplying high-quality commercial and military niche markets. Buzash, a self-styled "Army brat," grew up around the world, living in places including Japan, Germany, and Formosa (Taiwan). It was always his dream to start his own business. After receiving his engineering degree at the University of Florida, Buzash became an employee of the Olin Corporation, working for the company in its Winchester division, as well as other divisions of the

Steve Buzash alongside a decorative light fixture manufactured using waterjets.

company. While working for Olin, Buzash began to gather skills and knowledge that would lead to realizing his dream. Building on what Buzash calls the "tool kit for success," at Olin he learned about operational and financial planning matters crucial to keeping a company successful and prosperous.

During his time at Olin, Buzash was transferred to the corporation's home building

company in Maryland, where he was placed in charge of 300 employees—allowing him to learn tremendous people skills. This valuable experience taught Buzash what makes for loyal and committed employees. At the same time, Buzash was trying his hand at running one-man businesses such as a storm window hanging business and a small sand casting foundry where he moonlighted making aluminum casting. Each of these experiences went into Buzash's "tool kit for success," giving him all the skills needed for becoming a successful entrepreneur.

In 1977, Buzash became aware that the Standard Foundry Company and its 20,000-square-foot building were up for sale to settle an estate claim. Formed in 1903 by the McDonough family, the Hartford business included a sand casting foundry and a regional distributorship for large aluminum rods, some brass and copper rod, and was a master copper water tube distributor for the state of Connecticut. Buzash bought the business along with a partner. The first part of the business he bought was the 10,000-square-foot sand foundry. Shortly afterward he purchased the building itself with the assistance of the Connecticut Development Authority, which had issued Industrial Revenue Bonds to enable financing the purchase. In 1978, Buzash and his partner bought the last remaining section of the business, including the actual assets of the warehouse.

By 1980, the partners had divided the business, separating the foundry from the metal warehouse. Buzash assumed ownership of the brass distributor side and immediately eliminated the water tube business and began distributing various bronze alloys, including high-quality naval-related alloys. 7,000 square feet of the building were devoted to the Standard Metals warehouse.

Standard Metals began to purchase its first naval-oriented bronze alloys in 1981, effectively moving the company

Standard Metals employees: (standing left to right) Kyle Bishop, Ken Rich, Dennis Clemens, Steve Buzash, Ed Kennelly, Tom Kaczenski; (seated left to right) Rosa Bazzano, Greg Rataic. Not shown: Carol Buzash director/corporate secretary.

One of two major storage areas for storing certified copper alloys for naval use.

from a regional, commercial distributor into supplying the national military market. That same year, Standard Metals formed an affiliate, Specialty Industries, Inc., which became the machining arm for the company, primarily manufacturing bushings from SMI stock for end use by their customers. In 1983 the company created its first quality assur-

Tom Kaczenski (14-year employee) overseeing a cutting job on a horizontal band saw.

Various shapes of heat traceable bar ends.

ance manual, allowing the company to sell heat-traceable alloys to the nation's boatyards—and more specifically to companies such as Electric Boat of Groton, Connecticut, manufacturers of naval submarines.

Standard Metals purchased its first capital equipment in 1984: a saw that could cut through 13-inch material. As business continued to grow, the company added alloys for a larger regional and national customer base, each year adding more and more of the alloys their customers required. From the beginning the company has made it a policy to keep a large inventory on hand for its

customers, which serves to cut competition and gives them the ability to fill customers' product orders immediately, versus depending on mill lead times.

Since the company's beginnings, major changes have occurred in the way it does business. It has progressed from manual purchase orders and product inventory books to a state-of-the-art computer system. Before, taking an inventory of the company's product could take weeks. Now, with inventory software programs, managers know at any given moment exactly what is housed in the warehouse.

Standard Metals has also experienced drastic rises in labor costs, but has seen its profits rise eightfold—no minor feat for a small business. Buzash credits the company's success to the amazing teamwork of his staff of nine employees, many of whom have been with Standard Metals since it began. Ed Kennelly serves as the company's vice president, and was the first person to be hired by Buzash back in 1977. Dennis Clemens was hired shortly after that and is currently the company's quality manager. Greg Rataic, the company's sales manager, has been with the company for 21 years.

The loyalty of employees such as Kennelly, Clemens, and Rataic is a testament to the way Standard Metals treats its staff. Training each of his employees to be his or her own general manager, Buzash stresses that bestowing confidence, trust, and responsibility in a person makes them more productive, loyal, and trusting in the process. It also assures the employee that he or she will always be treated as part of the team. Buzash reinforces his commitment by offering his employees a profit-sharing plan in the business. In addition, once year-end profits have been tallied, Buzash distributes a part of those profits as bonuses to his workers. Such practices reinforce a sense of responsibility in the company's employees, Buzash feels, making

Ed Kennelly, Steve Buzash, Dennis Clemens: 82 years of combined knowledge.

mestic suppliers. And, to make sure he won't let his customers down, he has gone one step further. Stephen is very concerned that America is losing its industrial base. He makes a point to buy domestic, including when it comes to purchasing company vehicles.

Standard Metals went to People's Bank, with whom they have shared a long relationship, and secured a major loan. Buzash used the funds to buy up all the alloy stock he could find at a mill exiting the product line in order to prevent a shortage for his customers. Taking this action was the result of years of experience and knowledge, which Buzash again credits to his "tool kit." Buzash's foresight also gave his company a leg up on the competition.

When he noticed that submarine construction was dropping from a high annual count of six per year—finally down to one submarine a year—Buzash's knowledge and experience again served him well. To counteract the drop in demand for alloys from the naval builders, Buzash introduced value-added processes to the company early in its history. They began turning and milling in 1982, and then took a major step in 1999 by adding sophisticated precision metal-cutting

Quality Assurance Manager, Dennis Clemens checking machined parts during final inspection.

clear that if everyone has done their share and revenues are high, they will all reap the reward.

Another area to which Buzash and his company have a strong commitment is buying and selling domestic product: 99 percent of product bought by the company is domestic. This commitment has proved to be challenging, but Buzash believes it is central to the company's continuing success. Standard Metals has seen many of its suppliers of forged and extruded materials fold under the pressure of having to compete with cheaper, foreign-made product. Concerned that there was a potential for being left short of products that his customers needed, Buzash cultivated strong relationships with other do-

waterjet equipment, which immediately brought sales up. Standard Metals is now one of fewer than 10 percent of companies in the business which offers waterjetting. Facilitating plate cutting and shape cutting, the waterjet can hold relatively tight tolerances with significant precision. The machining has also made it possible for the company to sell custom-cut products as part of its service, moving beyond the simple sale of a sheet of metal and into specifically cut pieces, which can measure several inches thick. In 2000, the company added a second water jet machine capable of making precise cuts in up to eight-inch thick steel plates, as long as six feet by 12 feet.

Inside sales "nerve center" (left to right) Greg Rataic, Ed Kennelly, Dennis Clemens and Steve Buzash.

well as bridge cranes and forklifts. Its most recent entry into the market place is QQN 286G.

Specializing in niche markets such as alloys for military applications and waterjet cutting are two of the reasons why Standard Metals continues to grow in today's sluggish economy. The other secrets of the company's success are its president and founder, Steve Buzash, and the invaluable teamwork of the company's loyal and devoted employees.

One hundred and thirty years of experience waiting to serve you.

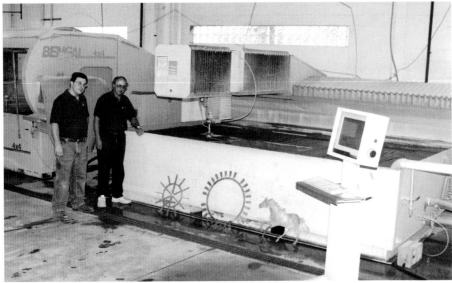

Six foot by twelve foot water jets in operation.

Today Standard Metals carries one of the largest selections of domestic "red metals" in the country, which includes brass, bronze, and copper, as well as 12 different Ampco-type specialty alloys. The company's military line includes copper-nickel (C715, C706), nickel aluminum-bronze (C630, C632), bronze (C903, C922, C934) as well as Monel equivalent NO4400 (nickel copper) alloys, which are often used for marine applications because of their resistance to the corrosive effects of saltwater.

As of 2003, the company uses a variety of processing equipment including two milling machines, three hand lathes, three vertical saws, a horizontal saw, two cut-off saws, and a Mazak CNC turning center, as

TANKWORKS REMOVAL AND REPLACEMENT, LLC
TEDDY'S OIL & ENERGY, LLC

Vision, integrity and an entrepreneurial spirit build companies, industries and prominence. Spotting a business niche that needs filling is the beginning of success stories such as Tankworks Removal and Replacement. In less than 10 years, it has grown to become the leading company many Connecticut homeowners and businesses turn to for meeting needs they didn't know they had.

Tankworks removes and replaces underground fuel tanks and cleans up oil contaminated soil. Many existing tanks date to the building boom that took place in the 20 years after World War II. Space restraints and fuel needs led to burying oil storage tanks outside. Having been in the ground for four decades or more, these tanks have begun to leak, a condition that has led to liability for property owners under state and, in some cases, federal rules.

A wave of installations came in the 1970s, when some homeowners fought widely fluctuating oil prices by putting in larger tanks underground.

Rose Viola Rainville, owner and founder of Tankworks, had to deal personally with the problem in the early 1990s.

A real estate agent since 1979, Rose Viola purchased an investment property in 1982. In 1910 it had been the site of a Tydol gas station. Later, it was a six-family apartment building. Rose wasn't aware that there were

Forming a full-service heating oil company was a natural expansion for the tank removal business.

Since June 1994 Tankworks has handled thousands of tank projects throughout Connecticut and bordering towns in New York.

six empty gas storage tanks buried there.

Pipes attached to these tanks came to light when the garden area was cleared and Rose realized she had work to do. Environmental concerns were becoming stronger, and she knew from transactions she'd been brokering that these were impinging on real estate deals, in some cases delaying—or even blocking—sales and refinancing.

"Local lenders were making removal of tanks a mortgage condition," she recalls.

In 1993 she hired an engineering firm to do an environmental study on her property. The assigned engineer, Kevin Rainville—her future husband—advised her as she conducted the tank removal.

Rose found there was no company that removed residential and small commercial tanks. "People did parts of it, but there are 30 to 40 steps to accomplish—from filling out forms, to removing and disposing of the tanks, cleaning up and installing a replacement if needed. No one did it all. I saw a whole niche where no one was working," she says.

Rose, entering what most would consider a man's business, moved to fill that niche. Initially, she and a project manager set out to educate potential clients about the risks and the need to remove old tanks. This included presenting seminars on tank regulations and deadlines for Realtors, bankers and attorneys.

"We told people that these tanks weren't meant to last forever. In fact, they had life expectancies of 15 to 25 years and many had been in the ground 50 years or more.

"We helped get people used to the idea that they had to do something about them."

In its first year, Tankworks pulled some 50 tanks. The challenge became keeping up with demand while maintaining high standards of service and top quality workmanship.

To spread the word about Tankworks, Rose drew on her real estate experience. In addition to advertising statewide and through billboards on buses, Tankworks put up yard signs at work sites. These signs led to the company working two-dozen or more homes on some streets.

Today, the company performs hundreds of tank projects a year.

The urgency of the need for Tankworks' services was revealed in its first year. That pressure came from the banks that didn't want their mortgage borrowers to inherit environmental problems.

"Home buyers are simply not willing to inherit a tank," says Rose.

A federal law was implemented in 1988 requiring all regulated tanks of more than 2,100 gallons to be removed or upgraded by December 1998. In general, the Federal Environmental Protection Agency concentrates on larger commercial tanks, leaving the regulation of smaller underground tanks to the states, which

Located in a former Packard automotive dealership Tankworks & Teddy's Oil enjoy the benefits of sharing customers.

second complementary venture. Kevin runs Teddy's Oil and Energy LLC, which distributes heating oil to 28 towns in the Greater Hartford area alone, along with the installation of new boilers, furnaces and central air conditioning.

Tankworks' employees figured in the decision to establish the new firm, Rose says. "They'd been after me to buy an oil delivery truck. Finally, they convinced me."

The new business is operating to the same standards as Tankworks.

"Honesty, integrity and one-stop service are what make us successful," says Rose. "We grew because we do what we say we will, and use the best materials. If you own a business, you have to stand behind your work and never cut corners.

"Teddy's is growing rapidly, but on the same basis. People understand that they are two companies, but one family you can count on."

Countless referrals are generated from the lawn signs throughout its service area.

This 1,000-gallon underground oil tank was in service since the 1930s when the property owner converted from coal to heating oil.

in many cases left the problem to the cities. In Connecticut the Department of Environmental Protection set criteria, and specific rules varied from town to town.

Insurance companies also applied pressure. In July 2002 some began demanding that tanks be removed before they would renew policies.

"The older the tank, the more likely it is to leak," says Rose. "Probably 85 percent of those 45 or more years old are leaking."

"The thing that causes leaks in tanks is Mother Nature. The old tanks had given excellent value for their cost—every penny's worth—but it's time to replace them. Plus technology has changed. Today, tanks are filled at a rate of 70 gallons a minute, and that's a lot of pressure."

In 2000 the Rainvilles, who have two children—Lily, 6 years old, and Teddy, 4—set up a

THERMODYNETICS, INC.

The founding of Thermodynetics, Inc. proves that necessity is not the only mother of invention—sometimes the best inventions happen through a plain and simple mistake.

It was a twist of fate in 1966 when a metal tube was placed in a lathe, the wrong controls activated, and the tube formed a distorted, fluted shape in an Oklahoma manufacturing plant. That mishap led to a patent being secured and the process was purchased and perfected by Massachusetts' Waltham Industries in 1969. Waltham saw the potential that this approach offered and invested several million dollars to form a new division of the company called Turbotec, Inc. in South Windsor, Connecticut.

The company worked hard to improve the process and the machinery to create the product. However, in the first two years of business, Turbotec was limited to applications that were mostly decorative, creating table legs, lamp bases, hat racks and depart-

Headquarters of Thermodynetics, Inc. and the principal manufacturing facility for Turbotec Products, Inc. with 55,000 square feet.

ment store displays. As a result, the new division generated only $50,000 in aggregate sales.

Waltham Industries was overextended in several areas and was forced into bankruptcy. In 1972 at an IRS auction, Robert Perkins, a New York consultant, purchased what remained of Turbotec, including machinery, equipment, patents and files. Perkins recognized the opportunity the process held and formed Spiral Tubing Corporation (STC) with just four employees.

Perkins' timing was fortunate, because in 1973, the Arab Oil Embargo resulted in a growing need for unique tubing, as the cost of energy was becoming an important factor. The applications quickly broadened from ornamental to utilitarian when the fluted tubing became instrumental in manufacturing tankless water heaters for residential furnaces, plumbing connectors, marine engine oil coolers, and even heat exchangers for blood oxygenators used for open-heart surgery.

By 1975 Spiral Tubing sales had reached $200,000 annually. Perkins continued to have vision for the company, and determined

that through further financial support, the type of growth he forecasted was certain.

In 1976 Perkins sold the company to Stampede Energy Corporation. A new, forward-thinking management team was hired to make the acquisition not just seamless, but profitable. Industry consultants Robert Lerman and John Ferraro were contracted to assist in managing the company's operations.

Spiral Tubing was positioned for growth. The company, which originally was housed in 8,000 square feet in New Britain, Connecticut, quickly doubled its space requirements. In 1978, Turbotec Products, Inc. was formed as a wholly owned subsidiary of Spiral Tubing, and Lerman and Ferraro joined the company in a permanent capacity as treasurer and secretary, respectively. Also in '78, the company sold its first coaxial condensers to the heat pump industry and expanded the applications of its tubing into new exchangers for the biomedical industry and bendable connectors for plumbing applications.

Establishing Turbotec was a progressive step for the company. It was created to work

A variety of tubing and tubing assemblies produced by Turbotec Products.

with customers in the effort to improve the use and efficiencies of thermal energy in a wide variety of applications.

Growth was rapid in terms of plant size, product offerings and sales. In 1981 Spiral Tubing Corporation merged into Thermodynetics, Inc. The company conducted an initial public offering (TDYN) on July 16, 1981. The $3.3 million raised allowed the company to construct a 40,000-square-foot facility in Windsor, Connecticut.

In just 12 years, the company had evolved from a small manufacturer of decorative items, to producing applications for the tubing, which included condensers and evaporators for water source heat pumps in addition to a variety of other heat-exchange applications including heat recovery and refrigeration.

The early 1980s brought great success for the young company. With revenues in the range of $3 million in 1984, a second public offering was held. The company used the $4.125 million raised to pay down debt, buy out holdings of Stampede Energy and explore new possibilities. The funding allowed Turbotec, the operating division, to grow its engineering and sales capabilities. The company began to offer tubing and tubing assemblies.

The early '80s also brought new opportunity: Thermodynetics acquired National Energy Savers Products, Inc.—a St. Petersburg, Florida, company that manufactured small residential and commercial heat recovery systems. Thermodynetics began to build large-scale heat reclaimers for residential and commercial use, which led to sales of large-scale heat recovery units for food processing plants and resort communities. The operations of National Energy Savers Products were eventually merged into the company's Windsor facility. With this acquisition, the company grew to revenues of $5 million by 1986.

Due to high standards and excellent customer service the company continued to progress despite the turbulent economic climate of the early 1990s. Thermodynetics moved forward, expanding its product line to offer refrigeration, heating, air conditioning, swimming pool heat pumps, plumbing connectors, marine air conditioning, soft drink dispensers, ice-making machines, aerospace and biomedical equipment, as well as energy conservation approaches.

The company was growing and a second manufacturing building, housing 28,700 additional square feet, was added to the main facility in 1991. The mid 1990s saw more growth for the business and revenues increased into the $6 million range.

Thermodynetics remained on the cutting edge of technology. But the 1990s brought with it a change in corporate culture. While many in manufacturing resisted the shift, the company embraced the new ideals. Total quality management was introduced and every employee became part of the team. Instead of seeing the company's mission statement as only valuable to upper management, all employees were included in the vision and guiding statement for Thermodynetics. As a direct result, a significant revenue increase occurred during the next few years.

In another industry-leading move, Turbotec made the conversion to cellular manufacturing and demand flow scheduling in 1999. These management tools created greater operational efficiencies and increased productivity for the company.

With a new millennium, Thermodynetics put maximum effort into not just keeping up with the industry, but setting the pace. In August 2003 the company purchased Vulcan Industries, Inc. of Sturgis, Michigan. Vulcan manufactures metal tubing assemblies for the automotive, appliance, and furniture industries in quantities into the millions. By combining Vulcan with Turbotec, a unique opportunity arose as they began to share resources and technical knowledge.

With a specialization in automotive-quality stainless steel tubing assemblies, Vulcan primarily serves as the sole source to its consumers in automotive manufacturing.

With this focus and state-of-the-art production, Turbotec is poised to expand its sales activities. In turn, Turbotec's stellar reputation and quality products will serve Vulcan's sales potential.

With the failure of the dot-com industry and the very real impact of terrorism, the early years of the 21st century presented their own unique problems. However, in 2000 the company invested in an upgraded computer system, which allowed for a fully integrated information-processing platform. The new system provided real-time data to better manage the reporting and control systems of the company.

In 2001 a 15,000-square-foot addition to the 40,000-square-foot main building was completed. This new structure allowed for Turbotec's manufacturing operations to be consolidated under one roof.

Today Turbotec's products are sold nationwide, as well as in Canada, Europe, Asia and Australia. The fluted tubes—usually made of copper, copper-based alloys, carbon and stainless steels and aluminum—are especially suited for flexible, space-saving and energy-efficient uses. The tubing offers dramatic increases in heat-transfer efficiency, providing up to four times the efficiencies of smooth tubing.

Thermodynetics, under the presidency of Robert Lerman, continues to call Windsor, Connecticut—the state's first town—its home. Keith Briggs serves as general manager of Vulcan and Robert Lieberman is president of both Vulcan and Turbotec.

The company contributes to the town's economic viability with its solid reputation in manufacturing and sales, as well as serving as a place of employment to many residents. The company currently provides many jobs and hopes to expand staffing in the near future.

Over the years, the company has maintained the goal to provide the best product with the best customer service possible. It is for this reason that Thermodynetics has established and maintained professional relationships with many clients for 10 and 15 years.

What was once considered by some to be an accident created more than three decades of success, numerous satisfied customers and millions in sales for Connecticut's Thermodynetics. The company has remained a leader through changing times by constantly building on the desire to innovate.

Thermodynetics, Inc.'s 28,700-square-foot manufacturing facility built for Turbotec Products.

HARVEY & LEWIS OPTICIANS

Harvey & Lewis Opticians is one of Hartford's oldest retail companies, and the first optical business, to be located in the city. James Lewis, the current president of the company and the great grandson of one of the company's founders, represents the fourth generation of Lewises to lead the company. Harvey and Lewis Opticians comprises a main Hartford store in addition to six other branches in central Connecticut.

The founders of the business, Foster Harvey and Robert Harris Lewis, both worked in retail as young men and then decided to specialize in optics. They opened for business at 11 Asylum Street in Hartford on Feb-

The Harvey & Lewis Building.

STORE & OFFICE BUILDING
FOR
the HARVEY & LEWIS CO.

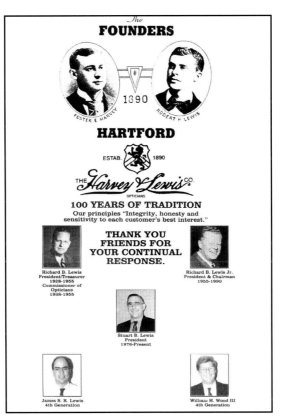

The Family.

ruary 24, 1890. Their first store offered eyeglasses and over the early years expanded to include cameras, watch repair, greeting cards, weather instruments, microscopes and telescopes. The two associates decided in 1920 to divide the company. Lewis kept the New Britain and Hartford stores, and Harvey kept the stores in Springfield and Worcester, Massachusetts—and Bridgeport and New Haven, Connecticut.

The Harvey & Lewis Building was built by Robert Harris Lewis in 1927 and was located on the corner of State and Main Streets where the Pavilion at State House Square now stands. Throughout the years, the main Harvey & Lewis store in Hartford has remained within a block of the original storefront. Lewis was well known for real estate development in Hartford. He built the City Club, a men's social club that is now a hotel, and Westerly Terrace, a residential area. Lewis's second wife, Lista Lincoln Jarvis, generously donated the Lincoln Theater to the University of Hartford's Hartt School of Music.

After Robert Harris Lewis died of pneumonia in 1927, his son Richard B. Lewis, Sr.,

took over Harvey & Lewis. Very prominent locally, he served as commissioner of opticians under four governors. After his death in 1955, his son Richard B. Lewis, Jr., became the company's president. He had served in the Pacific in World War II with Hartford's Battery B.

The Hartford store received national attention in the mid 1950s, when artist Norman Rockwell chose it as the setting for a painting that was printed on the May 19, 1956, cover of the *Saturday Evening Post.* Variously titled "The Optometrist," "The Oculist" or "New Glasses," the painting depicts a young boy being fitted for eyeglasses. Rockwell came from his residence in Stockbridge, Massachusetts, to sketch, while one of the opticians and a young customer sat in the store as the models.

Richard B. Lewis, Jr., retired as president in 1976, and his first cousin, Stuart B. Lewis, became president. Stuart had been with the company since 1962, after completing duty as an officer in the U.S. Air Force. He served on the board of Business For Downtown Hartford and as president of the Contact Lens Society. He retired in 2000 turning Harvey & Lewis over to his son, James.

There have been modifications throughout the years as the Lewises have guided the company through a changing economy and business world. However, according to Stuart Lewis, the business's core values, integrity and honesty, have endured through the generations. Harvey & Lewis Opticians consistently strives to demonstrate a commitment to good products, honest service, value and community involvement. Stuart is proud that Harvey & Lewis has provided "a good living for good people" as well as "the best product for the medical needs of the customers."

Many people still expect personalized service. Harvey & Lewis's ability to meet that expectation is what influences its success as a company. This small, family-run business has thrived over the past 113 years with its combination of old-fashioned values, expertise and quality products.

TRINITY COLLEGE

Historic Beginnings: Trinity College was only the second college in Connecticut when it was founded by Episcopalian ministers in the spring of 1823 as Washington College (the name was changed in 1845). When the inaugural semester got under way the following fall, classes were held in a church basement and students lived in rented rooms in a private home. Today, partly because the College's very conception symbolized the end of a statewide Congregationalist monopoly in higher education, Trinity's charter prohibits religious standards from being imposed upon any student, faculty member, or other member of the College community.

A year after opening, Trinity moved to its first campus, which consisted of two Greek Revival-style buildings, one housing a chapel, library, and lecture rooms, and the other a dormitory. Within a few years the student body grew to nearly 100, a size that was rarely exceeded until the 20th century. In 1872 an important step toward the future was taken when the trustees sold the "College Hill" campus to the City of Hartford as the site for a new State Capitol. Six years later, the College moved to its present location.

Trinity College, circa, 1895.

Bordered on the west by a tree-lined bluff, and by gently rolling fields to the east, the new site was known in the 18th century as Gallows Hill because local legend suggests that several Tories were hanged here during the Revolution. The buildings surrounding the main quad, designed by noted English architect William Burges, are generally viewed as America's earliest examples of "collegiate Gothic" architecture. Together with the imposing Gothic chapel completed in 1932, they are a compelling reminder of the medieval origins of collegiate institutions.

Changing with the Times: The Trustees voted to admit women as undergraduates for the first time in the College's history in 1969. In September 1984 Trinity passed a milestone when it enrolled the first freshman class in its history in which women outnumbered men. Coincident with these developments, the College has acted to increase the number of black and other minority students on campus, as well as women and minority group members on the faculty and in the administration.

In 1995 the College began to devote increased attention to the needs of the surrounding neighborhoods, which are troubled by many of the social and economic problems common to American cities. Central to that initiative is the "Learning Corridor," which includes a public, Montessori-style elementary school, a neighborhood middle school, a math, science, and art high school resource center to serve suburban as well as Hartford students and teachers, a center for families and child care, the first Boys & Girls Club in the country to be located at a college, and a health and technology center. Trinity students and faculty have numerous opportunities to engage in volunteer work, internships, and research projects in conjunction with these institutions and other elements of the neighborhood initiative.

A group of students in an art class with Associate Professor of Fine Arts, Pablo Delano.

A Quality Liberal Arts Education: Amid continuing change, Trinity's commitment to liberal education remains steadfast. The College is consistently ranked among the top liberal arts colleges in the nation. As a residential college situated on the historic 100-acre campus in Connecticut's capital, Trinity offers extensive opportunities for combining classroom instruction with experiential learning in the city. Its rigorous curriculum includes the traditional liberal arts disciplines as well as outstanding science, engineering and interdisciplinary programs.

The heart of Trinity's educational excellence is the personal encounter between professor and student. With a 9:1 student–faculty ratio, this intellectual partnership opens a world of ideas and launches a lifelong pursuit of knowledge. With 37 established majors and 970 courses, as well as an array of special curricular options, students explore many different paths to self-discovery. They are challenged to think critically and creatively, and learn to develop effective communication and argumentation skills.

Making New Connections: Beyond its traditional strengths in the arts and the humanities, Trinity engages students in ongoing conversations through innovative academic programs like Human Rights, InterArts, Interdisciplinary Science, and the Tutorial College—"a college within a

Above: *The Downes Memorial Clock Tower on campus.*

Below: *Associate Professor of Physics Barbara Walden and students conduct an experiment in a class on electricity and magnetism.*

college"—where students and faculty from multiple disciplines explore the world from varying perspectives. Two-thirds of the students take advantage of Trinity's urban connections and extensive internship opportunities in government and nonprofit organizations, in global businesses and media companies. More than half study abroad—on Trinity's campus in Rome; at one of the College's seven global learning sites, including Barcelona, Cape Town and Moscow; or through other exchange programs around the world.

Trinity's 2,000 students come from 46 states and 35 countries, and quickly become part of the diverse campus community. They benefit from a wealth of extracurricular offerings, including critically acclaimed films, plays and concerts, as well as lectures by internationally known speakers. Students also participate in cultural and community outreach activities, and learn to celebrate differences. Trinity is the place where students can discover who they are and who they want to become.

For more information about Trinity College, visit the website: www.trincoll.edu.

VISUAL TECHNOLOGIES, INC.

The history of Visual Technologies, Inc. is a story of independent and revolutionary thinking. Not unlike the idealistic and adventurous Marquis de Lafayette, whose bronze statue in Hartford is located just down the block from Visual Technologies, this young technology company has defined the leading edge in software development, web development, office networking, and IT consulting and contracting. From its inception in 1995, Visual Technologies has forged its own path in business and the technology field, taking part in the revitalization of Hartford along the way.

Visual Technologies was founded by partners Richard L. Huebner and Gregory J. Smith, who serve as president and vice president respectively. A graduate of Lehigh University, Huebner has extensive experience in computer technology consulting and software development. He met Smith, a graduate of Pennsylvania State University, at Vantage Computer Systems in Connecticut, where both worked in research and development. Huebner and Smith started

Statue of the Marquis de Lafayette, the French nobleman and general who fought alongside the Americans in the Revolutionary War. The statue stands just down the block from Visual Technologies.

Visual Technologies in May 1995. The privately held company originally started out in information technology (IT) consulting and developed a reputation for forward thinking and sound project management that saved its clients time and money.

Since its formation Visual Technologies has continued to build on its reputation, offering services such as developing business and e-commerce websites, building customized software applications, designing surround solutions to legacy systems, setting up office networking systems, integrating wireless technology systems, implementing Virtual Private Networks, placing IT consultant and contractor resources, consulting on graphic design needs, and providing strategic IT direction for organizational development.

The company's phenomenal growth in recent years can be attributed to its revolutionary approach to information technology projects known as Total Project Delivery. In the early years of the company, Huebner and Smith made several observations that inspired this new approach. They noted that it was often better if clients did not hire or contract full-time staff to complete IT projects, because it is often difficult to adequately and efficiently staff an IT project's fluctuating workload. Huebner and Smith also noticed that a single person might not have the various skills needed to handle responsibilities ranging from very simple IT

Visual Technologies' co-founders Gregory J. Smith (center left) and Richard L. Huebner (center right) are congratulated for their company's expansion in Hartford's Frog Hollow neighborhood by Hartford Mayor Eddie Perez (left) and Harry Freeman (right), executive director of the Hartford Economic Development Commission. Visual Technologies celebrated its expansion into a second building on Grand Street with a ribbon-cutting ceremony on January 7, 2003.

duties to complex tasks suited to the most experienced professionals. These observations inspired Visual Technologies' approach to IT services— Total Project Delivery.

Under the Total Project Delivery approach, a client contracts with Visual Technologies, not with individuals, therefore allowing the client to complete projects more efficiently. Visual Technologies assigns its own IT staff and facilities to provide the services needed to complete each project, assigning resources to a project when they are needed most, but also matching programmers' skills, experience, and expertise to the various tasks as needed. Visual Technologies manages each project from design and development through implementation. Clients don't have to hire extra staff for workload spikes or keep people busy during down time, freeing them up to focus on core competencies.

Total Project Delivery also structures IT projects in a way that helps companies

A network administrator at Visual Technologies inspects and configures hardware for a client.

manage expectations and project scope. Frequently, IT projects take longer and exceed budget, because new requirements are added as projects progress. Rather than just accepting or ignoring these overruns, Visual Technologies' project methodology enforces proactive management of new requirements and project scope changes to clearly present value and impact. As new requirements are documented and existing requirements are changed, Visual Technologies with Total Project Delivery resets expectations within the company to assure project completion and project deliverables are known and accepted.

While Total Project Delivery has independently been a success for clients, Visual Technologies further enhances software development projects with its suite of reusable and scalable components. Reuse of software components helps control costs and minimizes risk of project scope increase by providing a significant jump start for new software development. Visual Technologies has found a unique way to package components resulting from Total Project Delivery—Corporate Data Integration or "CoDI" for short. CoDI is a bundle of software components, tools, and business modules developed by Visual Technologies that fosters reuse of a company's existing software assets, even legacy systems, by enabling disparate systems and disconnected data sources to operate as a unified system. Companies who utilize CoDI have realized better customer service systems, decreased time to market, and improved business operations.

The successes of Total Project Delivery and CoDI have not only driven Visual Technologies' growth, but also its ability to fulfill its mission: to provide clients with cost effective, leading-edge technological solutions to business challenges. The company's diverse clientele includes Pfizer's international operations; Principal Financial Group headquartered in Des Moines, Iowa; Travelers Life and Annuity and Aetna in Hartford; and several small to medium-sized businesses in Greater Hartford and across Connecticut.

Visual Technologies has criss-crossed the country serving these clients, but it has been its location in Hartford, Connecticut, that has established the technology firm. Visual Technologies credits its 1999 move from Portland, Connecticut, to Oak Street in Hartford as a major part of its success. Moving from the suburbs into the city was part of a successful strategic plan to expand business lines and offer competitive technology services.

The company initially renovated a circa 1900 brick and brownstone building on Oak Street in Hartford to meet the 21st-century technology needs of its clients. The building was updated to include amenities not previously found in the area, such as a hi-tech conference room, Internet and network connectivity via DSL and T1 line data ports, and a fiber optic backbone. At that same time the seeds of a major citywide revitalization were just beginning.

Visual Technologies continued to develop and grow, and after just a few years the company was bursting at the seams of the Oak Street building. In the spring of 2002 the company decided to expand its roots in Hartford by buying and beginning renovation on a building on Grand Street. This building dates back to the 1950s and is located on an adjacent side of the same city block as the Oak Street office. (The company operates a third office in New York City in order to make networking services staff more conveniently available to clients in that area.) The company currently employs about 40 people.

While Visual Technologies' growth has been good news for the company founders, employees and clients, its expansion in Hartford is also great news for the city. Hartford Mayor Eddie A. Perez has formally recognized Visual Technologies as one of Hartford's "Rising Star" companies and was on hand to dedicate the opening of the Grand Street building on January 7, 2003, also known as "Visual Technologies Day" in Hartford. City officials believe Visual Technologies' expansion contributes to the revitalization efforts in Hartford and is attracting other companies to the area.

Software developers and a business analyst at Visual Technologies consult about the design of a client's web-based software system.

CANTOR COLBURN, LLP

Law firm Cantor Colburn, LLP, intellectual property attorneys, is in the business of protecting its clients' creativity. Safeguarding ingenuity can be demanding, considering a client's expertise can be anything from biotechnology to toys. But the growing, Connecticut-based company is more than meeting the challenge.

Cantor Colburn, whose main office is just eight miles from downtown Hartford, covers all aspects of intellectual property law, the law of intangibles. It specializes in patent, trademark, copyright, unfair competition, computer, trade secret and related licensing and litigation.

Cantor Colburn was founded in 1963 as a two-partner law firm, Fishman & Van Kirk. Partner Dave Fishman was also a professor at the University of Connecticut, where he taught Patent Law. It was there he met ambitious student Michael Cantor, who had already earned his bachelor of science degree with honors in chemical engineering and materials engineering from the University of Connecticut. He received his law degree from the same university in 1983. When Professor Dave Fishman invited him to join the established Connecticut-based firm, it was only natural that Cantor would say "yes."

By then, Van Kirk had left the firm, another partner had joined and the firm was renamed Fishman & Dionne. In 1988 Cantor became a partner and his name was added to the title. Fishman retired in 1997. Just two years later, Dionne moved to another firm, and Philmore H. Colburn II made partner, creating Cantor Colburn.

Phil Colburn's credentials were as impressive as Cantor's. Colburn graduated with honors with an electrical engineering degree from Northeastern University. He received his law degree in 1991 from the Western New England College School of Law. With a design engineering background, Colburn practiced in the areas of digital design, software, control systems and optical communication.

In addition to sharing Cantor's strong and diverse background, Colburn also shared his philosophy. "We wanted to stay on the cutting edge of intellectual properties, but we also wanted to maintain our boutique status," says Cantor. In order to accomplish this, they refused to join with a larger, general practice law firm—a temptation for other small patent law offices. Instead, they decided to hire lawyers who had strong technical and engineering backgrounds for Cantor Colburn's growing intellectual properties practice. "We hired highly skilled specialists who also managed to get law degrees," quips Cantor.

Multiple academic degrees in varied back-

Michael A. Cantor on the left and Philmore H. Colburn II.

grounds seem to be the norm at Cantor Colburn. After all, if a biologist wants to protect his latest find, it is important that his attorney knows something about biology; better still if he has a degree in it. Cantor Colburn meets its clients' demands by hiring attorneys as diverse as the clients: their staff consists of mechanical engineers, electrical engineers, software specialists, chemists and biologists. These expert attorneys have grown from a mere 10 in 1999 to approximately 50. The firm boasts 100 employees including partners, associates, patent agents and administrative assistants.

But growth, especially this quickly, does not come without growing pains. With the technology boom in the 1990s came the greater need for intellectual property attorneys. Cantor Colburn had to stay on the move to keep up with the expanding number and pressing needs of their clients. This sudden hiring demand meant an instant requirement for more capital. Cantor recalls a time in late 1999 when he made a memorable phone call to his wife Shari to empty out the savings accounts. Colburn took similar measures, and the company survived the frenetic transition from small patent office to a tightly run, full-service boutique.

Cantor Colburn headquarters.

The partners of Cantor Colburn, LLP, from left to right: Michael A. Cantor; Philmore H. Colburn II; Leah M. Reimer, Ph.D.; Michael J. Rye; David A. Fox; Pamela J. Curbelo; Keith J. Murphy and William J. Cass.

Not only do clients benefit from the creative and diversified atmosphere at Cantor Colburn, so do employees. New recruits are ready to join the firm, with flex hours, part-time opportunities and the ability to work from home being some of the incentives. One of Cantor Colburn's valued partners, Leah Reimer, takes full advantage of her flex schedule: "I'm still in my PJs and it's almost noon!" This accomplished attorney, who earned a Ph.D. with honors in organic chemistry from Stanford University, works diligently, but on her own schedule. "I'll drop my daughter off at soccer practice, and then I'll come home and work for the rest of the afternoon."

Reimer fits in nicely with Cantor Colburn's philosophy of balance between work and family. "It might sound cliché, but we really are a family-friendly firm," says Colburn, who has three young children. Cantor has four.

Even with this healthy balance of home and office life, employees find opportunities to give back to the community. Several employees, for example, participate as judges for the annual science fair, the Connecticut Invention Convention, which encourages submissions from elementary to high school students.

Cantor himself is an adjunct professor at the University of Connecticut—where he was first noticed by Fishman years ago. He gives back to that same institution by teaching classes in Patent Law. But it is a mutually beneficial arrangement: this is where he found Leah Reimer and other outstanding students, whom he has subsequently hired to join the firm.

Cantor Colburn's impressive client roster ranges from IBM to Denmark-based LEGO Toy Company. With technology and the ease of Internet communication, the company could be based anywhere. Why does Cantor choose to stay in rural Bloomfield, Connecticut? "The cost of living is lower here, and that savings is reflected to our clients. Plus, it's just a really great place to live with a great quality of life."

Headquarters at 55 Griffin Road, South Bloomfield, Connecticut.

J. F. FREDERICKS TOOL COMPANY

J. F. Fredericks Tool Company of Farmington, Connecticut has been in operation for over 50 years. Joe Fredericks started his tool and machine shop out of a two-car garage in 1951; today it manufactures components used by companies in Europe and Asia as well as the United States. J. F. Fredericks Tool is known as one of the most technically advanced facilities in the world, with clients in aerospace, medical and commercial fields.

When Joe Fredericks started his tool company, it was not his first venture into running his own business. He preferred working for himself and tried several times in his early years, sometimes even with partners, to build his own business. Joe was strong-willed and a hard worker, but over the years he grew ill and was exhausted from his efforts. In 1948 he had a nervous breakdown. Three years later, at the age of 41, he tried again with J. F. Fredericks Tool Company. His primary client was Pratt & Whitney, a large aerospace company with headquarters in the neighboring town of Hartford. He started out with simple manual machines, making tools and gauges that were used in the building of jet engines.

His son Roger Fredericks, now chairman of the board, worked in the shop and helped his father nights and weekends while attending high school. Cleaning the toilets,

Founder of J. F. Fredericks Tool Company, Joe F. Fredericks.

sweeping the floor and cleaning machines were his initial duties. After high school and serving in the Army, Roger came to work for his father full time. He served an apprenticeship and had the wonderful opportunity of learning a great deal from an older retired man his father had hired. His mentor knew a great deal about tool and diemaking and took Roger under his wing.

Through the years, technology in the tool and machinery fields has made vast improvements. Roger Fredericks has always been on the leading edge when it comes to research-

ing and learning about new equipment. As the company grew, so did the new technology and machinery they used. Roger was running the business by the mid-1960s, about 10 years before his father retired in the late '70s.

Roger transitioned the company from all tooling to manufacturing component parts. In the late '70s a new machine called Computerized Numerical Control (CNC) was available for manufacturing component parts. J. F. Fredericks Tool Company was one of the first to buy this equipment. Each year technology enhancements created faster controls, improved memory and higher quality, they are at the forefront in learning and utilizing this new machinery.

Today J. F. Fredericks owns three of the five 8-axis CNC mill/turn centers in the United States, enabling them to manufacture specialized components faster, with even more precision, and at competitive prices. Using this machine means only one setup and one process for what can potentially be a 16-process job.

J. F. Fredericks also creates prototypes for their clients. Most parts are made from exotic materials such as titanium, nickel and cobalt. Among the components they manufacture are those utilized in fuel systems, surgical applications, electronics, industrial air conditioning units and machinery used in oil exploration. They also support their customers' engineering staffs, offering their expertise and assist in designing components or prototypes.

In 1998 Roger approached David Derynoski, a man he had known in the business for over 25 years. He convinced David to join J. F. Fredericks Tool. As president of the company, David has made tremendous strides in broadening the customer base to international markets.

More than 50 percent of their business is in the international marketplace. Volvo Aerospace of Sweden says, "J. F. Fredericks Tool Company has the best quality, and has the most technically advanced facility of any vendor that we deal with." There may be other companies that can do what J. F. Fredericks does, but Fredericks works on higher levels. They have an excellent reputation in the industry for manufacturing numerous complex parts correctly, on time and at a competitive cost. "People in the industry know

Eight Axis TMA-8 mill-turn center.

Chairman Roger Frederick.

Five Axis, 40 pallet, 240 tool Horizontal machining center.

our capabilities, performance and quality," says David Derynoski. "Word-of-mouth gets our name out, and clients come to us."

Besides having the most sophisticated equipment, J. F. Fredericks has a staff that both David Derynoski and Roger Fredericks are quite proud to have on their team. Having 72 employees and very low turnover rate says a great deal about the positive management style of the company from the top down. Roger Fredericks believes the success and growth of the company has been, and will continue to be the result of their high-tech equipment as well as the quality of those running the operation. Like his father, he tries to treat people "fair and square." The majority of his employees have been with the company 10 years, and a handful have worked for him for 25 and 30 years.

Roger works alongside his employees, and makes sure he recognizes their hard work and dedication. When a group of his engineers had been working overtime and Saturdays for several weeks on end, he showed his appreciation by giving them $200 in food

gift certificates. The company also sponsors an employee of the month award. The first winner was the only female machine operator out of 40, who runs five machines effortlessly.

Through the years, J. F. Fredericks Tool Company has faced a fair amount of obstacles, one of the biggest being the terrorist

President David Derynoski.

attacks on September 11, 2001. Because so much of their business is supplying jet engine components, when the flights stopped—and later, when flight schedules were drastically reduced—there was a 25 percent reduction in order volume. However, David Derynoski says that the industry is showing signs of recovery.

The roots of J. F. Fredericks Tool Company were firmly planted by a man who had an amazing drive to run his own business and a work ethic to persevere. His reputation for working hard and treating people fairly are principles that still guide the business today. Because the company is strong enough to weather a downturn in business, move forward in creating a bigger customer base in the international markets and invest in technology and equipment, David Derynoski and Roger Frederick know the company will continue to thrive.

SAINT JOSEPH COLLEGE

In 1932, 63 women entered the halls of Connecticut's Saint Joseph College seeking further education because of the determination and foresight of the Sisters of Mercy. The order, founded in Ireland, dedicated itself to establishing a much-needed broad-based liberal arts college for women in Hartford.

The early 1930s were a time of profound economic strife for the country, but the Sisters, guided by their principles of service and leadership, understood the need to provide higher education to the young women of the area. These dedicated Sisters worked tirelessly, armed by their beliefs and courage, to establish a private, four-year college that offered an excellent academic curriculum in an atmosphere centered on the Catholic faith.

Their mission was to cultivate an environment that encouraged women to become not only educated in practical studies, but also learned in leadership, humanity and the importance of service to others. It must be noted that the Sisters desired to make this experience available to people of all ages, races, religions and cultures.

In the past 70-plus years, Saint Joseph College has mindfully maintained its focus, never wavering from the founders' dreams for the school. The college has grown to be a nationally recognized institution, offering more than 30 majors including nursing, economics, environmental science and religious study.

A view of the 84-acre campus shows the College's signature building, McDonough Hall, built in 1932.

Saint Joseph College also offers pre-professional programs including dental, law, medicine and veterinary studies. Also, the school is one of 12 women's colleges in the country certified to train professional chemists by the American Chemical Society, placing the College among a select group of institutions recognized for excellence in science education.

Beyond the school's undergraduate women's program, Saint Joseph College serves the adult learner through a degree completion program and The Graduate School.

The College has continued to receive rewards and honors for its excellent curriculum through national recognition. In *U.S. News & World Report's "America's Best Colleges"* list, Saint Joseph College has ranked in the top tier of regional universities for several consecutive years—and has been named one of the best values in the region.

Students can round out their collegiate experience by participating in more than 20 clubs. The student-governed organizations range from music, dance and business to service-oriented clubs such as Best Buddies, a group dedicated to working with children with special needs.

Athletics are always an important part of college life,

and that fact is no exception for SJC students. Students can participate in the eight varsity sports at the award-winning Division III school including soccer, tennis, cross country, basketball, volleyball, swimming and diving, la crosse and soft-ball. The College's strong sports program is centered on developing the team, not just individual players, while focusing on sportsmanship.

In the tradition of the Sisters' of Mercy wishes, service to others is incorporated in the SJC experience. Each and every student is encouraged to volunteer in the area of her choice. More than 90 percent of the students find time in their schedules to give of themselves, helping those in need.

Saint Joseph College is the only four-year women's college in Connecticut. While continuing positive growth, the College has held steadfast in the ever-changing world and its society over many years by holding fast to the ideals upon which it was founded.

Today, thousands of graduates have departed from those same halls that the first 63 women entered decades ago, with not only baccalaureate degrees, but also a better understanding of the world that awaited them. With each graduation, and each confident young women that goes out on her own into the world, the Sisters' of Mercy mission continues to be honored.

Students work in one of the College's state-of-the-art chemistry labs.

A TIMELINE OF HARTFORD'S HISTORY

1611–1614 Dutch explorer Adriaen Block explores the Connecticut River from Long Island Sound as far as the future site of Hartford, calling it "de Versche Rivier," or the Fresh River, perhaps because of the rush of fresh water it sends into the Sound.

1634 After a theological dispute between the Reverend Thomas Hooker and the Reverend John Cotton, the Massachusetts General Court grants a group led by Hooker permission "to seek out some more convenient place" for settlement.

1635 July Six men explore westward to the Connecticut River Valley, reaching a place the Indians call Sukiaug, at the confluence of the Connecticut River and the modern-day Park River—the future site of Hartford. Late that summer, 12 men travel to Sukiaug, which is named for the Indians who live there, to make final preparations.

October A larger party of 60 men, women and children arrive in Sukiaug.

Winter 1635–1636 Winter comes early and the Connecticut River freezes by November. Thirteen men return to Massachusetts; one dies on the way back, but the settlement survives.

1636/1637, February 21 Magistrates change the name of the settlement from Newtown to Hartford, after the English home of the Reverend Samuel Stone, Hooker's assistant.

1637, May 1 Elected delegates meet in the new meeting house in Hartford as the first Court of Election. They decide no religious test will be required for people to live in Hartford. The first General Court also fixed the price of Indian corn, declared wampum to be legal tender, awarded a monopoly for the fur trade, and declared war on the Pequot Indians.

1637 Connecticut raises a force of 90 men—61 from Hartford—to attack the Pequots on the Mystic River. As many as 600 Pequot men, women and children are slaughtered. The Sukiaugs are grateful for the Pequot defeat and grant the English what today are Hartford's North Meadows. The war leaves Connecticut with a debt of 620 pounds, cause for levying the colony's first tax.

1638 Ship *Desire* carries Pequot captives to West Indies, and returns with black slaves—the first in New England.

1638, May 31 Thomas Hooker preaches his famous sermon in which he declares that the

Trinity College, 1840s, by Charles Kuchel. (CHS)

foundation of governmental authority lies in "the free consent of the people." By early 1639, the colony adopts the Fundamental Orders, the first constitutional document to set forth the principle that the foundation of government authority is in the free consent of the people.

1639 With more settlers arriving from Massachusetts and England, a Body of Proprietors is created to determine who has a right to share undivided lands.

1643 Launching Hartford's retail trade, the General Court grants authority for a weekly market in Hartford, a combination of an English cattle fair, a 20th century flea market, and a roadside vegetable stand. The Court forbids the sale of alcohol to whites or Indians by any unlicensed person.

1644 Hartford's first inn opens.

1647 Thomas Hooker dies July 7, victim of an unknown epidemic that grips Hartford. When Elder William Goodwin marries Hooker's widow, the Hartford congregation splits into two factions, one favoring Reverend Stone, Hooker's former assistant minister, and one favoring Goodwin.

1659 Hartford's white population is extremely homogeneous. When a peddler named "David the Jew" enters a house while the owners are absent, he is fined and ejected from the community. The town meeting passes an ordinance allowing only such transients as are "concented to" by the meeting. Hartford's white population is to remain almost completely English until long after the Revolution.

1662 John Winthrop, Jr., obtains a royal charter for the Connecticut colony, solidifying the colony's legitimacy.

1666 Hartford's importance as a legal center is fixed as the colony is split into four counties, with Hartford made the seat of Hartford County. Hartford would remain the capital of the colony until 1701, when legislative sessions would begin to be shared with New Haven.

1675 King Philip's War. Hartford plays a role in the war against Philip, a Massasoit, who was trying to unite the North American Indians in destroying all English settlements.

1687 To prevent the colony's charter from being seized by a representative of King James II, Connecticut's leaders hide the precious document—by tradition, inside a huge oak that stood in Samuel Wyllys' yard. The incident leads to one of Connecticut's great legends, that of the Charter Oak.

1690 A Connecticut law orders the creation of free schools for teaching Latin, Greek, reading, writing and arithmetic. Hartford already has a Grammar School on what is now Main Street.

1701–1713 Queen Anne's War brings profit to Hartford's merchants, who sell food and other supplies to the British Army and colony government.

1706 Connecticut legislature adopts qualifications for voting: a man must be of legal age, hold at least 40 pounds of property, and be acceptable to the ecclesiastical authorities and a majority of the town's voters. During the early 1700s, all blacks must carry identification passes, and cannot hold public office.

1716 Trustees from Hartford of the school that is to become Yale University bid to locate the institution in Hartford. But trustees vote to fix New Haven as the permanent location. A Hartford town meeting votes to offer 1,000 pounds to the school, should trustees decide to relocate to Hartford.

1720 Samuel Thornton builds Hartford's first wharf on the Connecticut River. What is now Main Street is becoming a business center, as old home lots are being divided and newer mercantile buildings are being built side by side. The first State House, a wood structure, is completed.

1741 The spiritual turmoil of the "Great Awakening" that began with the preaching of Jonathan Edwards in Northampton splits the Congregationalists and allows the Church of England to gain a first foothold in central Connecticut, as Anglican parishes are established in surrounding towns and, later, in Hartford.

1745 Almost 100 Hartford men participate in the surprise capture of the supposedly impregnable French fortress on Cape Breton Island, raising economic hopes for a great expansion of the Nova Scotia trade for New England merchants.

1748 Expansion hopes are dashed when the Treaty of Aix-la-Chapelle returns Cape Breton Island to the French. Hartford's economic uncertainties continue.

1761 Hartford is not a particularly wealthy town. The tax list for the year gives the town's entire property value at about 40,000 pounds, a figure that ranked Hartford tenth among Connecticut towns. A census of that year counts 3,938 persons, including 109 blacks.

1764, October 29 Thomas Green prints the first issue of the *Connecticut Courant*. The paper rapidly becomes an influential—and vehemently anti-British—voice as one of the largest circulation newspapers in the colonies. Now *The Hartford Courant*, it is the nation's oldest continually published newspaper.

1765 Thomas Green, through the *Courant*, speaks out against the Stamp Act passed by Parliament, which required all almanacs, calendars, dice, newspapers, pamphlets and playing cards to carry a British stamp.

1766, May 23 Hartford celebrates Parliament's repeal of the Stamp Act, but festivities are

Corner of State and Main Streets, circa 1848-1849. (CHS)

marred when six people are killed and more than 20 injured in a gunpowder explosion.

1774 First Continental Congress. Colonial census figures show 5,101 enslaved black people in Connecticut. Connecticut bans importation of slaves.

1775 May A month after hostilities begin in the Revolutionary War at Lexington and Concord, Hartford is the staging point for the Ticonderoga Expedition as General Samuel Holden Parsons gathers men and provisions.

1778 A paper mill that provides the *Courant* with paper is destroyed by fire; Hartford Whigs say local Tories are to blame. The General Assembly authorizes a lottery to raise money for a new mill.

1780, May 19 Hartford experiences the "Dark Day," when darkness falls at 10 a.m. following a thunderstorm. Some think the end of the world is at hand, but it turns out a forest fire west of the city is to blame.

1780, September 20 The Marquis de Lafayette meets with General George Washington and Governor Trumbull in Hartford.

1783 Hartford's public leaders favor strengthening the Articles of Confederation after the Revolutionary War, but townspeople feel differently, as a town meeting opposes any "encroachment upon the sovereignty and jurisdiction of the states."

1784 In an effort to modernize government, Hartford is incorporated as a city by the General Assembly on May 24. The original

boundaries of the city, encompassing only 1,700 acres, are only a little larger than the present-day downtown. Thomas Seymour is elected the first mayor, an office he was to hold for 28 years.

1785 The new city buys its first fire engine, and an informal company, The Proprietors of the Hartford Aqueduct, attempt to set up a public water system.

1788 Connecticut becomes the fifth state.

1789, October 19 As part of a tour of New England "to cement the bonds of union," President Washington visits Hartford and stays at Bull's Tavern. Thrifty Hartfordites are pleased when Washington makes clear he is paying for the tour himself.

1790 Connecticut's Anti-Slavery Society formed. There are 2,648 slaves in Connecticut, according to the first U.S. Census. Hartford's first Baptist congregation is formally organized.

1792 The Hartford Bank, the city's first bank, opens for business. With Congress changing the nation's monetary standard, it is the first bank in the U.S. to set aside the old system of keeping accounts in pounds, shillings and pence, issuing its first bank notes in dollars.

1796 Hartford completes its new State House, an effort that began with a $500 contribution from leading businessman Jeremiah Wadsworth. The Old State House, which still stands at Main Street and Central Row, was designed by Boston architect Charles Bulfinch.

1803 The Marine Insurance Company is chartered, one of the precursors to

Hartford Fire Insurance Company Building, corner of Pearl and Trumbell Streets. (CHS)

Hartford's insurance industry.

1814, December 15 Federalists convene at the Old State House in Hartford to oppose the War of 1812. The convention is quickly rendered moot by American victory in the war, and the Hartford Convention is sometimes called "Federalism's last gasp."

1817 *The Hartford Times* is founded by John M. Niles, later a U.S. senator. It competes against the *Courant* until its demise in 1976.

1818 First Connecticut constitution adopted. Only free white males can vote.

1819 The Aetna (Fire) Insurance Company of Hartford is incorporated. Society for Savings is founded, the first mutual savings bank in Connecticut.

1820s and 1830s Hartford is the textbook publishing center of the U.S., with more than 30 firms engaged in the business. By the 1880s Case, Lockwood & Company is the largest printing house in the U.S.

1821 Hartford industry takes a new turn as the Hartford Iron Foundry opens on Commerce Street near the river. Other heavy industry follows.

1822 What is now the Institute of Living, a renowned psychiatric hospital, is founded as the Hartford Retreat for the Insane.

1823 Washington College is founded in Hartford, Connecticut's second college. It is renamed Trinity College in 1845.

1830 The first large group of non-English

immigrants to come to Hartford, Irish workers who helped build canals and railroads in and around Hartford, lead to the founding of the city's first Roman Catholic Church, the Church of the Most Holy Trinity. The Irish face intense prejudice in Hartford, and "No Irish Need Apply" signs are common on factory doors for many years.

1833 Two black schools are set up as part of the Hartford public schools; the black schools are closed in 1868, when the full system becomes integrated.

1834 A three-day race riot breaks out as Irish and blacks compete for jobs.

1839 The railroad arrives in Hartford, which quickly becomes a railroad center, as the Hartford and New Haven Railroad reaches Springfield in 1844 and New York City in 1849. African captives sold into slavery revolt aboard schooner *Amistad*. The ship is seized off Long Island and brought to New London. Trials in Hartford and New Haven and an appeal to the U.S. Supreme Court eventually free the captives.

1840 Immigration and the growing acceptance of the idea of Hartford as a manufacturing center double the city's population between 1820 and 1840, to about 13,000.

1842 The Wadsworth Atheneum, America's first public art museum, is founded in Hartford.

1843 Jews gain the right to worship in public, a right not included in the 1818 state constitution. Hartford's first Jewish congregation, Beth Israel, is organized with about 200 members.

1847 Samuel Colt, the inventor of the revolver, begins production in Hartford using rented quarters, first on Pearl Street and later on Grove Street.

1853 Aetna Life Insurance Company started in Hartford.

1854 A boiler explosion kills 21 people and seriously injures more than 50; citizens are appalled by the city's inadequate facilities for caring for large numbers of injured people. Hartford Hospital is organized several months later as a result. All services are free until 1892.

1855 Samuel Colt completes the blue onion dome-topped armory in Hartford's South Meadows, perhaps the largest individually owned factory in the world; within two years the factory is producing 150 guns a day. The dike that protects the factory from the Connecticut River is the largest flood-control project then undertaken east of the Mississippi.

Mid-1850s The Reverend Horace Bushnell leads one of American's first urban renewal projects, as Bushnell Park is created on the site of railroad tracks, tanneries and a soap factory in downtown Hartford.

1860 Hartford's population has doubled again over 20 years, to 29,152 people.

1861 The start of the Civil War. More than 4,000 Hartford men serve in the Union Army and Navy; almost 400 die in service.

1862 Samuel Colt dies, but his widow Elizabeth Jarvis Colt continues to oversee the Colt industrial empire.

1863 The 29th Regiment, a black Civil War unit, is formed. The 29th fights in several battles and is one of the first Union regiments to enter Richmond after the fall of the Confederacy. James Goodwin Batterson, a Hartford architect and builder, forms the Travelers Insurance Company, the first accident-coverage company in the U.S. Within a few years, Travelers enters virtually every type of insurance, becoming the nation's first real multiple-line insurance company.

1869 Black men gain vote in Connecticut. Gideon Welles, returning to Connecticut after eight years serving as secretary of the Navy under Lincoln and Johnson, sees a changed Hartford: "A new and different people seem to move in the streets."

1870 The 15th Amendment grants the right of suffrage to black males; added to Connecticut constitution as 23rd amendment

The first electric trolley car. The Wethersfield Horse Railway Company car barn is on the left. (CHS)

in 1876. Hartford's population reaches 37,743. More than a quarter of the city's population is foreign-born, with Irish immigrants by far the largest group.

1871 Samuel L. Clemens, better known as Mark Twain, moves to Hartford to be close to his publisher.

1872 In order to keep the state capital in Hartford, city leaders agree to buy the Trinity College campus for $600,000 as the location for a new state house. Trinity moves to a new campus off Vernon Street.

1878 Hartford's first telephone is installed. Albert A. Pope begins producing the Columbia bicycle in Hartford, the first American-made bicycle. The Columbia bicycle catches on and becomes a national fad.

1880 The new state capitol building is completed, at a whopping cost of $3 million. Hartford is thriving as a banking, industrial, insurance and wholesale-distribution center. During the year, more than 500 steam vessels and 270 barges deposit their freight on the Hartford docks.

1883, April 7 The Hartford Electric Light Co. begins service.

1884 The Open Hearth Mission begins caring for homeless men; guests sawed cordwood in exchange for shelter.

1888, September 21 The first electrified street car makes the run from the car barns on Wethersfield Avenue to Main and Church Streets in Wethersfield in 20 minutes, a run that took an hour with horse-drawn street cars. Horse-drawn street cars are quickly replaced by electric street cars, paving the way for development of middle-class neighborhoods to the far boundaries of the city and into the suburbs beyond.

1895 Albert Pope gives the city the 75 acres that become Pope Park. Pope and other inventors produce their first gasoline-engine car, the Pope-Hartford, marking the beginning of the American automobile industry.

1899 An English technical journal declares that Hartford is "the greatest center of activity in the automobile industry today," but Pope elects to concentrate on the electric, rather than the internal combustion, engine. The Pope Company is defunct by 1912.

1901 Hartford is well-established as an insurance center, as the roll of companies already, or soon-to-be, operating includes Aetna, Connecticut, Hartford, National, Orient, Phoenix, Travelers Fire, Standard, Mechanics and Traders, and the American office of Rossia, the largest insurance company in Czarist Russia.

1905 The U.S. Bureau of Labor reports that of the cities it had studied in regard to housing conditions, Hartford was the worst of cities its size. Most working-class homes are without bathtubs and the occupants of tenements bathe in commercial bathhouses in the poorer sections of the city, the report says.

1907 Following the "City Beautiful" movement that stemmed from the World Columbian Exposition of Chicago in 1893, Hartford creates a City Plan Commission to study land-use and urban beautification.

1910 Hartford's population stands at nearly 99,000 people, comprised two-thirds of immigrants or the children of immigrants.

1917, April 6 The U.S. declares war on Germany, and Hartford's workforce immediately swells as factories rush to supply the government's needs. Colt's pre-war workforce jumps tenfold to 8,000 workers.

1919, March 2 Amid anger over the postwar state of the economy, about 2,000 people gather to hear speeches from the International Workers of the World (IWW) condemn capitalism and praise Russian Bolsheviks. Soon thereafter, Hartford city leaders forbid the Communists or the IWW from holding public meetings.

1920 Fueled by immigration during World War I, Hartford's population reaches 138,036 people, making it the 46th largest city in the U.S., and more densely populated than Washington, D.C.

1921 As a result of flood control work that opens up the South Meadows for development, Brainard Field opens, the second municipal airport in the United States.

1925 Pratt & Whitney brings Hartford into the air age as its small plant begins to produce small, air-cooled Wasp engines for the Navy and commercial use. Within 10 years, the workforce grows from 25 to 2,000 and the company moves to East Hartford. The Hartford Foundation for Public Giving is formed, one of the nation's oldest public community foundations. By 2003, the Foundation had assets of $500 million.

1932 To save money during the Great Depression, the city eliminates every third street lamp, and 19 of its 80 traffic signals. Hundreds of unemployed people surround the state Capitol to demand a state appropriation of $12 million for unemployment relief.

1933, September 19 On National Recovery Authority Night, a parade of 20,000 people—virtually all the city's employed people—march in Hartford. Marchers sing "Happy Days are Here Again," but they aren't back yet.

1935 Creation of the Works Progress Administration (WPA) is a boon to Hartford. The city's unusually large population of unemployed musicians are put to work as the WPA creates the Hartford Symphony Orchestra.

1936 March The Connecticut River floods much of downtown Hartford, reaching a record 37.5 feet above its normal level, causing $35 million in damage. At the Bond Hotel,

Class at school—North Main Street, West Hartford, circa 1900. Photo by A. W. Howes & Co. (CHS)

bellboys in hip boots splash through two feet of water.

1938, September 21 A severe hurricane leaves the city in shambles, causing a second disastrous flood and city leaders move forward with plans to wall the city off from the river.

1941 Hartford completes a series of dikes from the North Meadows to the South Meadows, ending the city's face-to-face congress with the river. Hartford's rapid industrialization after the U.S. entry into World War II brings thousands of people to the city. In 1941 alone, an estimated 18,000 newcomers to the city came.

1944, July 6 In perhaps the greatest tragedy in the city's history, the tent covering the Ringling Brothers Circus catches fire, killing 168 people, many of them children, and injuring 500 more.

1946 Dissatisfied with the political favoritism and patronage of city government, the Democratic and Republic parties revamp city government. Hartford is to be run by a city manager and a nine-member city council, elected at large and without political party designation.

1950 Hartford reaches its peak population of 177,397, according to the U.S. Census. Except for the 1980s, the city's population would decline in every decade of the second half of the 20th century, as the suburbs grew rapidly. During the 1950s alone, the city's share of the population of Hartford County declined from a third to a quarter.

1957 Hillyer College merges with the Hartt School of Music and the Hartford Art School to become the University of Hartford.

1958 The city announces plans for one of the largest urban renewal projects ever attempted by a city. The Italian East Side will essentially be wiped out, to be replaced by office towers, with the residents and small businesses scattered to other Hartford neighborhoods and the suburbs.

1960 The new Census shows that a wealth gap is opening between Hartford and its suburbs: in 1950, Hartford residents' income was 98 percent of that of the overall state. By 1960 as middle-class people leave for the suburbs, Hartford's income is just 79 percent of the income of the state.

1962 Constitution Plaza, partly funded by Travelers Insurance Company, opens. It wins design acclaim, but lacking any housing—and built at a grade level above the surrounding streets—it is seen by many a generation later as an object lesson for what not to do to revive a city. One of the city's newest ethnic communities, its West Indians, launch an annual independence and emancipation parade that becomes a Hartford tradition.

1963 College students and seminarians organize the North End Community Action Project (NECAP), tutoring black children, registering voters, picketing slumlords and city hall. NECAP threatens a school boycott unless the city schools—black in the North End, white in the South End—are integrated. The board turns to Harvard for an integration plan, but fierce resistance scuttles it.

1964 The Hartford Stage Company, a professional, non-profit repertory company, begins operations in rented quarters in downtown Hartford.

Liberty Loan Parade (one-man sub), circa 1917. (CHS)

1966 Project Concern begins busing minority students from Hartford schools to West Hartford, Farmington and other suburban districts.

1968 Hartford is rocked by race riots after the assassination of the Rev. Martin Luther King, Jr. Over a hot Labor Day weekend, rioters around North Main Street set fire to a branch of the Hartford Public Library and prevent firefighters from fighting the blaze. The library is destroyed.

1969 The Hartford Foundation for Public Giving launches a series of crash social programs to help residents of the North End, an effort to buy time until better, long-range programs could take over. "The democratic way is slow and fumbling, but eventually tolerance and faith in the basic decency of most Americans, black and white, will win out, and a better society will emerge," the Foundation says in its 1970 yearbook.

1970 In another large project aimed at turning around downtown, city voters approve a referendum vote spending $30 million to build the Hartford Civic Center coliseum, while Aetna agrees to invest $35 million to build a downtown.

1973 In an early stirring of the group's

Asylum Street, circa 1924. (CHS)

political identity, Maria Sanchez becomes the first Puerto Rican elected to office in Hartford, winning a seat on the board of education.

1975, January 5 The Hartford Civic Center, a combined mall and sports arena, opens in downtown Hartford, and the following week, the New England Whalers hockey team plays their first game at the new coliseum before a sellout crowd of 10,507. The Whalers defeat the San Diego Mariners in overtime.

1977 The Hartford Stage Company moves to a new 350-seat theater on Church Street. An arts controversy erupts when sculptor Carl Andre is paid $87,000 to create a minimalist sculpture that consists of 36 large boulders in six parallel rows. Some people don't see it as art.

1978, January 18 At 4:19 a.m., under the weight of snow and ice, the Civic Center Coliseum roof collapses. No one is hurt, but just hours before the collapse, 9,000 fans were watching a University of Connecticut basketball game. City leaders immediately vow to rebuild the Civic Center "bigger and better."

1979 As a member of the city council, Nick Carbone has been the dominant force in Hartford politics during the 1970s, but he loses

his bid to unseat George Athanson as mayor, effectively ending Carbone's political career.

1980, February 6 After an absence of two years and 19 days, the Whalers—now the Hartford Whalers and members of the National Hockey League—return to the Civic Center. The Whalers come back from a two-goal deficit to defeat the Los Angeles Kings 7-3 before a sellout crowd.

1981, April 6 Riverfront Recapture incorporates, launching the formal effort to reconnect Hartford with the Connecticut River. It will take nearly 20 years for Riverfront to restore that connection, but ultimately, the effort succeeds.

December 1 Thirman L. Milner is sworn in as Hartford's first black mayor, and the first popularly-elected black mayor in New England.

1982 The year opens with downtown Hartford experiencing its biggest building boom since World War II. Under construction is CityPlace, soon to be Connecticut's tallest building at 38 floors, and a half-dozen other office towers are either in construction, newly completed or are in the planning stages.

1984 The Connecticut Department of Transportation agrees to restore public access to the riverfront when it reconstructs I-91. Plans are completed for improvements to Hartford's Riverside Park, East Hartford's boat launch area, and a site beneath Charter Oak Bridge in Hartford.

1986 Hartford celebrates its 350th anniversary.

1986 April "Whalermania." The Hartford Whalers, perennial NHL doormats, go on an improbable 12-3-2 run to gain their first playoff berth in six years.

1987 The Cutter Realty Group announces plans to build a 59-story office and condominium tower capped by a gold dome near Bushnell Park—New England's tallest building. Carrie Saxon Perry is elected mayor of Hartford, the first black woman mayor of a Northeastern city.

1989 April Starting a school desegregation battle that was to last a decade, parents and civil rights advocates sue the state, contending that Hartford's mostly-segregated public school system denies children the quality of education guaranteed by the state constitution. The Sheff vs. O'Neill suit does not

People boarding a bus at Asylum Street, circa 1950. (CHS)

argue that conscious policies led to the segregation of Hartford's schools, only that the situation is illegal and must be changed.

1990 Six banks force Colonial Realty into bankruptcy, saying the giant real estate firm could not repay $40 million of debts; what some call "The Colonial Recession" rips through an economy already slowed by defense cutbacks, over-inflated real estate values, bank failures and a national recession.

1991, January 6 Connecticut Bank & Trust, one of the most prominent banks in the city's history, is seized by the FDIC in the largest banking failure in the history of New England. A dozen banks fail in and around Hartford in a two-year period.

1992 November The corporate parent of G. Fox & Company announces that it will close the iconic Hartford department store, ending 146 years of retail history on Main Street. "This is the grande dame of department stores," says Don McGee, the cashier who rang up the store's final sale on a cold January day, "and it's a shame the times have been unkind to her."

1993, December 7 Ex-firefighter Michael P. Peters becomes mayor.

December 31 Travelers completes its merger with New York-based Primerica Corporation. The $4.2 billion deal is one of a wave of mergers and acquisitions that alter life for a city that once called itself "The Insurance Capitol of the World."

1994 Hartford is suffering through a wave of gang-related shootings that lead to a record 57 homicides.

October 4 The Hartford School Board signs a contract with Education Alternatives, Inc., a private for-profit company, to take control of the entire Hartford school system. As the first city ever to turn over management of public schools to a private company, the move garners national media attention.

December Judge Harry Hammer rules the plaintiffs in the Sheff vs. O'Neill failed to prove their case. They appeal to the Connecticut Supreme Court.

1996, April 22 Demolition begins of the Charter Oak Terrace housing project, as the city begins a campaign to raze its sprawling public housing projects. The federally- funded $46 million Charter Oak Terrace project will replace more than 900 barracks-style apartments with suburban-style detached homes.

July 9 The Connecticut Supreme Court finds against the state in the Sheff vs. O'Neill desegregration lawsuit, saying racial segregation in Hartford schools violates the state constitution, and directs the legislature to find a remedy. By 2002 the state will authorize more than $1 billion to build regional magnet schools and for other desegregation efforts.

1997, March 26 A low-water mark for downtown Hartford as the Whalers announce they will end the professional hockey team's two-decade stay at the end of the 1997 season.

April 13 The Whalers finish 18 years of NHL play in Hartford with a 2-1 victory over Tampa Bay. The team moves to North Carolina.

April 16 A low point for city schools, as the Connecticut General Assembly votes in an unprecedented move to dissolve the Hartford School Board and take control of Connecticut's largest school system. "Desperate times call for desperate measures," says Senate President Kevin B. Sullivan. The state is to run the Hartford schools for the next five years.

1998, March 19 Seeking to give momentum to his urban agenda and to revive economic activity in downtown Hartford, Rowland proposes a record $350 million development plan to build Hartford's long-postponed convention center, 1,000 units of housing, to develop more parking and make other improvements. "I think we all recognize, from across the state, 169 cities and towns, that we need to do something in Hartford. It's been stagnant too long," Rowland says.

May 13 Several hundred people pack City Hall to hear Robert W. Fiondella, president of Phoenix Home Life Mutual Insurance Co., present a $1 billion plan to develop the city's riverfront, using money Rowland has earmarked for a convention center and other uses. Adriaen's Landing marks the most ambitious effort in more than a generation to remake downtown.

November 19 Concluding secret negotiations, Governor John G. Rowland and New England Patriots owner Robert Kraft sign an agreement to build a state-funded, 68,000-seat stadium that will be a centerpiece of Adriaen's Landing on Hartford's riverfront. "We really wanted to be in an urban setting," Kraft says. "This is a historic day for the

Hartford community," Rowland says. "Touchdown!" the *Hartford Courant* proclaims in an extra edition.

1999, April 30 Fumble! New England Patriots nix Connecticut's $374 million plan to build a new stadium in downtown Hartford for the NFL team, as owner Robert Kraft decides to keep the team in Massachusetts. Kraft said he was worried about environmental and engineering problems on the site. Adriaen's Landing is in doubt.

2000 April Hartford has become the second-poorest large city in America, trailing only Brownsville, Texas, for having the highest poverty rate, according to the 2000 Census. The city has suffered wholesale population loss during the 1990s, losing 11 percent of its population. Hartford has the second-lowest rate of homeownership among large cities, and a majority of city residents now punch in at jobs in the suburbs—nearly unthinkable in a city that once made everything from pay telephones to bicycles, revolvers and typewriters, and bottled everything from A-1 Sauce to vodka. For the first time in the city's history, Hartford's black population dropped during the 1990s, as middle class blacks joined the move to the suburbs.

May 2 Lacking the euphoria that came with the New England Patriots, the state legislature nevertheless bestows final approval on a $771 million plan for Adriaen's Landing. "This is our defining moment," Rowland says after the vote. Still, there are reservations among lawmakers. "We'll be feeding this white elephant for years, but we won't be feeding it peanuts. We'll be feeding it millions and millions in state taxpayer money," says one state senator.

2001 November Hartford's grand old theater—the Bushnell Memorial Hall—completes a $45 million expansion that adds a second 907-seat performance hall. The Bushnell rechristens itself the Bushnell Center for the Performing Arts. Other expansion efforts are underway at the Wadsworth Atheneum Museum of Art, the Mark Twain House and the Connecticut Historical Society.

December 4 At the age of 44, Eddie A. Perez becomes Hartford's 65th—and first-ever Latino—mayor. Born in Corozal, Puerto Rico, Perez had moved to Hartford as a young boy in 1969.

2002, November 5 Hartford voters adopt a strong-mayor form of government, revamping the city's system of government. Under the new charter, an elected mayor—rather than an appointed city manager—will be the chief executive officer of city government. Hartford will elect its first "strong mayor" in a half century in November 2003.

BIBLIOGRAPHY

A Hartford Primer & Field Guide, including statistics from the Hartford Police Department, the Connecticut Department of Labor, U.S. Census Bureau, by Ivan Kuzyk, Trinity College Cities Data Center, 2001.

Aqui Me Quedo: Puerto Ricans in Connecticut, by Ruth Glasser, 1997, Connecticut Humanities Council

Capitol Region Council of Governments, median sale price records, published yearly, and CRCOG Census trend report, published 2003

Connecticut Department of Banking records

Hartford Courant clips, 1980-2003

Riverfront Recapture, Inc., chronology of organization's history

"The Connecticut Economy" Quarterly newsletter, the University of Connecticut

The State of Black Hartford, 1994, The Urban League of Greater Hartford

U.S. Census records from 1970, 1980, 1990, 2000

Live Interviews by Mike Swift with:

Arnold, Rudolph, deputy mayor and city council member 1979–1983

Farley, Bill, CB Richard Ellis

Ludgin, Robert, deputy mayor and city council member, 1977–1981

Milner, Thirman, mayor of Hartford, 1981–1987

Perez, Eddie A., mayor of Hartford, 2001–present

Perry, Carrie Saxon, mayor of Hartford, 1987–1993

Peters, Michael P., mayor of Hartford, 1993–2001

Rosario, Edna Negron, regional director of the Puerto Rico Federal Affairs Administration for Connecticut and Rhode Island

Russell, William, former head of real estate for Aetna Life & Casualty, 1980s and 1990s

Walsh, Andrew, urban historian, Trinity College in Hartford

Index